Geeks, Mush Heads and the IT Revolution

How SRA International Achieved
Success Over Nearly Four Decades

Ernst Volgenau

Rowman & Littlefield

Lanham • Boulder • New York • London

Photographs contained herein
are used with permission.

Published by Rowman & Littlefield
A wholly owned subsidiary of The Rowman & Littlefield Publishing Group, Inc.
4501 Forbes Boulevard, Suite 200, Lanham, Maryland 20706
www.rowman.com

16 Carlisle Street, London W1D 3BT, United Kingdom

British Library Cataloguing in Publication Information Available

Library of Congress Cataloging-in-Publication Data
Volgenau, Ernst.
   Geeks, mush heads and the IT revolution : how SRA International achieved success
over nearly four decades / Ernst Volgenau.
      pages cm
   ISBN 978-1-4422-4280-7 (cloth : alk. paper) — ISBN 978-1-4422-4281-4 (electronic)
1. SRA International, Inc.—History. 2. Electronic industries—United States—History.
3. Information technology–United States—History. 4. Volgenau, Ernst. I. Title.
   HD9696.A3U58 2015
   338.7'610040973–dc23
                                                              2014027559

Contents

Preface and Acknowledgments

I began writing this book more than ten years ago with the objective of compiling a history for the twenty-fifth anniversary of SRA International in 2003. I asked others to provide their recollections. Having received several pages from each of about ten contributors, I added my comments and began editing nearly a hundred pages into a consistent style. Sue Austin, my loyal and highly competent executive assistant, typed these drafts while performing many other tasks. However, other corporate events diverted my attention (continued rapid growth of SRA, an initial public offering, changes in leadership, and various challenges). Therefore, I set aside the manuscript.

In 2010 several events caused me to revitalize the effort. For years, as a hobby, I had worked on a historical novel based on my experiences in science and engineering and thought about publishing it. I discussed the idea with a friend, Bruce Sanford, who is an eminent First Amendment and publishing attorney. Bruce introduced me to Jed Lyons, who, as president of Rowman & Littlefield, has published many books. When the three of us met, Jed recommended a firsthand account of my experiences in building SRA International, reminding me that I had no credentials in fiction writing and that more people would be interested in how SRA evolved from me working alone in the basement of my home to a New York Stock Exchange company with a revenue of nearly $2 billion and 7,000 employees.

Jed's arguments were convincing. The book could be a history and a business reference. As such, a first person account could illustrate the lessons that we had learned over a span of more than three decades. With some misgivings, I stopped work on the novel wondering whether I would ever publish anything. I had coauthored a successful engineering textbook, but that was many years before. We had to get on with the SRA book. Many of the original contributors had retired or died, and memories of important events were fading from the minds of the rest of us.

There was another reason for urgency. After years of success, SRA growth had stalled, and the company was experiencing other problems. At the same time, I was conscious of my mortality. I had passed my seventy-seventh birthday and needed to move on to a lifelong ambition to contribute more to charities. It became clear that SRA would have to be sold, and this process would bring a whole new set of business challenges. I and others could provide a full gamut of business experiences: start-up, beginning with one person; infancy, where sales had to be achieved and basic infrastructure was put into place; rapid growth; a successful initial public offering; acquisitions; a transition to a new management team; problems and stagnation; and sale of the company. This, indeed, was fertile ground for business lessons.

I began again to dictate and edit events in our history. At the same time, I engaged Anita Huslin, a former *Washington Post* writer, to perform functions that I could not because of a demanding workload. Beginning with the original version, she conducted interviews and composed them into sections. Meanwhile, I prepared other sections and edited the emerging book. Others helped in the preparation: Ted Legasey, Renny DiPentima, Gary Nelson, Stu Rubens, Sherman Greenstein, Barry Landew, and Anne Donohue. Throughout all this confusion and change, Kathy Jones, and later Thia Kim, patiently and professionally typed draft after draft.

The story of SRA begins long before its incorporation. My parents instilled in me the desire to live a life based on honesty, service to society, and hard work. After Sara and I married and began to raise three small daughters (Lisa, Lauren, and Jennifer, all of whom continue to be an inspiration), Sara bore the brunt of my long work hours in the military, the Nuclear Regulatory Commission, and SRA. During those endeavors, many military officers and government and business executives inspired me, and I mention a few of them in this history.

I am very grateful to many people who helped make SRA a success, and I have tried to recognize some of them in this book. But this is not a comprehensive history; it is a series of vignettes intended to illustrate some of our successes and frustrations and the lessons we learned from the experience. Not everyone is properly recognized. Examples include the SRA award winners listed in appendix B; much more could be written about each of them. Other contributors are not even mentioned. My apologies in advance.

We learned a lot during more than thirty-five years working together, and some of the lessons are at the beginning of each chapter and in appendix A. These conclusions are divided into two categories: (1) people, values, and culture, and (2) business. The two categories are closely related, and it is difficult to combine or list them in priority order, but they are illustrated in the chapters.

SRA has been a wonderful experience, not only for me, but for many others. Some of these old friends are still in the company; others frequently return for visits. They all say it was a special place. Our mutual hope is that it will continue on the path to greatness.

Ernst Volgenau
Fairfax, Virginia

Idealism and Information Technology

⋯⟫ Values are vital; capable people want
to be part of something great.

⋯⟫ Noblesse oblige implies leadership for
the good of society.

⋯⟫ If you want to be successful, expect
long hours of very hard work.

⋯⟫ Information technology will always
be a growing endeavor.

"Plastics" was the advice emphatically given to Dustin Hoffman about a promising business profession. The year was 1967. My wife, Sara, and I were watching *The Graduate* in a movie theater near Washington. I was a member of a Pentagon team that developed nuclear war scenarios between the United States and the Soviet Union. We used every type of computer we could find—mechanical desk calculators, a teletype connected to a new small computer at the Rand Corporation in Santa Monica, California, and (whenever time was available) large mainframe computers in the Pentagon basement.

I whispered to Sara, "Plastics were the 1940s and '50s. Electronics and computers are the future!"

Sara squeezed my arm and raised her forefinger in front of her lips. I stopped mumbling and enjoyed the rest of the film. Later that evening, I reflected on the fact that virtually none of my friends knew or cared anything about computers or technology, and yet I was fascinated by these subjects.

About ten years after we saw that movie, I founded an information technology company called SRA International that, by the year 2012, would employ more than 6,000 employees and reach nearly $2 billion in revenue. Over the course of more than three decades, SRA met many challenges, including how to grow, be profitable, and persuade Wall Street of its value. We stumbled at times, most often when we forgot our values and business principles. Our emotions ranged from euphoria to dejection. And now, SRA is beginning a new chapter as a privately owned company. It seems fitting, therefore, to reflect on the past.

Many of the principles for the company emanated from a small farm in Western New York. My parents, struggling like so many others during the deprivation of the Great Depression, decided to move there with their four small children (soon to be five) from a little apartment in Buffalo, New York. With a $10 down payment, we moved into an old farmhouse about twenty miles east of the city. My parents thought the fresh air would be good for the children, and they could supplement their meager incomes with a garden and perhaps animals. My father had part-time jobs as a night watchman and salesman, and my mother was a substitute teacher. The house had been abandoned for some time. Appliances and plumbing did not work. A cistern collected rainwater. An outside well and hand pump provided water not suitable for drinking. Electricity was available, but the utility demanded regular bill payments.

Mom and Dad, both college graduates, vowed that their children would be well educated, but one teacher for fourteen pupils in eight grades in a one-room schoolhouse presented a curriculum challenge. So they formed an association of parents, hired an excellent teacher, and arranged for part-time student teachers from a college in Buffalo.

At an early age, I learned how to work hard. Before and after school and on weekends, we three boys and our two sisters tended animals and planted, weeded, and harvested a large vegetable garden. At one time or another, our family had three milk cows, assorted heifers and calves, geese, pigeons, chickens, pigs, and sheep. The labor was manual, not much beyond the Stone Age. One of my father's few luxuries was hiring a nearby farmer to plow the garden in the spring using draft horses. There were always chores. Farm animals require constant attention; cows must be milked twice a day. All of the animals had to be fed and watered and their stalls cleaned. In summer, the large garden added to the work; in winter, heavy drifting snow was a burden. The farm taught me the value of hard work, responsibility, and perseverance.

I learned from my father and older brother the meaning of service to society. At the beginning of World War II, my father's National Guard unit was activated. He was forty years old and, with five children, could have easily obtained a deferment. But he left for war, participated in Pacific battles, and did not return until five years later. His letters were intermittent and arrived in a compact form called V-mail. It was an early equivalent of photocopying and saved shipment weight, which was scarce because of the war. When the mailman brought a V-mail, we ran with it into our farmhouse. We gathered in a circle around my mother as she opened it and read it out loud. We usually cried several times during the epistle.

My older brother, Coleman, was determined to serve as well, but because of his age, Mom had to sign a special dispensation allowing him to enlist in the Marine Corps, which at the time was suffering horrific casualties in battles such as Guadalcanal, Tarawa, and Iwo Jima. When my father and brother went off to war, the responsibilities of running the family farm fell on me. I was eleven years old.

Douglas, my younger brother, helped but he was only seven. Later he graduated from the United States Naval Academy, became a commander of nuclear submarines, and retired as a rear admiral. Coleman returned from the Marine Corps, graduated from Harvard Law School, and became a successful lawyer and judge. My sister, Gretchen, taught me about the courage to be different. Dorothy showed me how to persevere in building a family.

One of the many things I learned from my mother was truthfulness. When I lied (as all children do occasionally), she punished me severely; but when, in spite of a big mistake, I was forthright, she forgave and praised me. It was these two lessons from my parents—honesty and service—that formed the basic values of SRA.

In grade school, I resolved to be a scientist. In high school, biology was interesting, describing plants and animals that surrounded me. Chemistry also seemed important, but I was not sure why. Physics was fascinating because it explained other natural laws, and one could build machines using its principles. To keep my options open, I became quite serious about academics in my third year. I graduated in 1950 at age sixteen. I was too young for college, so I took advantage of that extra year by attending a "cram school."

Aside from a few family trips to nearby relatives in our old Ford, I seldom traveled. I was alone and nervous when I boarded the 20th Century Limited train in Buffalo. My parents had given me a long list of advice, including warnings. I feared that danger lurked everywhere in New York City. When the train stopped, I picked up my old, battered suitcase and eagerly climbed the stairs to the concourse. There it was, just as described in the radio drama: "Grand Central Station! Crossroads of a million lives."

Following my father's instructions, I got into a Yellow Cab, gave the driver the address in an authoritarian voice, and then sat back and marveled at the commotion in the streets as we drove. When I arrived at my destination, 589 West 57th Street, I took the elevator to the thirty-seventh floor and looked out the window. I had never been so high. I knocked on the door—once, twice. Finally, someone turned the knob from the other side, and I found myself staring down at a little man, barely five feet tall.

"Yessss?" he hissed in a deep voice.

"I . . . I . . . I'm Ernst Volgenau. I'm here to see Mr. John C. Martin."

"That would be me. Welcome to the School of Ten."

There were eighteen of us under his tutorial that summer, most preparing for entrance exams to the service academies and to a few other top schools. It was called the School of Ten because Mr. Martin accepted no more than ten students applying to each academy and a few other universities. I spent the summer studying math, physics, and English.

Because of the planning and preparation learned from my parents, I had several alternatives for college. The two most attractive were to accept an appointment to the Naval Academy at Annapolis, Maryland, or enter the Massachusetts Institute of Technology to study nuclear engineering under a small scholarship. Although somewhat studious, I never regarded myself as an intellectual. In high school I had all the usual distractions (sports, girls, and friends), although my activities were limited by unrelenting farm chores in the morning and evening.

In those days, the news was dominated by the growing Cold War and the promises and dangers of nuclear energy. MIT would provide the opportunity to understand the strange forces of quantum mechanics. On the other hand, the Naval Academy emphasized engineering, liberal arts, leadership, and service. My interest in science and technology has always been more practical than theoretical, and I wanted to be a leader like my father. (I still have a picture of him, with General Douglas MacArthur, showing a rocket that he and his team installed on landing craft to suppress enemy fire during attacks on the Pacific islands.)

The Naval Academy, therefore, was my choice. I did not know it at the time, but there was a French phrase that captured my desire to serve—*noblesse oblige*—which means roughly: obligation of the nobility. Those who have had the good fortune to be well educated and raised with values have an obligation to help those less fortunate. To me it means the best type of leadership.

The four years at the Naval Academy were demanding and fulfilling. The academy reinforced the ideals of honesty and service gained from my parents. The curriculum was primarily electrical engineering, with a substantial portion of liberal arts. I had only two electives: language and a great books course. For language, I chose Russian and learned a lot about the Soviet Union, which was our country's primary nemesis in those days.

At age three, I nearly drowned in a small pond. I was afraid of the water and never learned to swim. The academy requires that every midshipman become a proficient swimmer. The tests begin in the plebe (freshman) year, and become steadily more difficult. Midshipmen must swim roughly one third of a mile in a certain time, using a variety of strokes. Each year, the time becomes progressively shorter. There are other trials as well, such as enduring a simulated airplane crash with the cockpit inverted in fifteen feet of water, and jumping feetfirst from a high diving board. Swimmers must then remove the outer layer of their uniform while treading water and use the clothes to prepare a makeshift float.

Midshipmen who did not pass the tests were relegated to the sub squad and had to march to the swimming pool each day for practice. They continued this special education until they passed. I could not bear the humiliation of being on the sub squad, so I often practiced alone, with occasional advice from classmates. During the first test, the midshipmen in my group soon outdistanced me. But I continued and, with my classmates cheering at the side of the pool, finished the test in just under the prescribed time. In subsequent years, my swimming improved so that I finished well ahead of the test time. Everyone has different levels of tolerance for frightening or painful situations. Learning to swim helped me overcome a lifelong fear of the water and reinforced the habit of perseverance.

At the Naval Academy, I became fascinated by the exquisitely designed mechanical analog computers used to control naval guns and also the advanced radar systems. I had heard that a new type of computer was being developed based on discreet (digital) rather than continuous (analog) signals. In 1952 a digital computer predicted the outcome of the presidential election prior to human experts.

When I graduated from the academy, because of poor eyesight I was qualified only for restricted duty in the Navy. I wanted to command a combat unit, so I accepted a commission in the Air Force, which offered me immediate guided missile training, an assignment to a missile squadron, and the possibility of early graduate education. I attended guided missile school at Lowry Air Force Base in Colorado. My assignment from there was to a Matador tactical missile squadron at Orlando Air Force Base, Florida.

The Matador was designed to carry conventional and nuclear warheads, and we guided it to the target by radar. Its computer was similar to the mechanical analog computers that I studied at the Naval Academy, but the circuits were electronic and used vacuum tubes. Surprisingly, the Matador had many of the capabilities of modern unmanned aerial vehicles that are used today to attack terrorists and other enemies. However, it was not very reliable. Managing a launch team and later a guidance team of about twenty enlisted men helped me hone leadership skills I had learned at the academy.

In the mid-1950s, IBM was making mechanical office calculators, cash registers, and other similar devices. But big electronic digital computers were beginning to receive attention, and I believed that IBM would soon dominate that area as well. Through an advertised Merrill Lynch program, young professionals could invest a fixed amount each month in several stocks. I contacted a broker and told him I wanted to invest $40 each month in International Business Machines. For twenty-five years I continued the monthly investment. The IBM stock largely paid for the college education of my three daughters, and I still have some through a dividend investment program.

My next assignment was to the Air Force Institute of Technology (AFIT) at Wright Patterson Air Force Base in Ohio. There, I earned a master's degree in electrical engineering, specializing in automatic control, which is an advanced form of automation. My career in computers (later called *information technology*) was developing well, although I did not realize it at the time. I wanted to go to MIT, but orders were orders. AFIT was difficult and depressing, and I had never heard of it, but the graduate school prepared me well for future events.

The highlight of this period of my life was a blind date. I and Hugh Seborg, a fellow officer in graduate school, were introduced to two young ladies for an evening of dinner and dancing. I was matched with an affable young woman by the name of Lucile, but by the end of the evening, I was taken with my friend's blind date, a second-grade teacher named Sara Glen Lane. She had been homecoming queen and a popular undergraduate at Morehead State University. We spent a lot of time talking and realized that we had similar goals and values. We married four months later on a Sunday afternoon in 1959. The next day, we drove in Sara's car toward Los Angeles, where I was assigned to the Air Force Space Systems Division. Our friends on the double-date have long since forgiven us. Lucile and Hugh Seborg married a few months after we did and have remained friends over the years. Sara has been a wonderful wife and mother; she consistently provided support and stability during trying periods of my military career and the founding and growth of my company.

In my new job, I was assigned to prepare a development plan for a satellite system to detect clandestine Soviet nuclear detonations in space. The project was called Vela Hotel, and my team included scientists from nuclear laboratories in Los Alamos, Livermore, Sandia, and other places. The plan was approved and later, after I had been reassigned, the satellites were placed in orbit and detected what appeared to be a nuclear explosion. Detailed review of the data indicated that the radiation was gamma ray bursts from exploding stars in deep space, a new scientific discovery in astrophysics.

I had one more assignment before my work for the military turned in a different direction. In 1962 the Air Force created an astronaut course for selected graduates of the Air Force Test Pilot School at Edwards Air Force Base. The course was called the Aerospace Research Pilot School, and the commandant was Colonel Chuck Yeager, the first person to fly faster than the speed of sound. Two instructors in the program (Majors Thomas McElmery and Robert Buchanan) had attended one of my engineering lectures at UCLA, where I was teaching at night. They asked if I would agree to help develop the full program. Since the astronaut school was to consist solely of volunteers, I said I would be glad to, provided I could also attend the program as a student. This caused some concern in the Air Force because I was not a pilot, much less a talented test pilot. However, the Air Force agreed to modify its policy, and I participated with others in rigorous training, including centrifuge tests that exerted fifteen times the force of gravity on its oc-cupant, as well as zero-gravity flights; I spent many hours in fighter jets. I applied for Air Force flight training and, later, the NASA astronaut program. But because of my poor eyesight, I was rejected by both. It was a major disappointment to realize that I was not destined to fly in space like many of my colleagues at the Aerospace Research Pilot School. Nevertheless, I did gain a private pilot's license, and I learned a great deal from my colleagues, some of whom went to the moon.

I never considered plastics as a professional specialty. Instead, I gained a PhD in electrical engineering at the University of California at Los Angeles in 1966. My studies were automation, computer design, and operations research, which is the application of mathematics to societal problems.

About that time, Secretary of Defense Robert McNamara established a new office in the Pentagon called Systems Analysis. It was directed by a talented economist named Alain Enthoven and consisted of care-fully selected civilians and a few military officers. The media referred to the group as the "Whiz Kids." The name was a double-edge sword. The work was often controversial, and some seasoned military officers resented the fact that relatively young analysts (many with little experi-ence in the services) were making recommendations about some of the military's most important programs.

I was selected for the office and assigned to analyze the entire U.S. continental air defense system. At the time, it consisted of a huge ar-ray of fighter airplane bases, airborne and ground radar stations (in-cluding a distant early warning line in the Arctic), and nuclear-tipped surface-to-air missiles around major U.S. cities. All of this was controlled by stations containing advanced computers and communications.

After a lengthy study, I concluded that this system, which cost billions of dollars a year, was outmoded and should be dramatically reduced. It had originally been designed to combat a huge bomber attack, but the Soviets never developed such a force. Moreover, they were deploying intercontinental ballistic missiles, which outflanked the system. Even if air defense was very successful against bombers, damage to our nation from their intercontinental ballistic missiles would be devastating.

The generals disagreed with my conclusion, but my thinking was recognized as valuable and I continued to be promoted. My time in the Pentagon system analysis office resulted in an idea that would lead to the creation of SRA International eight years later. I left that job in 1970 and had three others before starting the company in 1978.

Of all my professional experiences, four themes seem stronger than others: idealism (high ethics and service to society), leadership, perseverance, and information technology. As an engineer, I relate to technology. In this regard I have sometimes felt isolated from my friends and colleagues. For example, Sara and I were at a small dinner party in 1973. Our hostess invited the guests to speak about their backgrounds. Each elicited questions and comments from the others. I waited my turn, and when the time came, I discussed the activities of my computer development team. The other guests nodded politely but had no comments. They had no background or interest in engineering. Information technology did not regularly touch their lives, although many computers existed at the time. Computers were remote objects used by banks and utilities. Most people received bills prepared by the machines, and they remembered the errors and sterility of the process. It was like a replay of *The Graduate* six years earlier. On the way home from the party, Sara tactfully suggested that I avoid the topic in social gatherings.

After my company had been in existence for a few years, we used nicknames for two types of employees. *Wire heads* were computer experts, later called geeks. *Mush heads* were those who specialized in the softer disciplines and understood the business of our customers. I came to realize that I was both a geek and a mush head.

Recently Sara and I waited for a plane at Dulles International Airport. People all around were using laptops, BlackBerrys, iPhones, Kindles, iPads, and many other devices. They were speaking, texting, and emailing. Facebook, Twitter, YouTube, Google, and other applications had billions of users. Countless other computing and communicating devices were embedded in the machines that people used every day. Individual entrepreneurs were developing programs to sell all over the web. Thousands of hackers were attempting to break into networks for theft, sabotage, or simply the fun of it. I reminded Sara of those many other computer events that had touched my life for the past sixty years; and in the habit of old people, spoke about past events, of plastics and electronics, and life on a small farm.

I sometimes feel like the *2,000 Year Old Man* who emerges into modern society after many centuries in seclusion. This was a comedy sketch that Mel Brooks and Carl Reiner developed in the 1960s. However, the routine should have referred to the 50,000-year-old man who lived in the Stone Age when people first began developing information technology tools. To him and many of us today, the advancements are accelerating at an incomprehensible rate. Despite a lifetime immersed in science and technology, I am just as ignorant as the rest. It is with this perspective of historical humility that I submit the following saga about one man and his fellow workers who tried to do their part in the vast architecture of space, time, and humanity.

2

Prologue

⋯⋗ **Plan ahead, influence destiny.**

⋯⋗ **Technological euphoria can be expensive.**

⋯⋗ **Your vision must fulfill a definite
market need.**

S ome people are content to let fate dictate their futures. I am
not one of them. From the time that I was commissioned in the
Air Force in 1955, I developed plans for career alternatives and
adapted them throughout years of military service. I meticulously responded to assignment preference questionnaires that the Air Force
sent to officers, and sometimes stopped by the personnel office to express my preferences in person. Many of my colleagues seldom thought
deeply about their careers and often completed their questionnaires
with short-term goals in mind, such as the opportunity to fly a particular airplane or serve overseas. The journey toward SRA began when
I knocked myself off the military fast track, a move that some friends
considered career suicide. I would soon be promoted to full colonel at
age thirty-seven, the youngest on the promotion list for that year. But
I chose another road, one that was not yet paved. If I hadn't, it is likely
that SRA would not exist today.

In 1970 I resolved to one day start a company. I had spent four years
as a "Whiz Kid" in the Pentagon Systems Analysis office, when a new
assistant secretary of defense took over. He asked me to resign my commission with the Air Force and become a deputy assistant secretary of
defense overseeing land, sea, and air tactical forces. Although the ap-

pointment that was offered to me was a civilian position, it would have been an immediate promotion, equivalent to becoming major general.

At the same time, I was growing tired of analytical work and had read about a very large computer system being developed in the Air Force Logistics Command (AFLC) at Wright Patterson Air Force Base. The command, located near Dayton, Ohio, consisted primarily of civilians and was regarded as a career dead end for military officers. But it had more computers than any other organization in the world and the project would produce a business system that, by some measures, would be the most complex ever undertaken. The Advanced Logistics System represented one of the first large-scale conversions from first and second generation mainframe computers (punch cards and tape) to third generation hardware and software, random access disc storage, a huge central database, thousands of remote terminals, and high speed communications. After carefully contemplating my options, I declined the Pentagon job and volunteered for an assignment at the AFLC. Rather than career suicide, it turned out to be one of the best things that happened to me professionally.

I was assigned as chief of a software division on the Advanced Logistics System (ALS) project. After a few months, I received word that the Air Force promoted me to colonel. Then I was named director of data automation and put in charge of all of the Air Force Logistics Command computers around the nation. In addition, I was given the title of deputy project manager for the ALS development. One of my first jobs was to take a team of about eighty military and civilian specialists to Sunnyvale, California. Our objective was to test the ALS hardware and software. The AFLC bought the hardware from Control Data Corporation, which at the time built the world's fastest supercomputers. My programmers were developing software that would enable users to access and manipulate the data within this new global computer system and interact with other users. Even by today's standards, it was a formidable project.

We needed the best people on this team, and I had many candidates. One of them was a promising young lieutenant named Ted Legasey. A distinguished graduate of the Air Force Academy, Ted went to the University of Pennsylvania where he earned a master of science degree in operations research. Then he was assigned to my organization.

Ted's talents were immediately apparent. He was smart, analytical, collegial, and tough—perfect to help me manage and motivate a team of mainly civil servants operating around the clock in three shifts. Ted is one of the best problem solvers I have ever seen. We share a way of dealing with people and getting things done. Even then we knew that we wanted to continue to work together. And in the way that these things happen in life, we became friends and business partners. He later joined me at SRA, and we worked together nearly forty years.

I needed another top-notch deputy, this one to oversee the technical details of the project. I found him toiling in professional purgatory on a minor project. Emerson Thompson started as a computer operator at AFLC in the early 1960s but quickly gained a reputation as a talented programmer. However, he quit government service to start a company. When that venture failed, Emerson returned to AFLC as an application programmer. In effect, it was a demotion because he was assigned to a lower pay grade than before he left. Emerson worked nights and weekends as a consultant to make up the difference. His talents were not being fully exploited and he was not paid what he was worth. So I found a way to get him reinstated to his earlier Government Service Level 13 status, and he took over all of the technical aspects of the test team in Sunnyvale. Emerson also would later join me at SRA.

The testing process began immediately. The computers failed often and we could not always determine whether the cause was our software or the vendor's. After a few days, Emerson gave me his assessment: "This will never, ever work." Emerson was noted for his blunt comments, and I knew he was tired and probably blowing off steam. Nevertheless our lack of progress was troubling.

After about three weeks we were visited by my boss, Major General James A. Bailey. He was in charge of the project—a good man, intelligent and hardworking, but he knew nothing about computers or large scale system development. He, Emerson, and I met in the small sitting area of my tiny apartment.

Emerson and I gave General Bailey a frank status report and attempted to answer his questions. The meeting ended after about two hours. Just before leaving, the general looked directly into my eyes and said, "Colonel Volgenau, I expect you and your team to get this system working!"

For a moment my thoughts flashed back to my first year at Annapolis and a reply that every plebe understands—"Aye Aye, Sir," meaning, "I understand and will comply." Failure would be unacceptable.

Over the next eighteen months, initially at Sunnyvale and later at

Dayton, I and many others worked hard to fulfill the general's command. However, despite our best efforts, the problem was beyond our capabilities. Two years later ALS was canceled after several hundred million dollars in expenditures. Ted was transferred to Edwards Air Force Base to work on the B-1 bomber. Emerson remained at Wright Patterson working on other systems.

ALS was a bitter lesson for all of us. Over the years, I have often reflected on what went wrong. Information technology has accelerated since the dawn of civilization; and, for the last fifty years, has moved at a frantic pace. As a result, people sometimes overestimate its potential impact on society. However, social processes usually change slowly. The result is sometimes great disappointment and wasted time and money. The ambitions for ALS were about thirty years ahead of the technology available at the time. One formidable problem was inadequate software, but the basic challenge was that a lot of business processes had operated independently for decades (so-called silos or smoke stacks), and they could not be easily consolidated. They were social inhibitors. Trying to combine them led to very ambitious technical specifications, and the government processes for procuring such systems were terribly inadequate. The result was a huge failure.

I learned a lot while on the Advanced Logistics System project. Certainly the techniques of computer system development were important, but the more meaningful lesson was how people and technology interact on a challenging project. The old saying about playing the game well despite a loss certainly applied to ALS, and would work often as we built SRA. Perseverance and a positive attitude under duress are very important.

By the year 1974, I had been at the Air Force Logistics Command for four years. It was time to leave. I called a former colleague from the Office of Systems Analysis. William K. Brehm had been appointed as Assistant Secretary of Defense for Manpower and Reserve Affairs, and he had a special project from Secretary of Defense James R. Schlesinger. The United States was still engaged in a prolonged Cold War with the Soviet Union and other communist nations. Bill Brehm's mandate was to examine the entire military command structure for efficiency and effectiveness. Headquarters were high on the list because they were expensive and bureaucratic. Bill hoped to streamline operations by decreasing the number of people in the headquarters.

Bill wanted to see the command structure personally, so he organized a worldwide tour. Our first stop was Ramstein Air Force Base, in Germany, home of the U.S. Seventh Army and not far from the U.S. European Command (EUCOM). The next day, Bill and I set off in different directions. He went to talk to the generals and admirals about the military headquarters bureaucracy and how it could be streamlined; I visited mid-level officers, who understood the details of military operations. Our basic question was this: "What are all these people doing and are they all really necessary?"

One of the first offices I visited belonged to the director of data automation at EUCOM, a colonel who managed all of the computers. My job had been similar at the Air Force Logistics Command, so I knew what questions to ask and what to look for. The government had invested millions of dollars to purchase mainframe computers for EUCOM and the units that reported to it. Computers and communication systems provide information about enemy and friendly forces and make it easier to manage troops and resources. In using such command and control systems, more can be accomplished with fewer forces, at lower cost. I wanted to know how these computers were being used. The colonel described his organization—the number of people, types of computers, and their functions.

After our conversation, I asked to see the processing center. He took me to a room filled with large mainframe computers whirring away at their tasks. Next to them were disc drives, tape units, printers, card readers, and communications units—essentially, all the peripherals needed to operate a computer system at the time. The military had spent a lot for all of this equipment.

Several problems were immediately evident. At this and many other bases we visited, I found computer terminals still packed in their boxes, growing dusty in storage rooms. The systems were designed to allow people to sit at terminals and interact with the mainframes, testing various scenarios to improve plans and managing resources during war time. Even if the terminals had been working, I realized that there was no software infrastructure to accept, process, and share data, and no high-speed lines to connect computers to other bases. Instead, messengers brought boxes of punch cards and tapes to the computer room where operators placed them in long queues to be processed in batches.

In this so-called World Wide Military Command Control System, modern equipment was being used as if it were part of a decade-old system. This was akin to buying a new airplane and then taxiing it from one place to another instead of flying. This helped explain some of the bloat on the base. Machines that were designed to free humans to perform more thoughtful, analytical work were instead being served by a cadre of clerks. It was a waste of taxpayer money and a missed opportunity to make the military work smarter and leaner.

I felt that this problem could be fixed. But most senior military people knew nothing about computers, and the government did not have the insight or expertise to put it all together. The germ of an idea was growing for a company that could provide this expertise. In the meantime, I could help the military realign its resources to better serve its mission. Bill Brehm and I found that a combination of demands and incentives produced the best results.

At each base, I engaged in negotiations with colonels about staffs that had grown over the years, constituting most of what the Secretary of Defense saw as "bloat." The conversations went something like this:

Col. V: "We need to get some of these people out of headquarters and into combat units. I think we should reduce the number by 100. Here's how I would do it." Then I'd offer my suggestions.

Col. X: "I'll tell you what. I can get eighty positions out, but that's it."

Col. V: "I'll take them."

Then I would add the numbers to my report. From the perspective of the military brass, the carrot for going along with this kind of downsizing was that they could shift the positions to combat units or buy more planes, tanks, or ships.

When Bill and I completed our tour, we recommended cuts and efficiencies that eventually shrank the military headquarters by forty thousand people. And I came away with several important conclusions that would help me begin to plan a business.

The military and the rest of the federal government faced increasingly complex problems, such as how to maintain forces in a state of readiness and rapidly get them where they needed to go. Given the number of potential scenarios under which this might occur, there were no easy answers to such questions. And there was a significant financial cost to using what were essentially World War II procedures to support modern units overseas. But I saw the value in being able to provide information and systems that help people make good decisions.

Today, most professionals regularly interact with computers, and talk about hardware and software problems. However, in the early 1970s the word "computer" was rarely mentioned except among a relatively small group of engineers, scientists, and technicians. I knew that information technology would grow rapidly.

After nearly twenty years of military service, I came to believe that companies can do this work better than government, primarily because they are more agile and more open to risk-taking and innovation than a civil service bureaucracy. From the government's perspective, one of the great advantages of hiring a contractor is that it can fire the firm if it does not perform well and can end the contract (and its cost) when the job is done. Getting rid of a bureaucratic institution is much more difficult. I was confident that I could build a company that could succeed where government had not.

Over the next several years, I talked to old colleagues who had started businesses. I shared my ideas and asked them what they had learned. They became my informal council of advisors. I continued to organize my ideas, thinking about whom my customers would be and what kind of people I would want to hire. I prepared a plan for the business. It would incorporate a number of the lessons I learned in the military and government:

- Plan ahead; do not leave your future to chance.
- Hire outstanding people and inspire them with a noble goal. Give them opportunity to learn and advance rapidly.
- Insist that your team is the best in accomplishing its mission whether it is in the military, government, or business.
- Persevere. Despite your best efforts, there will be times when everything goes wrong. If you really crave the satisfaction of success, then keep going when most rational people would quit.

My company would use technology (particularly computers) and scientific analysis to solve large societal problems. It would employ an evaluative and development process called the systems approach that had become popular among engineers in the 1950s and 1960s when the United States was developing large military and space exploration systems. And it would operate with many of the values of our military, particularly honesty and service to one another and to our country.

After twenty years and seven months of service, I retired from the Air Force. It was January 1976. Eight years had passed since I first started formulating ideas for a business. This was much more time than I needed. I was ready to launch SRA.

3

Countdown and . . . Delay Launch

···⠗ **Your business vision must fulfill
a definite market need.**

···⠗ **Plan ahead; influence destiny.**

E arly in 1976, I took out a lined notepad and created a list of possible names for my new company. There were fourteen. Among them were Applied Technology Corp., Management Systems Corp., Systems Applications and Methodology, Systems Engineering Inc., and System Sciences Corp. The term "systems" had to be reflected in the name of the company. Systems theory views most phenomena in the universe as a network of relationships among elements, that is, interacting parts. A system can be electrical, mechanical, biological, or social. It can be a living cell, a complete human, a company, a nation, or all of humanity. It can be a car, the space shuttle, or a network of trains. Computers and communications in a company are often referred to as a system. Systems have common patterns and properties that can be understood. Systems theory brings together knowledge from a variety of disciplines: physics, engineering, computer science, biology, sociology, political science, and economics. The idea is to form general principles that apply to all types of systems in all fields of research.

The systems approach is the practical implementation of systems theory. Parts of the systems approach include systems analysis (defining what is needed), system design (creating the specifications for the desired entity), and system development (building something according to the specifications).

The systems approach became particularly popular in the engineering profession in the 1950s and 1960s when huge military and space exploration systems were being developed. Individual groups of engineers each designed components of a big system. These parts were sometimes called black boxes because their interior design was often a mystery to others. Engineers tend to be perfectionists. They did not stop after the first design but produced improved versions (smaller, more precise, etc.). However, their good intentions actually detracted from the project. In addition to needless costs, they often made the systems less reliable and too rigid; some systems operate better when they contain more slack. As a result of these experiences, project managers began to evaluate individual components within the context of the whole (the systems approach).

I wanted the new company to solve problems using the systems approach, while at the same time, employing computing and communications (now called information technology). Several other firms of this type already existed, but they focused on analytical and general engineering services, not information technology. Since then, nearly every company of this type has developed a strong IT capability. In any case, the logical name for the new company was Systems Research and Applications Corporation. It would use the systems approach to solve complex societal problems, it would conduct research to develop new technologies and tools in this area, and it would focus on a market that I knew was emerging—the application of computers and communications to business problems.

With the help of an accountant, I submitted an application to the Virginia State Corporation Commission and a few weeks later received a certificate. On February 11, 1976, Systems Research and Applications Corporation became an official, registered business.

The next step was to find some customers. One of the first people I called was William Anders, a Naval Academy classmate, who became an Air Force fighter pilot and veteran astronaut. He was one of three crew members on Apollo 8, who, on the first mission to the moon on Christmas Eve, read passages from the Bible. Later, after jobs with the National Aeronautics and Space Council and the Atomic Energy Commission, he was named chairman of the Nuclear Regulatory Commission (NRC). The meeting with Bill would significantly alter my plans.

During the 1950s and 1960s, our government fostered nuclear power. The Navy constructed aircraft carriers and submarines fueled by atomic plants. Concurrently, the Atomic Energy Commission tried to convince electric utilities to convert from coal to nuclear power. The rhetoric of the day was that nuclear energy would be so inexpensive that people would no longer need meters in their homes. Instead, they would be charged a flat rate and could use as much electricity as they pleased. By the mid-1970s, nuclear plants delivered roughly 20 percent of the electrical power in the United States, and additional plants were under construction.

Then the government abruptly reversed its policy because of safety concerns. The Atomic Energy Commission (AEC) was split into the Energy Research and Development Administration (ERDA) and the Nuclear Regulatory Commission (NRC). The new NRC chairman had to be a person who had high integrity and was objective, and he needed to understand nuclear power. Bill Anders was a good choice.

I knew that the new Nuclear Regulatory Commission would need contractors and thought that my company, with its prospective skills in systems analysis and computer technology, could be one of them. Ten days before our meeting, I sent Bill a copy of my resume and a description of the firm. Then I went to his office in Washington and explained the capabilities of SRA.

Bill listened carefully and said, "You can serve our country better at this time if you will accept the job of director of the inspection and enforcement for the NRC."

I was completely surprised and not inclined to give up the idea of the new company. But Bill persisted; he described an organization of more than seven hundred physicists, engineers, nuclear health professionals, and physical security experts who inspected all of the commercial nuclear power plants under construction and in operation in the United States. It also regulated hundreds of other licensees that produced or used radioactive materials—industrial, health care, research, and other organizations. He said I would report directly to him and the four other commissioners through an executive director for operations, who was mainly a coordinator. He emphasized that my authority in the new position would provide plenty of room for innovation. Then Bill added a final remark that he thought might persuade me.

"You just retired as a colonel. This position is the civil service equivalent of a three-star general. You only need to accept the job for two years. Think of the additional credentials your company will accumulate; you will be able to sell its services to the entire commercial nuclear power industry."

I told Bill I would think about it and drove home in a state of confusion. My carefully laid plans were in danger of being derailed. A few days later, Bill called and asked me to meet the other commissioners. They reaffirmed his offer. I discussed the idea with my wife, Sara, and finally decided to accept the job. I had already waited eight years to start the company and this offered an opportunity to make a significant contribution. Two more years would not make much difference, and the additional experience would improve my probability of success. I placed the SRA letter of incorporation and notes on starting a business in a folder and put it in my desk at home. I joined the NRC in March 1976.

Several hundred people worked for me in an NRC office on East-West Highway in Bethesda, Maryland. The rest occupied five offices around the country. Our job was to ensure NRC licensees complied with safety regulations developed by other groups in the agency and to levy penalties and other punishment if they did not.

Bill Anders and the other commissioners described a pro-industry bias that some people in the NRC brought with them from the old Atomic Energy Commission. He asked me to not only conduct the current inspection and enforcement program but also to devise significant improvements. Although the entire design of a nuclear power plant uses technology proven over many years, there are dangers that begin with the radioactive mining and production process, carry over in the manufacturing of machinery, and continue through the construction, testing, and operation of the plant. My office inspected these processes and products and paid particular attention to safety practices during power plant construction and operation. I set about designing a revised inspection and enforcement program.

I needed outstanding people with technical and management skills who would be industry-neutral. Some of them were already in the Office of Inspection and Enforcement. My deputy, John Davis, was particularly capable and dedicated, but I needed others as well. By this time, Ted Legasey had finished working on the B-1 bomber project and was considering whether to remain in the Air Force. The timing of my call turned out to be propitious.

I located Ted in Oklahoma City, where he had been summoned for a meeting. He was standing in the anteroom of his boss's office when the phone rang. The secretary answered and held out the phone. "It's a Dr. Volgenau for you." Ted replied, "I know a Colonel Volgenau but not a Dr. Volgenau."

"Hi, Ernie, how are you?" Ted said, with his usual engaging rapport.

Without prelude I asked him, "Are you ready to get out?"

I told Ted about my new government job and that I thought the Nuclear Regulatory Commission would benefit from someone with his skills. That night, Ted called his wife. He told her about the job. He pointed out that it would be a good career change, and they could move back East. Tricia, who never felt like California was home, did not hesitate. "I'll be packed by the time you get home."

At that point, I recused myself from the recruitment process, and Ted applied and interviewed with the NRC. "I had to convince the organization," Ted later recalled. "Ernie always does everything by the book." Once Ted was hired, I offered him the job of senior analyst in my office.

A few months after arriving at NRC, I was told that one of my additional duties involved emergency planning and response. During my military career, I was sometimes involved in the design or improvement of command and control systems for emergencies. Preparation and training for all types of contingencies are important aspects of military units. A great deal of effort is spent developing effective processes, conducting exercises, correcting deficiencies, and training in new techniques. It may be true that the military never fights a war according to plan, but the process of preparing for emergencies makes organizations much better able to deal with them.

I looked for similar nuclear emergency management systems at the NRC but was disturbed by what I found. There was little planning or effort given to this issue. A large conference room near my office had been equipped with extra telephone jacks, and there was a telephone call tree. If a person was called, he or she was supposed to go to the conference room, plug in a phone, and be ready to respond. But the directory of people to be called in an emergency was incomplete and out of date. Many were missing or had moved to other jobs. No one recognized that different scenarios would require people with varying skills, such as experts in physical security or health physicists. Such people worked at the NRC, but there was no organized inventory of them, much less training programs.

I knew how to solve the problem. We would construct a modest command center consisting of a mini-computer, work stations, displays, and seats where people could be briefed and confer. There would be one or two small adjacent conference rooms for work teams. I discussed this idea with my staff, and we prepared a request for proposal to contractors that contained a detailed description of what was required. Several companies submitted bids, and we selected a contractor to design the specifications, estimate the cost, and prepare a schedule to build the response center.

The contractor required several months to prepare its report. Then the Commission had to approve funds, and more time was required to build it. I did not want to wait that long. We had to do something soon.

With the Commission's approval, I sent a letter to all of the NRC offices announcing that we were going to have a two-hour emergency response drill. I scheduled a time well in advance, described the hypothetical emergency, and asked the office heads to designate people who would participate. Even having provided the scenario ahead of time, I was disappointed by the results of the exercise. Some offices did not even bother to send representatives to discuss how we could be better prepared. The response was symptomatic of the attitude of some senior NRC executives, who probably reasoned that a large nuclear incident was unlikely and that, in any case, all power plant operators (and some other organizations) were required to have emergency response plans approved by the NRC. They were essentially abdicating nuclear crisis response to the businesses that NRC regulated.

Months passed, and I defended the plan for the emergency response center and also the rest of a revised inspection and enforcement program before the Commission and in Congressional testimony. At the same time, we continued the usual business of conducting inspections, issuing notices of violations, and taking enforcement actions.

My professional life was in a fish bowl. Nuclear power was very controversial during the 1970s. There were frequent accusations of wrongdoing by utilities, other companies, and even the NRC. My name was occasionally on the front page of the *Washington Post*. It was not a pleasant experience. In addition, the budget was tight for fiscal year 1978, and my request for the response center had been steadily cut back. Nevertheless, the work was fulfilling. Construction finally began on a modest crisis response center. The NRC commissioners approved most of my recommendations for a revised inspection and enforcement program. However, they did not implement all of them. In May 1978,

I left the NRC after two years and two months. Less than a year later, the accident at Three Mile Island occurred, and NRC fell short in its response. The institution had not planned and prepared properly for emergencies.

The bonanza of contracts suggested by Bill Anders never materialized, but I have no regrets. The revised inspection and enforcement program and the emergency response system were steps in the right direction. The insights and expertise that Ted and I gained would pay off in unexpected ways in the not-too-distant future.

4

Liftoff! Building a Business Based on Ethics and Performance

⋯⋗ Hire outstanding people.

⋯⋗ Values are vital; capable people want
   to be part of something great.

⋯⋗ Quality work and customer satisfaction
   are essential.

S ystems Research and Applications Corporation opened for business on July 31, 1978. In order to keep costs low, we began operating in the basement of the small Volgenau family home in Reston, Virginia. Using an old desk tucked underneath the basement stairs, I shared accounting and administrative duties with Sara. Despite managing a household, raising three teenage girls, and caring for her ailing mother, Sara somehow found time to help. She kept the books and prepared the checks for employees, suppliers, and tax authorities. Most importantly, she provided moral support. The oldest of our three daughters (Lisa) would soon leave for college. Lauren and Jennifer were busily involved in school and extracurricular activities.

My ambitions were high, but straightforward: Build a technology company that would contribute to society. From the beginning, honesty and service was our underlying theme. Later, that became our official motto. I had in mind several people whom I admired personally and professionally and who lived by these principles; at the appropriate times, I asked them to join me.

William K. Brehm, my boss on the global military headquarters review, was the first. With a high-level understanding of military and government operations, he brought credibility to the company when we were trying to establish a reputation. Bill was not ready to become a regular employee but agreed to become chairman of the board of directors, which included Sara and me. These were unpaid positions.

We found our first work after I contacted two former colleagues from the Pentagon Office of Systems Analysis (the "Whiz Kids"). Charles Rossotti and several others had formed a management consulting company called American Management Systems (AMS) that focused on improving the operations of commercial and government clients. Years earlier, Charles had been my boss in the Pentagon and provided advice from time to time as I formulated plans for SRA.

I visited the AMS offices in Arlington, Virginia, which had a commanding view of Washington, DC, overlooking the Potomac River. After patiently listening to my marketing pitch, Charles said, "Starting a business is hard; it requires a lot of sacrifice. We can offer you a good position at AMS. Are you sure you want to do this?"

I thanked him for the offer, but said I was determined to try to create a successful company. Charles nodded and said, "Okay, I'll try to help. Of course you remember Paul Brands . . ."

Paul was another former Whiz Kid who had worked for me in the Pentagon. Charles explained that Paul was managing a large five-year contract with the United States Navy to help modernize its fleet of surface ships.

Charles continued: "You obviously have good computer system knowledge and, even though we're mainly a management consulting firm, computers are becoming increasingly important. We can use your skills."

Paul processed a $10,000 purchase order for SRA to work as a subcontractor on the project. It was a start and could be expanded if we did a good job. I was ecstatic. I knew we could do excellent work. I told Paul about Ted Legasey's skills and accomplishments and suggested that Ted also work on this contract. Paul agreed, so I went back to the office and called Ted. He became SRA employee number two on August 23, 1978. Over the succeeding years, Ted became my de facto deputy. A consummate problem solver and inspirational leader, Ted repeatedly helped define clear paths to success and then took a strong role in helping us follow them.

Our task on this first job was to determine how computers could be used to improve maintenance systems aboard Navy surface ships. This was Ted's kind of work. In his final Air Force assignment, he had helped test and refine new computer software on the B-1 bomber. The systems were the first of this type installed on an aircraft. They captured data about the plane's operation in flight, which enabled ground crews to identify operational problems immediately and analyze the patterns. From our perspective, it would not be difficult to show the utility of such a system on a Navy ship.

In one of those "small world" stories that weave through our lives, Ted ended up working with an AMS manager whose job was once offered to him. When Ted was at the Nuclear Regulatory Commission, a headhunter asked him to interview for a position at AMS. Ted declined, and the AMS person who ultimately took the job (Bill Purdy) supervised our work on the Navy ship project. Ted became the SRA project manager while I shifted my focus to developing additional business. Ted and Bill were a dynamic team. Both connected with employees and customers particularly well. They were warm, friendly, caring people who were always ready to roll up their sleeves to help. Perhaps because of their similarities, they clicked on this first project, which was followed by others. We developed a wonderful partnership, beneficial to both companies that continued for more than two decades. Ted and Bill deserve a lot of credit for this.

After thirty days on the project, Ted wrote a seventy-page report that his wife, Tricia, typed on a portable Sears electric typewriter at their kitchen table. The report recommended important changes in the way the Navy used computers on its ships. By the late 1970s, the military was finally starting to appreciate the enormous value of automation. Measuring ship performance data enabled crews to identify failure trends and isolate problematic equipment for reengineering. As a result, life-cycle costs of equipment were lowered. Ted's report suggested that instead of relying on mechanics to keep informal repair notes in their back pockets, standardizing all that information in a database would enable a mechanic anywhere to look up repair instructions. They would no longer have to rely on paper-based technical instructions that were often out of date. And a baseline repair and maintenance history could be used to train work crews. Computers would replace typewriters and smudgy mimeograph sheets and allow people to share information.

Today, combining systems analysis with computer technology is considered standard procedure, but at the time, most people did not realize how fast this type of professional technical service would grow.

Computers were beginning to be deployed outside of big machine rooms and were becoming more user-friendly. It was difficult for larger companies to adjust quickly to this new wave. In 1978 most of the big computer companies—IBM, Control Data, and Univac—were creating large machines and the software to go with them. Other companies used analytical techniques but did not have expertise in information technology.

Within about two years, we had (loosely speaking) two types of people—those focused on technology and others who understood business processes. We used to refer to them as "wire heads" and "mush heads." Later we stopped using the term "wire head," replacing it with the familiar expression "geek." Neither term was derogatory. SRA valued both types of people. Our strength and competitive advantage was in the ability to hire not only technology experts, but also those who understood the operations of our clients.

With this as a basis, we gradually developed a business methodology. We would become experts in the problems of our customers, perform excellent work exceeding their expectations, gain follow-on work, and leverage our qualifications to accumulate new lines of business. We would also continuously improve our business development, project execution, and administrative processes to support a growing organization. After completing the initial Navy ship contract, we analyzed Air Force maintenance systems to see if those processes might benefit the Navy more broadly.

Our third contract was facilitated by Bill Brehm. When Bill and I did a world-wide tour of military headquarters in 1975, it was clear that there were serious weaknesses in the military's ability to mobilize and deploy its forces. Before leaving the Department of Defense, Bill requested that the Joint Chiefs of Staff and the military services conduct a major mobilization exercise in order to get a clearer picture of what improvements were needed. The Army conducted an exercise in 1976. The results were so revealing that, in 1978, General David C. Jones, the new Chairman of the Joint Chiefs of Staff, decided that all of the Department of Defense (DoD) should participate in another exercise. Richard Danzig, a senior executive in the Office of the Secretary of Defense, wanted the simulation to encompass civil agencies as well as the military services. General Jones agreed. And so began the planning for exercise Nifty Nugget 78.

In 1978 the Cold War was at its zenith, and our country was seriously concerned about a major war in Europe. Prior to this time, the United States relied on its nuclear superiority to prevent conflict with the Soviet Union. But as the Soviets approached nuclear parity, the utility of the deterrent was questioned. Neither side would be likely to precipitate a nuclear war, but knowing this, the Soviets might invade Western Europe using their large conventional forces. A stronger NATO conventional war-fighting capability seemed necessary. The United States needed to be able to mobilize, deploy, and sustain its forces for major land combat in Europe, something that had not happened for more than thirty years.

Bill received a call from Danzig asking whether he would be willing to form a team to lead the design and evaluation of this "war game" to test military capabilities. By that time Bill was working at a company called Computer Network Corporation, which was a timesharing business. Bill believed that SRA, then three months old, could form the basis for the evaluation. He arranged for SRA to become a subcontractor to Comnet, which had much more mature systems for contracting with the DoD. Bill gained approval for SRA to form a team of recently retired flag officers, including Army General Walter "Dutch" Kerwin, to provide the experience necessary to observe and evaluate the exercise effectively.

The test began in a windowless, metal-lined room in the Pentagon. Known as a Sensitive Compartmented Information Facility (or simply a SCIF), it was impervious to electronic eavesdropping. More importantly, it was a command center where military leaders could engage in a simulated war game. Tables were arranged in a U-shape in the middle of the room, surrounded by displays and seats for observers. Representatives from each of the military services sat at the table, as did those from major civil agencies (such as the Departments of State, Transportation, Treasury, Commerce, and the Federal Aviation Administration). These agencies would be called upon in an actual mobilization.

The SRA team was part of this group in the Pentagon basement and spent six weeks preparing for the exercise, which then lasted another three weeks. We helped create the basic scenarios, and came up with unexpected changes to intensify the pressure. If done well, the exercise would provide an unvarnished assessment of the military's ability to make critical mobilization and deployment decisions leading to all-out war.

Four-star generals made the decisions, and others played the role of commanders of such bases as Fort Campbell and Langley Air Force Base. Military and civilian leaders also participated. They had to determine—in real time—how to adapt their strategies and resources to deploy forces and equipment as necessary.

At that time, the armed forces used an array of computers and communications called the World-Wide Military Command and Control System (WWMCCS). It was the same system that I had observed on my global headquarters evaluation assignment with Bill Brehm. WWMCCS ran what was officially known as the Joint Operations Planning System, or JOPS—a collection of data, including inventories of troops and equipment—that the military would use to plan campaigns.

All kinds of scenarios were thrown at the participants. Determine how to move a half million troops to Europe within a limited period of time. Find a way to move a heavy air division to Europe within days. Mobilize a dozen Army and Marine reserve divisions and as many Air Force squadrons and make them converge at a specific place and time to prepare for battle. Each command had a computer connected to the JOPS, which contained the sequence for deploying units. The scenario managers provided a challenge on one day, then changed it the next. A cacophony of protests erupted from participants sitting at the command center table; they could not adjust their plans quickly enough. Within a few days, commanders began to throw up their hands. As one general said, "We abandoned the computer system and went back to stubby pencils and paper."

In addition to deficiencies in the military's computerized information systems and planning processes, the Nifty Nugget exercise and our subsequent report revealed other problems: ships and ports were inadequately prepared to transport supplies to Europe; civilian agencies were not ready to respond to a national emergency; headquarters in the Pentagon were not capable of mustering equipment and manpower and had no mechanism in place to quickly call up reserves. In short, Nifty Nugget disclosed that our military was not ready to take on its most important mission.

Interestingly, computers were barely an afterthought in the planning for Nifty Nugget. A twenty-seven-page unclassified report noted that computer programs to manage complex manpower and logistics were virtually nonexistent. The reserves had virtually no computers, and those used by the services were unable to meet the demands of mobilization. This was not news to Bill Brehm and me. Nifty Nugget helped the DoD understand in very graphic terms the importance of computers in planning for war and national emergencies.

While the conclusions of the SRA Nifty Nugget report were disturbing, the secretary of defense was pleased with our work. We had helped the client define its problems, thereby achieving the first step in our growth strategy—executing our work with excellence. That put us well on our way with the second—becoming experts in our customers' work. Our next step would be to build out contracts that acquire follow-on work that provided value to our clients. And over time our Nifty Nugget work led to many initiatives to retool the nation's defense management, particularly in planning, conducting, and supporting military operations. In the wake of this exercise, SRA helped produce the master mobilization plan for all of the DoD, and we helped define a new command and control system. We also became involved in other military personnel issues, including the Selective Service System, the call-up and structure of the reserves, and reorganization of the Joint Chiefs of Staff.

The kinds of computer systems that could have solved some of the problems we observed from Nifty Nugget were some years away from development. We viewed our analysis work as a platform on which to build an information technology practice. In this way, SRA and the burgeoning world of information technology would evolve together.

Our contract with AMS continued to develop as well. AMS was pleased with the work we did on those early purchase order tasks and enlisted SRA as a subcontractor to take the next logical step for the customer: design and test a computerized maintenance information system that would be installed on more than four hundred Navy ships. Simultaneously, we developed a program management system for the Department of Energy nuclear fuel office.

An important requirement to successfully launching a business is to know key people in your potential client base who respect your work. This had been demonstrated in our early contracts and occurred again with the Defense Nuclear Agency. The director of the agency was an admiral who was familiar with my work in the Pentagon many years before. He introduced me to one of his project officers, who awarded us a small contract to study dual-capable aircraft. These were fighter bombers that could carry either conventional or nuclear weapons and were part of our deterrent force around the Soviet Empire. As mentioned earlier, one of the ways a war could have started in those days would have been a Russian invasion using conventional forces; presumably we would have responded conventionally. Another scenario was all-out nuclear war, and there were variants—a war involving tactical nuclear weapons, in which neither the Soviets nor we attacked the homeland of the others, but both parties continued to wage war in a theater. The objective of the study was to determine the best basing and arming of aircraft to produce the maximum deterrent for all scenarios.

My personal mode of operation in those days was to win the work, assign it to someone on staff, and then move on to find the next opportunity. One part of our early methodology was to hire exceptionally skilled and well-rounded people, not necessarily technicians for a particular job. Today, this might sound a bit backward because the general practice in information technology companies is to hire people to fill billets, and let many of them go when the contract is finished. However, we were building a company that had lasting value, not simply one that produced near-term revenue and profit. To form the basis of the firm, we wanted smart people who could react quickly and innovate in the face of a wide variety of problems. They had to be comfortable managing conflicting priorities, performing them all well.

Having won the dual-capable aircraft study, we needed a project leader. Stuart Rubens was a University of Michigan graduate with a master's degree in aerospace engineering. He spent four years as a junior officer in the Air Force where he worked to resolve a potential problem with the launch sequence for nuclear missiles. Stu then accepted a civilian position in the Pentagon Office of Systems Analysis. I did not know him there, but a friend of mine in that office (Bud Coon) praised him and told me that Stu had decided to leave government service. We often hired people because they were capable and held our values, even though we didn't know exactly what to do with them. This was the case with Stu, but only briefly.

I had assigned the dual-capable aircraft study to Herb Puschek, another Whiz Kid alumnus. Herb seemed to be proceeding well, and I became preoccupied with other issues. But in the middle of the study, he left to return to the Pentagon. Unfortunately, Herb had spent most of the project money. Stu now had an assignment. But with much of the work still left to be done, he also had a real challenge. That experience produced a story that became a part of SRA folklore.

Two hunters and trappers, Sam and Eddie, lived in a cabin in Alaska.

Like many hunters, they exaggerated their stories, drank too much, and irritated one another. One night in early spring, they were drinking and arguing over the paltry results of their winter's efforts. Sam was particularly critical, and Eddie responded by boasting about his hunting and trapping skills. Sam replied caustically, "You can't do any of those things. I can skin anything in ten minutes that you can catch." Eddie responded with a challenge: "Within three days, I'll bring you something that you can't skin in ten minutes."

And so the bet was on, with the winner getting all of the income from the past year. The following morning, Eddie rose early to go hunting while Sam slept in. After all, they had seen nothing in the previous three weeks, despite constant foraging and checking of their traps.

Suddenly, Sam was wakened by a commotion outside. Eddie was running as fast as he could toward the cabin. Cradled in his arm was a bear cub. Perhaps 30 yards behind him and gaining ground was an irate mother grizzly. Eddie burst through the cabin door, dropped the cub, and leaped out a small rear window hollering, as he continued his run to the woods, "Okay, I caught her, now you skin her, and do it in ten minutes!"

Stu was *our* bear skinner. The customer had the potential of becoming as irate as the mother grizzly. In the end, Stu completed the job, and our client was pleased with the results. In subsequent years, other people brought problems to Stu because he was good at solving them. Stu suggested that this story illustrates that the mark of a good leader is knowing when to get out of the way and leave people to their work. I think the story reaffirms my belief that if you hire the best people, they will be able to solve a variety of problems.

Based on the positive reviews we got on our dual-capable aircraft studies, the Defense Nuclear Agency asked us to compete on a classified request for proposal (RFP) that addressed whether advances in technology could improve conventional weapons so that they might "kill" some targets now targeted with nuclear weapons. In other words, could conventional weapons substitute for tactical nuclear weapons? We won the contract against some of the best known companies in the field: BDM, CSC, SAIC. Over a two-year period, we concluded that advances in guidance system accuracy, weapon configurations, software, and fusing could produce an entirely new generation of "smart" conventional weapons. Though we were not a manufacturer, such as Lockheed Martin and Northrop Grumman, our early studies influenced

Department of Defense decisions to begin intensive research on the conventional smart bombs and guided missiles used decades later in Iraq and Afghanistan.

In those early years, most of the company's growth and revenue came from the studies work of Stu's group. If we were to be successful in gaining more of this work and executing it well, Stu needed more help quickly. I found Sherman Greenstein, in late 1979, at my alma mater for graduate studies, UCLA. He was teaching and conducting research there and was recommended by one of my former professors. So began a relationship that would lead to interesting brainstorming sessions and later work on artificial intelligence. Everyone liked Sherman. Small in stature, perennially worried, but eternally optimistic, he often produced some of the most original and outlandish ideas in the company. He enjoyed the creativity and challenges of working for a start-up, and he believed that our focus on people was very important.

Sherman recalls one story to illustrate this. About a year after he was hired, we brought in Russell Murray II, a former Assistant Secretary of Defense for Systems Analysis (the head of the Whiz Kid office). Russ was known for raising concerns about the high cost of weapon systems. Not long after he arrived at SRA, Russ wrote a letter to the editor of *The Washington Post* critical of the weapons work of one of our clients. Before sending it, Russ showed it to Stu and me. We decided to discuss the matter with our client, General Dynamics (GD). When we did, the manager of one of our projects at GD threatened to cancel our contract if we allowed Russ to submit the letter. This was no small matter because the contract represented a significant percentage of our work. In the end, I decided that the corporate interests of SRA should not trump Russ Murray's right to free speech. I knew he was an objective expert. Russ submitted the letter, which was then published. Nothing happened to our contract with General Dynamics. But it sent a message early on that SRA valued its people and would support them, even at the risk of losing a client. This was one of the ways in which we enhanced our culture.

In the early 1980s, our nascent company was also involved in one of the most notable and constructive changes in the Defense Department during the second half of the twentieth century. Bill Brehm played a principal role in this success.

During two assignments in the Pentagon, I often dealt with officers from the four military services. Many of them were nominally assigned to the Office of the Joint Chiefs of Staff, but it was clear that most were motivated to protect the interest of their individual service, rather than to support unified action of all of the departments. Furthermore, they had little preparation for joint military duty. The problem was a relic of World War II, when there were two chains of command, one from the President through the Secretary of the Army and the Army Chief of Staff and the other through the Secretary of Navy and the Chief of Naval Operations. In 1947 the Secretary of the Air Force became a third line of authority. Creation of the Office of the Joint Chiefs of Staff (OJCS) did not improve the situation because officers from the services were loaned to the JCS, and they also had duties with their services. As a result, problems with unified action continued through the Viet Nam War and then the 1980 failed attempt to rescue U.S. Embassy staff members held hostage by the Iranian revolutionary government.

The Goldwater-Nichols Act of 1986 immensely improved the unified command structure. Now when there are wars or other military conflicts, the chain of command flows from the President, through the Secretary of Defense, directly to the military officers in charge of combatant commands, greatly streamlining management. Service secretaries and chiefs no longer command forces engaged in conflicts; they are responsible for training and equipping the forces, and they provide advice to the President and Chairman of the Joint Chiefs of Staff. Furthermore, in order to qualify for promotion to flag rank (general or admiral), officers must have served in a joint assignment such as OJCS. As a result, they have a much broader perspective and are less inclined to be parochial. These constructive changes became evident during the first invasion of Iraq (Desert Storm) in 1991, when an Army general successfully commanded forces from all of the services: Army, Navy, Air Force, and Marine Corps.

A lot of credit for the passage of the Goldwater-Nichols Act should go to General David Jones who, in the early 1980s, was Chairman of the Joint Chiefs of Staff and had the courage to overcome strong opposition from some in the services. David was ably assisted by Bill Brehm, who was chairman of the SRA Board and who had joined our company as a full-time employee. He was helped by Jerry Burcham, a retired Army colonel who had experienced Nifty Nugget as an officer in the JCS. Bill prepared a paper that was very influential among leaders in Congress and the military. It was titled "Organization of the JCS" but commonly called "The Brehm Report."

About ten years after retiring from the Air Force, David Jones joined the SRA Board, served on it for many years, and became a good friend. In 2011, David told me that of all his accomplishments in over forty years of military service, he was proudest of his contributions to Goldwater-Nichols. Since then, I have talked to many active duty and retired military officers in all of the services who regard the Goldwater-Nichols Act as very constructive.

5

Fiscal Prudence and the Search
for Leg Room and Talent

┈┈▷ Get money when it is available;
don't wait until you really need it.

┈┈▷ Frugality is more than a virtue.

┈┈▷ Information technology will always
be a growing endeavor.

┈┈▷ Your business vision must fulfill
a definite market need.

T he early years of a company's existence test its mettle. Statistics
from the Small Business Administration indicate that more than
95 percent of new companies fail within five years. Some companies cannot sell enough of their services or products; others fail to
control costs; and many are unable to raise enough capital. By the end
of our first year, we needed a bank loan, referred to as a line of credit.
After getting a contract, we had to perform the work and then wait
thirty to sixty days to be paid. In the meantime, there were many costs:
employee payroll, consultants, supplies, equipment, office space, and
so on. The loan had to be big enough to pay these costs over a ninety-
day period. Several hundred thousand dollars was a lot of money in
those days, particularly if your income and assets were limited.

I knew that bankers were discerning. So I carefully reviewed the business plan that I had prepared and then asked a friend to introduce me
to a loan officer at the Bank of Virginia. I sent the plan ahead of time
and brought in detailed charts to brief the officer. It was clear he had
reviewed the plan. I had no problem answering his questions.

Finally, he paused and said, "This is certainly a good plan. It shows
a lot of care."

I nodded hopefully.

Then he continued, "A sound plan is important, but we also need financial security. Do you have any personal assets?"

I thought for a moment. There was our home and, over many years, Sara and I had invested in three town houses in the Washington suburbs. This nest egg was intended for our three daughters' college education. The first (Lisa) would leave for college the following year. We had some stock and other savings that would support her college costs for a year or two. Sara and I had loans on this real estate, but during most of the previous years, the property had appreciated in value. I told him about that, explained that SRA already had government work and pointed out that other companies routinely borrow money using their contract invoices as collateral.

The officer replied that the bank loan committee would not approve this practice for a new company that had no credit history. It was clear that, in order to get this loan, I would have to find some other way to pay for my daughters' education. I reluctantly submitted an application using our home and the town houses as security. I had learned a business lesson. Banks do not like to lend money to people who really need it. Plan ahead and make arrangements for funding long before it is needed. The bank approved the loan, and we had the money to run SRA. Financing the company with personal assets provided one more reason to make SRA successful.

We also had to pass an audit by the Defense Contract Audit Agency to qualify for Department of Defense work. To prepare, I gathered our company accounting records, vouchers, payments, receipts, and time cards, and organized them neatly in separate piles. I had other supporting documents ready, just in case. When the auditor arrived at the global headquarters of SRA, I escorted her downstairs to our partially finished basement. She was self-confident, quirky, and given to occasional outbursts. She sat on a couch in our improvised family room, while I tried to work at the desk in my tiny office under the stairs. The audit lasted about three hours and was punctuated by the auditor's exclamations and sometimes laughter. Each time, thoughts of doom flew through my head: "If we fail this audit, the government won't pay and we won't be able to pay our bills. The bank will call in the loan, and the company will go bankrupt along with the Volgenau family."

That didn't happen. SRA passed the audit but, after that experience, one of the first tasks I delegated to an outside firm was accounting, which included dealing with government auditors.

As Nifty Nugget wound down, it was time to relinquish the space the Pentagon provided for us while we were working on the exercise. To do our American Management Systems (AMS) work, Ted and I were offered an office there with one desk and two chairs. Whoever arrived first each morning got to sit behind the desk, where there was leg room. The latecomer sat on the other side, knees knocking against the desk front. More leg room meant that we would soon need to lease office space.

I was continuously looking for work and was convinced that as long as we followed the plan, we would grow. As we picked up one contract and then another, I knew we would need more people and a place for them to work. Bill Brehm found office space in a building owned by the Association of the United States Army (AUSA) at 2425 Wilson Boulevard in Arlington, Virginia. In view of the small size of SRA (we ended the first year with six employees and $192,000 in revenue), we were not sure that we could actually qualify for a lease. So Bill arranged for his employer, Comnet, to rent space from AUSA and sublet it to SRA. Bill then leased 3,300 square feet—a warehouse, compared to the 150 square feet we had occupied at AMS and the small office in my basement. It was about twice as much room as we needed, but it reflected Bill's confidence in our firm. It was also a leap in our operating expenses.

Knowing that overhead has swamped many a new business, I relentlessly tracked how we spent our money and our hours of work. The underlying economic model of our business was that of a professional services company. Simply put, we were hired on contracts to provide a service or create a computer program, and we billed our labor and other costs to clients. Our contracts allowed us to add to each direct labor hour a factor called overhead, which accounted for indirect expenses, such as paid time off and office space. Always seeking to be competitive and profitable, I constantly preached our fundamental business challenges:

- provide a steady stream of new jobs, extensions to current contracts as well as new work;
- maximize the time spent on direct labor, and minimize adminis-

trative costs that did not produce or contribute to revenue and, therefore, came out of profit; and

- employ indirect labor strategically, using it to develop new business and maintain a good infrastructure for the company.

My attentiveness to these principles prompted many jokes over the years. For example, I was accurately accused of waiting three years to authorize an outside coffee service. Until then, we brought in jars of instant coffee. When we moved into new space at 2425 Wilson Boulevard, we thought it was better to avoid the cost of buying a copier and paying for maintenance. Instead, we negotiated access to the landlord's machine and paid five cents per page. When we did need equipment, we usually bought used machines. In those days, specialized word processors were replacing electric typewriters, and our used machines cost us a fraction of their original price.

There was a tax advantage to company cars. Our first car was a relatively modest but necessary expense. We bought it for Ted who owned a 1970 Fiat Sport Spider. It was a rust bucket. One day when Ted was driving on the Capital Beltway, his seat fell through the floor to the frame. He repaired it by bolting galvanized metal (fashioned from the slide of his son's swing set) to the floor of the Fiat. Then he reinstalled the seat. Ted was surprised when I suggested that this might be unsafe and sent him out to buy a car. He chose a white, used Volkswagen Rabbit. Eventually I bought myself a car—a used Buick that was generally reliable and, beyond the purchase price, only required an occasional oil change or tune-up.

I wanted to introduce computers into our company as soon as possible. In 1980 I bought an early version of a personal computer. It was a Radio Shack TRS-80, which cost $4,400 and became informally known as the Trash 80. I used it and a programming language called Basic for financial planning. When IBM announced its personal computer, we knew it would become a worldwide standard. We could not afford to buy personal computers for the executives, so we encouraged them to buy their own and reimbursed them for the hours used on business.

Personal computers would not be enough to turn SRA into an information technology company. Mini-computers were assuming many of the functions of mainframes, and we found a used Data General for $80,000. The owner had paid $120,000, and the mini-computer was almost as powerful as a slightly older mainframe. The power of electronic integrated circuits doubled every eighteen months with concurrent price declines. My expectations for computing, dating from the 1950s, were being realized. SRA could benefit greatly from these advances.

The challenge, then and now, was continuing to grow. We did not yet have the revenue to hire a separate sales and marketing staff; everyone was expected to pitch in. Whether working on studies with Stu or on technology problems with Ted, everyone was constantly networking, looking for new ways to sell our expertise. This habit was important even after SRA became much larger.

As time passed, professional technical services companies began to specialize into various categories of work. Consulting and systems work was evolving into a large, complex industry that is sometimes described as a value chain. At the top of the chain are firms such as McKinsey that provide consulting support to the most senior managers of commercial companies. Such service firms charge very high rates and avoid more pedestrian work, such as implementing large information technology systems. A step down in the value chain are companies such as Accenture (formerly Andersen Consulting) that develop client information systems. At the bottom are companies that merely sell the time of technical people. These so-called "body shops" generally are the least profitable and their work is less interesting and challenging.

From the beginning, we aimed at the higher end of the value chain by understanding both the business of the client and information technology. This meant that we were always looking for executives who had worked in high levels of government or military. Bill, Stu, and I were familiar with government business and knew many people in the Pentagon. Our network on the technology side was smaller.

Whenever we found someone who had customer knowledge and technical expertise and seemed to fit into our culture, we hired him as quickly as possible. Rolland Fisher was one of them. In 1969, when Lieutenant Ted Legasey was assigned to the ALS project at Wright Patterson Air Force Base, he replaced Captain Rolland Fisher, who headed to the University of Illinois to work on a PhD in operations research. He was also experienced in computer systems analysis. Rolland joined as senior associate in July 1979. As was often the case, we did not have a specific job for him, but we were confident that he could work in a variety of areas.

Many of the people with the most current knowledge of technology were university students. In the summer of 1980, Ted drove to Baltimore to meet some of them at Johns Hopkins University. He discovered Barry Landew, twenty years old and a month away from graduation. Barry was an economics major, but he was also interested in business and had written several papers on national security. It became clear to Ted that Barry was an irrepressible debater who loved to provoke and challenge. He and Ted spent the entire interview intellectually jousting. Barry challenged Ted's views and competed to declare the best solution to problems they discussed.

"I was pretty sure I had him hooked," Ted recalled. When we offered him a job, Barry was unfazed by the fact that we didn't really know what he would be doing.

Barry recalls, "I don't think Ted knew what he was looking for, but we hit it off." Ted arranged for him to meet other SRA people to get a sense of the culture and the work. "I wasn't thinking about government information technology and SRA didn't even do any IT work at the time, just policy analysis and planning. But I liked the people I met and the programs they were doing. So I said yes."

Barry spent his first several years at SRA splitting his time between IT project work for American Management Systems (AMS), associations, and as a proposal manager and writer. He became the prototype for our potential recruits—someone who could read between the lines of a request for proposal, understand what the client was looking for, and then write a response that would clearly set SRA apart as high-level thinkers who solved problems creatively.

By the end of the second fiscal year in July 1980, the permanent staff of SRA had increased to twenty. Sales topped $1 million, based on the early Department of Defense contracts and our first commercial jobs with the National Association of Truck Stop Operators and two other large associations. We also won work with the Department of Education, creating automated computer systems to evaluate student loan and grant programs.

Bill Brehm and I believed that we could do much more to help improve government information systems and the way the military planned and managed its operations. We reviewed notes from our earlier assessment of headquarters around the world and improved them with fresh details and observations from work on Nifty Nugget. Then we prepared and presented a paper to Charles Groover, Deputy Assistant Secretary of Defense in the Office of Manpower, Reserve Affairs, and

Logistics outlining the operational shortfalls the military faced, and recommending work that would lead to improvements. Charlie had worked for Bill a few years before, and they knew each other from the late 1960s as Whiz Kids under Secretary McNamara.

After reading our paper and hearing our presentation, Charlie liked our ideas and arranged for an RFP to conduct a formal study. It was known as the Mobilization, Deployment, and Sustainment Information System project. SRA was awarded the work in 1982. This put our firm at the center of what would become a groundbreaking effort by the DoD to modernize its systems for responding to large-scale conventional war. And it became the seed for our work in designing new strategic command and control systems for the next fifteen years. We had positioned SRA to fulfill a definite market need using information technology, which was growing explosively.

We celebrated the win—for a moment. Virtually overnight, we were swamped. At just the right time, Gary Nelson called me. He was leaving the federal government. Ivan Selin, one of the founders and chairman of AMS, told Gary about our company and extolled our virtues as a boutique firm with a reputation for high-quality work. That opinion was confirmed by Groover, who, as it happened, was Gary's successor in the Pentagon. Gary joined SRA and took over as project manager for the mobilization study.

Gary was an expert in both national security and government personnel, and he had extraordinarily strong quantitative and analytical skills. He was a PhD economist and a veteran policy analyst at the Institute for Defense Analyses, the Rand Corporation, and the Congressional Budget Office. He had served in two executive positions within the Carter administration. In the first, Gary oversaw the analysis of military and civilian manpower and logistics as a deputy assistant secretary of defense. In the second, he was responsible for the government civil service retirement system and for federal employee health and life insurance programs. We saw future business in both areas, and Gary had operated in the thick of it at very high levels.

Our mobilization and deployment study took place over eighteen months. First, Gary's team analyzed the existing processes for mobilizing fighting forces and resources, and deploying and sustaining them in battle. They defined the key decisions that the National Command Authority (the President, Secretary of Defense, and military commanders) had to make in the event of war and outlined the information needed to do this. Then they created a framework for those decisions. Finally, they assessed the ability of existing and planned DoD information systems to provide clear, accurate, and timely data.

After about six months, Bill Brehm helped arrange a briefing of our work to the admirals and generals in the Organization of the Joint Chiefs of Staff. Gary made the presentation, which went well. Then he and Bill stayed to listen to another briefing, this one for the Joint Chiefs and the Joint Deployment Agency. The agency was brand new; it was created after both military and civilian mobilization plans fell apart in the Nifty Nugget command post exercise. The United States and its NATO allies actually "lost the war" in that simulation. Now, the Joint Deployment Agency was charged with overseeing the integration of the armed forces deployment procedures.

One of the problems with the existing war mobilization plan was that it contained a lot of information that was outdated, presented in difficult-to-integrate forms, and had no explanation of its purpose. At the time of Nifty Nugget, the military plan called the Joint Operation Planning System (JOPS) lacked an important component—a way to actually use all the mobilization data. If commanders needed to move a certain number of troops, with tank and air support, to a location by a specific date, how would they do it? Where would they get these units? How long would it take to get them there, and what kind of support would they have? The information concerning troops, hardware, and other resources was virtually useless if it did not fit into a decision-making process supported by computers.

Listening to the briefing about this, Bill and Gary immediately concluded that a new type of system was needed—the Joint Operational Planning and Execution System (JOPES). Not only was this work important and relevant to our overall study, but SRA possessed the analytical and technical expertise to help make the old computer planning system (JOPS) into one that could actually be used. This was an opportunity to get in on the ground floor of very important work.

We offered to provide support for the task force charged with creating JOPES. Our client in the Office of Secretary of Defense (Charles Groover), agreed to modify the contract to shift SRA over to the JOPES project. We temporarily stopped work on the study because we did not have enough people to do both jobs simultaneously, and we began to think about how to design JOPES.

As Nifty Nugget had done, our JOPES work provided insights not available to other contractors. As a result, we bid and won three other multimillion-dollar JOPES contracts. We continued to help the Joint Staff with the overall development of JOPES, and provided training in crisis planning processes and systems to the military forces around the world. This work expanded over the years, growing to a staff of nearly a hundred people, who worked in our new office in St. Louis, Missouri.

At the same time, JOPES laid the foundation for a new self-sustaining business unit created by Gary Nelson. He began weaving together "loose strands" of work, including the information systems contract through Groover, and a new crisis response job for the National Communications System, which handled emergency communications for the federal government.

Capitalizing on his years of work in the field, Gary also focused on finding business analyzing military and civil service manpower problems. Gary's demeanor was persuasive. He had a deep, resonant voice. He had never been in the military but carried himself with authority. Within six months, he was responsible for six new contracts and a dozen people. By 1983, his group's work helped SRA revenue grow to nearly $4.8 million a year and almost double a year later.

The JOPES project made SRA a player in strategic command and control systems, where large long-term contracts were available. As the Pentagon began to issue contracts to solve some of the problems our work had highlighted, we began to look beyond studies. Developing information technology systems had been our goal for some time, and it would not take long for us to find the opportunities.

In building SRA, we wanted our managers to be informed about every part of the business so they could make decisions based on the interests of the entire organization. We were collaborative, not hierarchical. Because almost all of our hours during the week were devoted to billable jobs, evenings and weekends were often the only times to work on proposals and develop new ideas and strategies. Saturday mornings became a time when managers gathered in the company conference room to describe their work and be tutored in various aspects of the business. It was not only important to be entrepreneurial, but also to learn the business fundamentals.

We reviewed every project to ensure the work was going well and that costs were under control. Since I did not want outside investors in the company, cash management was important. Therefore, we checked to be sure that we were submitting our bills and getting paid on time. We drew countless schematics and flowcharts that spelled out various business processes. The diagrams grew rapidly more complex.

Gary Nelson recalls the "spreadsheet Saturdays" as being excruciating. "There were eight or nine of us in a room and all of these spreadsheets; we would sit there for hours going over every number. I had come out of government, where I had a thousand people, and I didn't work like that. I remember walking down the hall to escape and doing a primal scream."

As the company got bigger, these meetings were shortened and focused primarily on big issues. Nevertheless, they produced several important results. We learned the value of allocating and tracking the time of our people. Charts showed the percentage of time that each person worked on a contract. In some cases, employees worked more than one job. Our objective was to ensure that everyone was making adequate progress. Our effort also helped make sure that employees who had completed a job were not sitting "on the bench" and thereby costing overhead while producing no revenue.

When Ted assumed the responsibility of poring over these spreadsheets, the rest of the management team was grateful. And they gained a new appreciation for the many hours he spent finding work for employees after a contract ended, to avert having to let them go. We did not believe in lifetime employment for our people; the company could not afford it, but we hated the personal trauma of laying off someone. Moreover, it was expensive to lose trained people. I doubt that other government consulting firms devoted such effort to taking care of their people.

Another thing we learned was that although we were winning contracts at a steady pace, the effort was exhausting and, ironically, limited our growth. A business having a maximum contract size of about $300,000 over an eighteen-month duration will not grow rapidly. We also recognized that our focus was on studies rather than the implementation of information systems, where the contracts were much larger and would make us more technically capable. Bill Brehm issued a challenge—to become a company of $100 million within ten years, that is by 1992. That, and our internal analyses, prompted us to raise our sights.

As we planned the company's fourth year during a spring retreat at the Wayside Inn in West Virginia, we decided that Ted Legasey, Gary

Nelson, and Stu Rubens would focus on "home run swings"—multi-year contracts that would each yield revenue of at least $1 million per year. There were about six opportunities. One of them was destined to become our first home run. The factors went all the way back to the days when Bill and I did our worldwide military headquarters review. The computers that I saw being used to do rudimentary calculations were part of the system that was supposed to contain all the data that military leaders needed to quickly and efficiently deploy resources and control them in emergency situations.

Gary learned that the Army was ready to issue an RFP for a contract called AWIS that would pull all of this together—data, execution plans, and command and control centers—into a new computer system. It would be a modernized version of the World Wide Military Command and Control System (WWMCCS). The Army wanted a contractor to design a new database system that would enable the five military services (Army, Navy, Marine Corps, Air Force, and Coast Guard) to share information, communicate, and make decisions.

I was initially skeptical, knowing that such projects can produce mountains of paperwork and no concrete results. I wanted SRA to do work that would benefit our clients and society at large. Ultimately, at the insistence of Gary and Ted, we bid for the contract. We described our deep understanding of military command and control and crisis management challenges. We emphasized our earlier JOPES work. Our competitors were a GTE Corporation team involving an incumbent (Xebec) and Computer Sciences Corporation (CSC).

Our proposal was a major corporate effort. The earlier team headed by Bill and Gary was now aided by Ted, Barry Landew, and Jon Hertzog, whom we had hired from CSC a year earlier. Jon was a Stanford-educated systems architect who was a strategic hire, brought on to help build our presence in information system design and implementation. They put personal lives on hold to create an outstanding proposal. Both Ted and Gary interrupted their vacations to fly back to Washington to give the oral presentation. After we submitted our final bid, the selection process took only three hours.

Informally, we were later told that the Army thought that SRA had knocked the ball out of the park with Ted's oral explanation. The technical approach was based on work we had done for AMS, designing Navy ship maintenance systems. The $7.6 million AWIS contract was awarded to SRA on September 19, 1983. The previous year the company had earned just $4.8 million in revenue. In that instant, the backlog of SRA work went from less than $2 million to nearly $10 million. SRA had its first flywheel contract.

In addition to giving us a victory over several large incumbent contractors, AWIS profoundly changed the course of our company; it signaled our first big leap from front-end analyses work to formal system requirements analysis and design. Because of this project, we gained people who strengthened and deepened the company's capabilities and expertise.

We had kept in touch with Emerson Thompson from the ALS project of the mid-1970s, asking him whether he was ready to work at our new company. It wasn't until Ted described the AWIS project that Em was finally tempted. He accepted the job of technical lead of the AWIS Project and joined SRA in 1983.

Emerson had the reputation for being a magician with computers, but when he first came to SRA and looked at the proposal we had written that won the contract, he was stunned.

"For two or three days, I felt like I'd made the biggest mistake of my life," Em recalls. "What was promised and committed to in that proposal was so far beyond what SRA could do. I realized why they had worked so hard to convince me to come on board."

We named Joe Newman, a smart, gruff retired Army colonel, as overall project manager. Prior to retirement, he headed the Army Command Center in the Pentagon. He understood the joint military command structure and had an appreciation for the entire process. Because he was an expert in the subject area, he was the perfect interface with the military.

The team eventually grew to about fifty people and included a broad range of domain expertise (customer business) and technical knowledge. Linda Skelton had these multifaceted capabilities and eventually led the team. At the same time, we hired Bill Crennan to help pursue similar Air Force work. He had retired from the Air Force and was an expert in aircraft data systems.

At its peak, the AWIS contract was about 25 percent of the work at SRA. Moreover, this was a predictable wedge of business that would enable us to look ahead. Over the next five and a half years, our revenue from this first systems architecture work was $30 million.

More importantly, AWIS and related contracts created the opportunity for SRA to become a recognized technology company in the field of strategic command and control systems. We were still making most of our profit from analytical studies, but we were also beginning to go after bigger federal contracts with new customers, and getting more of the technology work I wanted SRA to do. We met executives from many other companies, and were able to glean lessons from the practices of the major prime contractors.

Unprecedented events were about to lead SRA into a new arena of planning that would bring new talent to the company and expand our horizons. Military spending throughout the Cold War was driven by the fear of nuclear annihilation. If the Communist Block were to unleash its atomic weapons, how would our country respond?

6

Planning for Emergencies

····⫶   Plan ahead; influence destiny.

····⫶   If you want to be successful,
expect long hours of very hard work.

A t 4 a.m. on March 28, 1979, a major water pump failed at Three Mile Island nuclear power Plant 2 near Harrisburg, Pennsylvania, and the reactor core overheated. The power plant had cost well over $1 billion and had been in operation only about three months. Now, television newscasts and newspaper front pages carried ominous images of steam rising from the plant cooling towers. The steam was actually harmless and was emitted routinely every day as part of the process of electrical power generations, even on on-nuclear plants. But to the typical TV viewer, it appeared ominous; perhaps containing deadly radioactive elements. While scientists and engineers scrambled to prevent the nightmare of a nuclear meltdown and officials tried to calm public fears, more than a hundred thousand people clogged the roads radiating away from the power plant. A stunned nation watched for five days while officials sought to assess the damage of an event that once seemed unimaginable.

A presidential commission later concluded that the accident was caused by mechanical malfunctions in the plant and made much worse by human errors in responding to equipment failures. The operators, because of poor training, did not recognize what was happening. The result was a partial melting of the core. Some radioactivity was released into the atmosphere, but there were apparently no immediate or long-term injuries.

In my view, Three-Mile Island was an example of some relatively minor design shortcomings, but mainly poor management. Senior executives in the utility did not devote enough attention to nuclear safety. Lackadaisical is too strong a word. Overconfidence is a better description.

It had been barely a year since I finished working for the Nuclear Regulatory Commission as Director of Inspection and Enforcement. Had I still been there, I likely would have been at the Three Mile Island plant, leading the emergency response team. Instead, I watched events unfold from a new perspective—that of an executive of a company that specialized in evaluating government response to crises. It was clear that the ability of civil agencies to coordinate and communicate in such a situation was very limited and that the NRC had not made significant progress implementing changes I had recommended more than a year before.

Our Nifty Nugget report strongly urged the creation of a new federal agency that would organize and integrate the efforts of civil government agencies to support the Department of Defense in an emerging military crisis. It also identified the need for coordinating the entire federal government during all types of emergencies. On April 1, 1979, several days after the accident, President Jimmy Carter signed an executive order launching the new Federal Emergency Management Agency (FEMA). It was the first federal agency to serve as the nation's crisis manager, coordinating all civil agencies and military response to disasters and war.

On the day that FEMA was created, Bill Brehm had an appointment with the agency's new director, John Macy, who was a former colleague in the Army Secretariat. One of the agency's first tasks was to prepare a government-wide federal radiological emergency response plan, which was exactly what I had been trying to accomplish at the Nuclear Regulatory Commission. The plan would coordinate the activities of eleven federal agencies in preparing for and mitigating the consequences of a nuclear power plant accident. It was later expanded to cover other types of incidents, such as transportation accidents involving nuclear material.

FEMA issued a request for a proposal to create this plan. Ted and I had been steeped in these very issues. We knew what FEMA needed, and working with Bill Brehm, we won the contract that helped define the new agency. We asked Stu Rubens to run the project. During his time at the Pentagon, Stu served two tours in Geneva, Switzerland, negotiating with the Russians. He was familiar with the concept of "strained relations." But when Stu started working on the FEMA project, he was shocked to find that the animosity between federal agencies dwarfed what he had witnessed between the world's superpowers, United States and Russia. Nevertheless, he and his team got everyone working together to produce a plan, which was eventually published in the Federal Register.

SRA won another FEMA contract. It was not large; valued at less than $30,000, and was essentially a civil version of the military's Nifty Nugget exercise. But it opened the door for one of our newest team members to begin building a business at FEMA that helped SRA along the information technology path. We won the contract for the Rex 80 Bravo Exercise in 1980, just a few weeks after Ed McGushin joined the company.

I almost decided not to hire Ed. At the time, we were looking for engineers and analysts with strong, quantitative skills. Ed's degree was in history. His references were good, and he had been a speech writer for the Secretary of the Army so I felt that, at least, he could help improve our proposal and report writing capabilities.

I had greatly underestimated Ed during his initial interview. Although he had been a paratrooper and Green Beret with two silver stars earned in combat, he had no experience in business or computers systems. If he had chosen a different line of work, he would have been a great Irish bartender: full of stories and always ready with a joke. Ed proved to be a charismatic leader who was loved by his employees and not intimidated by technology.

For several years Ed performed well but was not on the list of key people marked for rapid promotion. He was a good manager but had not demonstrated skill in finding new business. One day the leader of a key team decided to leave the company. Ed worked on that team. He came to my office and said, "I can do that job." By then, Ed and I had developed a good rapport so I replied: "Ed, be reasonable. You're like a third-string quarterback. I think we need to draft a new leader."

Ed was persistent, and quickly got down to business. He described the project, pointed out issues to be addressed, and outlined what he planned to do if chosen to lead the team. I thought about it for a few days, discussed his capabilities with Ted and other members of the management group, and then decided to make him acting head of the team. It was a fortuitous decision. Ed's likability and attentiveness helped him build relationships with clients. Over time, his team created one of our largest and most successful groups during the 1980s, merging technology and mission to make SRA indispensable to his customers.

Personal computers at the time were new to the market. I showed our executives the TRS-80 that I used to manage company activities and encouraged them to use TRS-80s in their projects. The first time SRA produced its evaluation of the Rex 80 Bravo exercise, Ed did it the conventional way—taking notes and writing up a report evaluating civil agency performance in the exercise. When SRA won the contract to do the next version of the exercise two years later, Ed brought a TRS-80 (which we still jokingly called the Trash-80) into FEMA. Jon Hertzog, a member of his team, created a software program that made Ed a hero in the eyes of our client. Ed used it to track all of the assignments the FEMA director made to his staff during exercise planning meetings. At the end of each day, Ed delivered a report that he generated on the computer, summarized the exercise results, and listed actions to be performed. After a few days, that report became a vital management tool for FEMA. When the two-week exercise ended, so did the director's daily reports. Within a few days SRA was given a $10,000 purchase order, followed by a sole source contract for $90,000 to develop our first custom software application.

As the months passed, Ed's team took a lot of risks under early FEMA contracts, creating operations center software and using personal computers in a business setting before conventional wisdom acknowledged that this could be done. In fact, FEMA had nothing else available. The team's creation of a personal computer system for FEMA became a significant leverage point for our company. The effort engaged some of the most talented staff members, among them Bill Brehm, Barry Landew, Andy Cohen, Kemp Prugh, David Oppenheimer, Richard Shullaw, Rolland Fisher, Jon Hertzog, and others. Through their efforts, an important client had helped define SRA as an information technology company.

Our exercise work for FEMA was a logical extension of our earlier efforts on Nifty Nugget, and other opportunities begin to arise. In early

1981, two retired Army officers, Jeff Tuten and John Claybrook, offered to join SRA and help us bid on an exercise contract for the Army. The incumbent at the time was BDM, a technical services firm based in Tysons Corner, Virginia, which was far older and larger than SRA. But with our experience and success, we believed there was a good chance of unseating them. We hired Jeff and John as employees 44 and 45. We bid on that contract and won. The Army became our largest client at the time; and since then, SRA has remained its primary exercise contractor.

Over time, our FEMA exercise practice shifted into highly classified or "black world." Few people, even within that agency, knew such work existed. FEMA was responsible for developing plans and systems to ensure continuity of government in event of war or emergency. If the U.S. Capitol were attacked, what would the evacuation plan be? If key officials were missing or dead, who would be next in succession? In 1983, FEMA paid for the construction of a Sensitive Compartmented Information Facility (SCIF) where we could perform work classified above Top Secret. To do this, we moved all of our federal government support staff to an office at 1501 Wilson Boulevard in Arlington.

At the time, we were still the primary tenant in the building owned by the Association of the United States Army (AUSA). This situation worried both our landlord and us. The landlord was concerned about having so many of its eggs in one basket; and we wanted room to grow. We began to look for another location. Our search revealed that the Charles E. Smith Corporation was contemplating the construction of a fourteen-story office building, with an impressive glass exterior, near the Arlington County Courthouse, and just a few blocks from the AUSA building. Smith needed a lead tenant in order to get construction financing.

There was no doubt that the new building would be a prime location, with its proximity to the Pentagon; but could we afford it? We arranged for the senior SRA executives to go to the roof of the highest structure in that area, which at the time was the Arlington Courthouse. The panoramic view of the Potomac River and the nation's capital left no doubt in our minds. The gamble was as beautiful as it was bold. While construction was still going on, we leased the top three floors of the stunning new green-glass building, known officially as Arlington Plaza. We moved from the AUSA building to Arlington Plaza in 1985. It was our first custom-built office.

Sara and I had purchased an expensive new home in McLean, which was closer to our headquarters. I worried about SRA being able to afford the new building, and our family, the new home. It was probably not a coincidence that I contracted diverticulitis and spent ten days in the hospital while recuperating.

Fortunately, SRA continued to grow and prosper. We opened small satellite offices in Boston, San Diego, San Antonio, and Heidelberg, Germany, to better fulfill contract work for our clients in those locations. To SRA employees working elsewhere, Arlington Plaza unofficially became known as the "Emerald Palace." The contrast was particularly notable to the FEMA team that remained in old, somewhat seedy, offices at 1501 Wilson Boulevard. They reveled in the underdog status of that space and developed a unique subculture.

They worked long hours for months at a time, and their efforts were rewarded with even more tasks. To ease the tension of late nights and long hours, FEMA project team members constantly played practical jokes on each other. Once, they wrapped everything in someone's office in recycled paper, down to individual pencils in the pencil jar. Another time, they removed everything from a colleague's office, including the ceiling tiles. Later, they pulled the reverse of that prank, filling another person's office with empty cardboard boxes, floor to ceiling. In revenge for another caper, they filled a perpetrator's Volkswagen Rabbit with recycled paper. Then they put a "For Sale" ad in the *Washington Post*, offering the Rabbit for $250; it was probably worth $10,000. The unwitting owner of the car got 157 direct calls and 35 messages in response.

With so many engineers on the FEMA project team, the hijinks were hardly limited to clandestine sabotage. New technologies were added to the fray after someone discovered that a rubber band wrapped around a write-protect ring (a gizmo that came with 9-track tape drives) could be propelled at an unsuspecting target with appreciable velocity. After that, rubber band firefights periodically broke out in the hallways of 1501.

One day, as he walked through the office, Ed McGushin discovered about twenty staff members crouched behind the reception desk. Enemy forces were hiding everywhere, they explained; they were simply defending their territory. "Very mature," he muttered before passing, unscathed. A client who witnessed this kind of behavior might conclude that the inmates were taking over the asylum. But Ed enjoyed a good laugh as much as the next person and viewed all of this as a perfectly reasonable response to the demands of work. Ed and his hard working team taught all of us that letting off a little steam can produce better results.

"We were an island, geographically just a couple of blocks down the street, but spiritually a million miles from the Emerald Palace," Rolland Fisher once recalled. "We could afford to be renegades, understanding that the FEMA work served as a cash cow for the company."

To us a cash cow did not produce outrageous profits, but rather steady, reliable work.

Profit margins from our FEMA engagements were not substantially higher than any other government contract, but the volume of work was consistent year after year. This allowed us to hire more people and build technological capabilities in other management areas, including training, personnel, security, logistics, and finance. They began to develop a suite of software that automated checklists, journals, notification systems, and similar procedures.

All of this technical innovation was labor intensive; requiring painstaking coding that often involved long hours, which we called "all-nighters." FEMA teams would sometimes finish between 10 p.m. and midnight, giving them just enough time to assemble a program for a demonstration the next day. After one of these events, Rolland Fisher extemporaneously and brilliantly laid out to a client a plan that his team had developed for $15 million in future work. Then he started nodding off while the client asked questions.

Within a few years, SRA became the dominant provider of professional services for FEMA and other federal participants in the Continuity of Government (COG) program. But the constant renovation activity at the Wilson Boulevard offices never managed to bring comfort or beauty to the working environment.

One day, a visiting government client walked through the office, took note of its appearance, and said, "Well, at least, here's one contractor who's not spending a lot on fancy offices. This place is a dump!" Eventually, we knew this would have to change. But our frugality paid off by illustrating that SRA invested in the work, not decorative trappings. Fancy offices may be fine for lawyers, but they do not impress government clients.

We adapted many of the Cold War emergency response capabilities to planning responses for national disasters of all types, and we continued to do work in the nuclear arena after the Three Mile Island accident. In 1983, Stu's team designed, developed, and evaluated the nation's first full-scale radiological emergency exercise. All eleven federal agencies responded to a simulated nuclear power plant accident in Port St. Lucie, Florida. The exercise was a great success and helped us earn a reputation for doing difficult projects well.

Within a few years, our firm had become the command post-exercise contractor of choice for the Office of the Secretary of Defense, the Joint Chiefs of Staff, the Army, and FEMA. We conducted a wide range of exercises simulating worldwide nuclear war, major conventional conflict in Europe, and regional contingencies in the Middle East and Asia. This work proved valuable during the first Iraq War because many of the logistical issues encountered in preparing for that conflict had been addressed in earlier exercises we oversaw. And all of these contracts drew more national security experts to SRA and helped us earn a reputation for excellence within that community.

Ultimately, many of the programs that contributed to the end of the Cold War were themselves victims of its demise. What was left of continuity of government work dried up after the Berlin Wall fell in 1989.

The Exxon Valdez oil spill prompted Ed McGushin to suggest that other organizations, as well as the federal government, need command and control processes—high-risk industries such as utilities, for example. Ed created the Center for Response Ability (CORA). We marketed that work to about three hundred chief executive officers (CEOs) of large companies. Over a half-day meeting, senior corporate staffers listened to advice from experts in FEMA, EPA, DoD, and DoE concerning disasters. While the idea for such a program was original, it never gained traction and we shut it down. Shortly afterward, Ed retired. In 2010, we were shocked and saddened to learn that Ed had died. He had a fine career in the Army as a combat paratrooper, and afterward at SRA, where he and his wife, Sandy, made many contributions. They showed us that corporate life is about more than financial success. Human relationships are what we remember.

After more than thirty years, SRA remains at the forefront of national security exercise and emergency planning, which continues today under leaders like Tom Hutton. The size and content of this work changed significantly after the dissolution of the Soviet Union. In 1998, for example, we helped plan and evaluate a joint United States–Russian

theater missile defense exercise and hosted a related planning conference. Seeing Russian military officers in SRA buildings was a clear indicator of how much our company and geopolitics have changed with the
times. Still, our thoughts often return to Ed McGushin and his merry
team of nuclear holocaust survival planners. They did their part to help
end the Cold War.

7

Competing for Weapons Work

···⟩   Moving to a new offering or market can be risky.

···⟩   Values are vital; capable people want
       to be part of something great.

···⟩   A management team without focus invites chaos.

B
y our fifth year, revenue had risen to $4.8 million, from $200,000 at the end of our first year in 1979. Our success was fueled by the "whatever it takes" attitude of SRA employees. They often toiled late into the evening and through weekends to complete jobs, find opportunities for new contracts, and write winning proposals. The story could have been dramatically different if we had not put significant effort into relationships with other firms, particularly in those early years.

American Management Systems (AMS) provided good mentoring, free office space, and opportunities to work on some of its projects. AMS gave SRA the kind of support that we would later offer to other hardworking, promising start-ups. The corporate relationship between SRA and AMS was based on mutual respect and trust; together we demonstrated that joint capabilities can be formidable. We learned, however, that even with our best efforts, success can also be elusive. Nevertheless, several particularly intriguing opportunities arose from our relationships with people in other firms who respected our work. Although we did not always achieve the goals we had set, we were ultimately rewarded in ways that were far more valuable.

Two prospects, in particular, came as a result of President Reagan's 1981 decision to expand the size and capabilities of the armed forces.

Two years later, the president announced his Strategic Defense Initiative. That program was later dubbed "Star Wars," after the movie series. It called for the development of an anti-ballistic missile system shield to thwart a potential Soviet attack on North America and other measures for new weapon technologies. The Reagan plan included development of intercontinental ballistic missiles, which could be mounted on trucks and moved around the country, as needed, to avoid detection and attack by Soviet forces.

In 1983 Ted's counterpart at AMS, Bill Purdy, received a call from a sailing buddy. Jim Tomlin was the technical director for GTE, the prime contractor on a program to develop an intercontinental ballistic missile (ICBM) called the missile experimental (MX). Jim needed help developing the logistics and maintenance elements of its command and control system and had worked with Bill Purdy before. "Can you help us?" Jim asked. Purdy said, "Sure, as long as we have SRA on our team." Then Purdy picked up the phone and called Ted.

This was a good opportunity to build our credentials on military hardware. Working with AMS, we began to develop the technical requirements for the MX Command, Control, and Communications system. Specifically, our job was to help define the data needed to create computer programs that would enable MX operators to control the system. Later we provided support to the engineers who actually designed it.

Our effort was led by Ted Legasey and Barry Landew and a cadre of SRA analysts and engineers, including Rolland Fisher and Jon Hertzog, who made weekly trips to Westborough, Massachusetts (near Boston), where GTE was working on the MX. In an era long before long-distance commuting was commonplace, nearby Framingham's austere but quaint Koala Inn became a temporary office. As the work became more intensive, SRA and AMS opened a joint office in Westborough.

Around the same time, a former colleague of Stu Rubens from the Pentagon Whiz Kids days said that his company, General Dynamics (GD), had won a contract to work on a small ICBM, known as the Midgetman. Would Stu be willing to come out to San Diego and look at their plan? This job involved framing the general design of the system: its characteristics, method of operation, and defense. As a result of that conversation, SRA won a $1 million contract to help General Dynamics define the proposed missile system. Although this was a small job, we hoped it would lead to a larger piece of a subsequent $100 million Air Force contract to actually design part of the system.

For the first year or so of our work, the SRA people on the General Dynamics contract in San Diego were Stu, Ted, and Sherman. One of our GD bosses was a personable, African American slightly over six feet tall. About nine months into the contract, Ted, Stu, and Sherman gave an important briefing on logistics for the Midgetman. Most of the GD senior project team members were there, along with our boss. The briefing went well, and Ted asked if there were any questions. Our boss, the tall African American, asked a question: "Does SRA discriminate in its hiring?" Ted, Stu, and Sherman were all surprised. Why would anyone get the impression we discriminated in our hiring? Ted replied directly: "We don't discriminate against anyone because of their race, religion, gender, or personal preferences." Our GD boss then said, with a big smile, "No, but do you guys discriminate against tall people? I haven't seen a single SRA employee above five and a half feet." Everyone laughed.

Eventually we rented a house in San Diego and opened an office, where six to ten SRA people lived and worked. But it turned out to be a short stay. General Dynamics was competing with several of the other large defense contractors for the initial design of the Midgetman. Unfortunately, they lost and our San Diego work ended.

Nevertheless, we still had good relationships with the GTE people in Massachusetts from our work on the MX. We knew that the government would soon issue a RFP to define the concept for a small ICBM launch system. We had reason to be optimistic about winning a contract on this next phase. After all, GTE had done the Phase 1 work, and the Air Force had decided that they would award three contracts for the concept phase. The winners would subsequently compete for the full-scale development contract of the Small ICBM launch control system.

We took nothing for granted. We mounted a high-priority effort, with our best and most seasoned proposal writers, committing them full time to the work. Our team included Ted Legasey, Barry Landew, Sherman Greenstein, Ron Sherwin, and from AMS, a retired Navy admiral, Woody Rixey. Together, they represented more than a hundred years of experience in military and government contracting.

The GTE technical lead for the proposal was Jeff ("JR") Rydant, a twenty-six-year-old MIT graduate with a brilliant mind and a will to match it. He was hired at GTE right out of graduate school after a friend told him that the company had just gained a big contract and needed to bring in one hundred people in a month. With resume in hand, JR went to GTE and was hired on the spot. When he started work the next day, a supervisor directed him to a small cubicle. He said he would get back to him with an assignment. After about a week of doing nothing, JR started looking for work. He found a computer modeling project on nuclear weapons and inserted himself into the team. A day or two later, the supervisor told JR that he had an assignment.

"It was really dull," Jeff Rydant recalls. "So I objected." The supervisor told him, "Hey, I'm your boss and this is your assignment." JR replied, "I no longer accept your authority over me to make assignments." The stunned supervisor took the matter to his boss, who looked at what JR had been doing and said, "Don't worry about it, Rydant will work for me."

When JR was appointed technical manager of the small missile launch control system proposal, he had been at GTE less than two years, but the combination of JR and Barry Landew alone sparked epic brainstorming sessions. They and the rest of the GTE/SRA team devoted heroic effort to the fifty-page proposal which cost $500,000 to develop and write.

So confident were we that a contract would be forthcoming that we began working, at our cost, the day after we submitted the proposal. Three months later, we were told that a GTE executive should stand by to receive a call from a Massachusetts congressman. Rumors were positive. Everyone felt that the Air Force could not afford to lose the participation of the very engineers who knew the most about the system. We readied the champagne and eagerly awaited the verdict.

At 5 p.m., the call arrived. GTE had lost! We were stunned. There was silence in the hallways. Our team stopped work. Suddenly, we were relegated to spectator status as the three winners aggressively moved forward, with an eye on a big prize—full-scale development of the Small ICBM launch system.

A few months earlier, in the heat of the proposal process, our Red Team (created to evaluate and provide feedback) had warned that we had an Achilles' heel. GTE was known for its world-class communications engineering capabilities, but its software development team reportedly had experienced substantial cost growth and delays in the MX launch control project. We were powerless to change that weakness.

Another detail might have been relevant. Our proposal was built on the idea of categorizing the universe of launch control options into fifty-three mutually exclusive and collectively exhaustive concepts. In retrospect, Barry says, "It was absolutely accurate and precise, but it missed the KISS principle: Keep It Simple, Stupid." We were victims of over-sophistication and the earlier poor performance of GTE.

Just as we were putting this painful loss behind us, we got a call from GTE. Even though they lost the Small ICBM launch concept development contract, they had petitioned the Air Force and received permission to compete for full-scale development of the Small ICBM Weapon Control System. We knew that our chances were not good. Our three competitors had been working on the program intensively for six months. Moreover, we suspected that the reasons GTE had lost the competition had been neither forgotten nor forgiven. We decided to stay on the sidelines and not repeat the painful lesson from which we were still recovering.

But then SRA and AMS received a call from the GTE proposal manager, a sometimes cantankerous, outspoken, but insightful veteran named Lew Hadelman. He had masterminded the GTE capture of a big command and control program called WIS several years earlier and had high regard for our work. He was confident that he could overcome the perceived software development weakness of GTE by using a different group to perform that function. We reluctantly agreed and resumed our weekly trips to Boston to work on the proposal.

Several months later the winner was announced. The award went to Boeing. We had lost again. There was no ambiguity in this second defeat; the fate of GTE was sealed. Many of its most talented engineers and analysts sought employment elsewhere. The Small ICBM program was canceled about a year after the contracts were awarded. No launch control system was developed.

Despite the stinging defeat, our efforts ultimately were rewarded in an unexpected way. Some very talented people from GTE were attracted to SRA because of our values and culture. We began to realize that capable people want to be part of something great. The first GTE person to contact us was Jeff Rydant. In SRA, he saw many of the qualities that were lacking at GTE—a hard-charging leadership team, tolerance for dissenting views, a habit of working together, and opportunities for professional growth. In January 1986, he left that company and joined our corporate development group. He was SRA employee number 186.

When Lew Hadelman came to see me, I was already familiar with his background as an electrical engineer from the University of Pennsylvania and an MBA from Northeastern University. He had worked for twenty-seven years at GTE on the Minuteman, MX, and other ICBM projects. At fifty, Lew was still young, but eligible for early retirement from GTE. I said to him, "One of the things I'm concerned about is that you have been a manager for many years. Can you still roll up your sleeves and do engineering work?" Lew laughed and assured me that he understood that SRA was a place where everyone had to be a contributor. This was an important part of our culture.

Lew fit in well. We asked him to temporarily remain in Westborough to manage the SRA/AMS offices there and in San Bernardino, California. Lew was joined by Mike Fox, a twenty-five-year-old GTE marketer. At SRA, Mike went on to become senior vice president and director of marketing and sales. Soon after, Lew managed our capture of another large and important JOPES contract, which led to the creation of a new group within SRA and a new role for JR. Lew also recruited Gene Frank to manage an important task on the next big JOPES contract. Gene had worked for Lew at GTE, and he eventually became vice president and director of our western operations.

In one fell swoop, we had hired four of the best in the industry. Each of them went on to play a pivotal role in transforming us from a studies firm to an information technology company. Had GTE and SRA won the Small ICBM contract, it is doubtful that any of those future SRA leaders would have left GTE.

Our experiences on the missile projects reinforced my belief that partnerships provide not just contracting opportunities, but also knowledge about markets. Another such occasion came to us through a friend, James Kalergis, who was a retired Army lieutenant general, introduced to me by Bill Brehm. He was chairman of an American construction firm (Vinnell Corporation) that had won a big contract with the Kingdom of Saudi Arabia to modernize the Saudi Arabian National Guard (SANG). The mission of SANG was to protect the Royal Family. However, it had no automated information systems to manage its people and equipment.

Jim Kalergis introduced us to the Saudis and, with their approval, Vinnell hired SRA to assess ways of using computers and communications to improve the SANG. Ted recruited AMS as a subcontractor and led the team to Saudi Arabia at least six times to define and perform the work. Vinnell's domestic base of operations was in Baltimore, but the vast majority of its team was in Riyadh, Saudi Arabia. When the SRA team returned from its fact-finding visits, Barry started us off by building a computerized inventory tracking system. The Vinnell and SANG people liked it and summoned SRA back to Riyadh to discuss further refinements. SRA and AMS performed most of the requirements analysis and general design for an entire system that would manage the SANG inventory, track supplies, and plan logistic operations.

It was a gamble for us to divert talent from other work for such a faraway project; we knew little about the Saudi government and their contracting. We did not make a significant profit, but this was another opportunity to move into technical work. We evolved a strategy of analyzing client information needs and developing requirements for computerized systems. If that phase went well, we intended to develop designs, create prototypes, and build a complete system. The job in Saudi Arabia was the closest we had gotten to actually building a full scale system.

We knew it would be challenging to win this work but did not realize how many unexpected problems would arise. One evening, at a dinner in Riyadh, Ted encountered a guest who suggested that "the American companies should leave this work alone." As we later learned, the work was coveted by a number of Saudi contractors, including Adnan Koshoggi, a notorious Saudi businessman.

However Saudi competitors did not shut down our efforts to win this business. We prepared a proposal to the Saudi Arabian National Guard in which SRA and AMS could create the system they needed. Ted went to Saudi Arabia and made the final presentation. Vinnell and Saudi leaders agreed to hire SRA on a fixed-price contract to build and deploy the system. Ted returned to Washington with the news. Bill Brehm and I listened carefully as Ted described the work that I had craved for years.

To the astonishment of all who had worked so hard to win over the customer, Bill said, "We shouldn't do it." The stunned team protested: "Why not?"

"Because we can't do that work. It is too risky to deliver a complete system for the first time, with little sense of what the obstacles might be in such an unfamiliar environment. Furthermore, it has a significant opportunity cost." Bill was weighing the SANG job against other, more certain, contracts within our sphere of business.

Barry's initial efforts had given us the credibility to secure the work. However, even his considerable oratorical efforts failed to change the decision. But Bill Brehm was right: a management team without focus invites chaos.

Barry was disappointed that SRA would turn down a large, meaningful development contract that Ted had worked hard to secure and that the customer was ready to award to us. But Barry did acknowledge, "Back in those days we were enthusiastic and had more confidence than capability. We weren't bothered by that challenge."

During the early 1980s, we worked hard to find paths of success in a variety of markets. We fearlessly accepted almost any job. It did not matter whether the customer was government or business, domestic or international. The type of work was immaterial, as long as it involved either systems analysis or the application of computers and communications to business problems. Later we learned that such lack of focus can be risky. In fact, our failure to get weapons development work was not all bad because we gained people, capabilities, and experience that were to serve us well as we began to specialize in what would eventually be called information technology.

8

Growing Culturally and Administratively

⋯⇢ Values are vital; capable people want
to be part of something great.

⋯⇢ Get money when it is available;
don't wait until you really need it.

E
ven in 1979 it was clear that SRA would be more than a handful
of people. Business achievement was always on our minds, but
I wanted the company to stand for something more. We had to
be ethical and serve society. We discussed this subject in several meetings. Everyone agreed, but there was no obvious consensus on how to
articulate the idealism. Finally, I decided on *Honesty* and *Service*, and
we began to use the terms regularly. Honesty implies complying with
the letter and spirit of laws and regulations, not by lying or cheating,
and keeping your word. Service has three components: quality work
and customer satisfaction, taking care of one another, and serving society. These ideals have survived and inspired our professionals for more
than thirty-five years.

Our professional appearance was not polished; creating a corporate
image was low on our early priority list. Our first business cards were
printed on simple cream-colored stock, featuring in small, neat type-
face the employee name and title, and the company name and address
(the Volgenau home in Reston). Our business and home phone numbers were the same. It was primitive, and I was open to ideas.

One day, Ted started experimenting. He drew a circle around SRA
and fabricated a few cards. The symbol would have been a good cattle

brand. Then he tried lowercase letters: sra, streaking white horizontal lines through the letters. I thought that a creative group of people like ours might have other ideas, and we opened this little project to the entire staff as a competition.

Ted submitted the only entry. It was a forward-slanted capital S placed in front of the name Systems Research and Applications Corporation. Intended to convey SRA as a forward-looking, action-oriented company, the new logo nevertheless was not likely to warrant a second look from clients. But within the company, it produced an immediate reaction.

"It looks like a pregnant penguin to me," said JoAnn Fargo, SRA employee number 6 and manager of our administrative functions. "Add a beak, eyes, and little stick feet, and the 'S' will become a penguin." In the absence of any other options, I reluctantly declared Ted the winner.

If we had been looking for a corporate mascot, the more likely candidates would have been a sleek and a ferocious predatory beast, such as a lion or a hawk. But once the association was made, the image stuck. Ted's stylized "S" waddled across the bottom of the page of the company's first underground newsletter; the "SRA Penguin."

The flightless bird was embossed on the company softball and volleyball team shirts, and inspired sporting contests at company picnics, thereafter known as Penguathalons. For years, the penguin was also prominently featured on the programs for many SRA corporate celebrations. As a matter of fact, despite its docile image and vulnerability to predators on land, a penguin under water is aggressive and astonishingly graceful. And its coloring is handsome, not unlike a tuxedo.

While Ted's "S" eventually was retired, the penguin survives as our corporate mascot and has occasionally served as our goodwill ambassador. In the mid 1990s, we sent a stuffed penguin to our stressed staffs in many states where SRA teams were installing new computer systems for tracking Medicare and Medicaid claims. We held a photo contest with the stuffed animal. The winning entry was submitted by an SRA employee who bungee-jumped with the penguin in Las Vegas.

Despite its abundance of serious type A personalities, SRA was also a place where most were ready for a good laugh. My fiscal restraint frequently provided fodder for this. In the early days, I enthusiastically joined pickup basketball games with other SRA employees on Wednesdays after work. At six foot two, I was probably the tallest person on the court, although far from the most agile. To this day, Sherman Greenstein, a dynamic and formidable five-foot-six guard, claims to have blocked my shots. One day Ed McGushin ceremoniously presented me with a T-shirt that pronounced me as "Captain Overhead" for my emphasis on reducing indirect costs. For years, I wore that shirt with pride, and it became my uniform for basketball games, picnics, and other SRA events.

I believe that cultivating a culture of innovation can occur within the process of professionalizing a company. Creativity, improvisation, and a good sense of humor were important parts of life at SRA. There was no system of well-defined career ladders. We hired people with widely different professional and educational backgrounds, and they navigated their way through the firm often in a process of trial and error. New college graduates somehow found their way. Retired military professionals generally came with broad subject-area knowledge, such as command and control, logistics, or computer science. Regardless of their backgrounds, employees learned that collaboration was key to professional advancement and company success.

Matthew Black attributes his success in moving to SRA to the tutelage of Gary Nelson, who hired the young PhD because he was an expert in econometrics. Gary assigned Matt to work on a government manpower project. One day, Matt accompanied Gary to the Pentagon to help brief a Department of Defense (DoD) commission whose chairman was a two-star general, Stuart Sherman. Matthew, preoccupied by the presentation he was about to give, turned to Gary as they walked toward the briefing room and asked, "What's his first name?" Gary shot him a steely look and, in his best authoritarian voice, barked, "His first name is *General*."

In the middle of the briefing, Matt forgot. So when the chairman asked him a question, Matt replied, "Well, Stu—" and then realized the room had gone deathly quietly. It ultimately was a harmless breach of protocol, but Matt credits the presence of Gary and Dick Hunter, his deputy, with saving face for the team that day.

The benefits of collaboration also worked in reverse. Because Ted, I, and other early SRA managers had quantitative backgrounds, we tended to expect that skill set of any person we hired. Eventually, we realized that was unrealistic, particularly if someone had spent an entire career in the military working on issues that did not require competencies in such areas as mathematics and technology. Ed McGushin excelled in customer relations and managing employees, but math was never his strong suit. To compensate for that, we named Mike Duffy as Ed's deputy. Mike had a PhD in mathematical economics. Together they were a formidable team.

A good sign of corporate strength occurs when managers spend time working with employees and observing their aptitudes. We recognized that some people have capabilities not displayed on resumes. This has enabled us to hire and cultivate employees who worked productively in the company for decades. Anita Stolarow was a young political science major who wanted to move from an entry-level job at another company. She was introduced to Andy Cohen, who in turn arranged for her to be interviewed by Judy Sakowitz and Barry Landew. She was hired and worked productively on our important Pentagon projects for years. To this day, she leads an important team.

Another example is Diane Pulliam who, in the early 1980s, was by far our best typist on word processors—fast and accurate. During one of our conversations, Diane told me that she hoped to become a programmer. She had no background or education in computers, and I did not want her to be disappointed. Diane persisted and became a good programmer and leader. She worked at SRA for more than thirty years. While we were discerning in hiring, we believed that it is a supervisor's responsibility to watch for signs of someone hitting a ceiling in capabilities—the so-called Peter Principle, and if an employee failed, we tried to find another place in the company where he or she could work productively. SRA was not, however, a lifetime employer. People who could not perform were separated from the company, as gracefully as possible.

In the first decade of our existence, a growing network of people in their twenties developed friendships that revolved around work but often extended into their social lives. Anita Stolarow remembers "a young person's mafia," which met several times a week for impromptu lunches of Japanese food or fried chicken. Andy Cohen also recalls the group being joined on occasion at lunch by "old-timers" like Sherman Greenstein, who had broad interests in international relations and politics. Sherman sometimes pontificated, on a range of subjects such as world history and entertainment. He also did an excellent imitation of Marlon Brando, blurting out a line from *On the Waterfront*: "I coulda' been a contendah!!!!" Such comments sent the table into roars of laughter.

Anita Stolarow recalls lunches out "with the boys" and credits that camaraderie with providing a sense of support to the cadre of young SRA people, regardless of their backgrounds or where they worked. Others, who joined the company around the same time, such as David

Kriegman, Mike Duffy, and Richard Spires, all rose to become corporate leaders within the firm.

Judy Kaplan was hired out of graduate school and created our first quality assurance program. She met her future husband, Michael Sakowitz, at SRA. He and Barry Landew often provided social glue to the group. Barry organized lunches and get-togethers. He managed the company softball team and sometimes assigned me to contribute beer to corporate events that he hosted at his home after games. Sherman and Andy were good athletes and kept the SRA team competitive. Mike Sakowitz and Barry organized our early holiday parties held in the main conference room. Their specialties were Chinese pepper steak, walnut chicken, and sweet-and-sour meatballs.

SRA employees were known not only as smart, creative people but also as straight shooters who were discreet and loyal to customers. We treated our employees with the same respect, paying competitive wages, above-market bonuses, and offering them opportunities to grow professionally. For much of the first decade, Ted took it upon himself to help employees "on the bench." They were people whose contracts had ended and were at risk of being separated from the company. Ted helped them find new work within SRA, instead of simply laying them off.

We were a $15 million company with 150 employees, and our internal systems for measuring work performance needed to become more formal. SRA was long past the "spreadsheet Saturday" phase, and although we held annual retreats where managers reported on their business units, we decided to add monthly and quarterly reviews. These would provide clear assessments of how we were managing projects and costs, and developing new business. We also used these reviews to develop "business literacy" among managers and to identify candidates for a leadership track. Later, we decided to expose intermediate managers to high-level profit and loss decision making, so they could see how their efforts fit into the big corporate picture.

By 1985, we also needed a more formal approach to compensation. I believed that rewards should be proportional to results and not simply based on seniority. Our system was primarily for key managers and had a base salary and a bonus. Salary was competitive with the industry, but through bonuses, the total compensation could be much better if performance was above market norms. We wanted the company to grow fast, and we rewarded people who could make that happen—by doing excellent work for clients and by securing new business. Providing other competitive benefits was also important and, when combined with cash compensation, helped us recruit and retain capable people. We became an early adopter of the relatively new concept of retirement known as the 401(k) savings program.

The market for talented people was very competitive. We provided generous cash bonuses to anyone who recommended more than one person whom we hired. Those who were particularly effective in the referrals had the opportunity to win a classy new car in a raffle.

Perhaps our most important motivator was a program of granting stock options based on our assessment of someone's future performance. Providing the opportunity to own stock in SRA was a privilege, something that would reward an employee for helping to move the company forward and incentivize them to cooperate with others in this endeavor. We prepared tables for our key executives showing their payoff if the individual and the company performed well. An executive would have stock options granted at a low price; someday the price would be much higher, and he or she could make a lot of money. Gary Nelson remembers buying SRA stock at seven cents per share when he first arrived. There were several stock splits, and the price increased by a factor of 100.

SRA began publishing an annual report in 1985, which contained financial information about the company (revenue, profit, earnings per share, etc.). This enabled our employees, partners, and others to compare our performance with other companies. To set the price of the stock, we created an internal system. We began by using the book value of the shares, which is determined in the simplest case by taking the difference between the assets and liabilities of the company and dividing by the number of shares of stock. While this worked for a few years, it also undervalued the stock. Therefore, beginning in 1992, we engaged an outside financial firm to perform independent valuations. This compared our financial factors with those of comparable public companies. We offered opportunities for employees to sell their stock back to the company if they needed money to buy homes or pay for their children's college educations. Later, the value of our company estimated by investment bankers was much higher, and it led to our decision to have an initial public offering.

Our banking relationships were usually quite good. But in December 1984, a banking problem threatened to ruin the company. Each year, the Bank of Virginia routinely approved a new line of credit, but then it unexpectedly refused to renew the loan. Our loan officer had suffered a heart attack, and no one else at the bank knew much about our account. At the same time, the nation was going through a credit squeeze.

I suggested that we apply to other banks, but Bob Russell, our vice president for finance and accounting, reminded me that they would assume that the Bank of Virginia's refusal reflected a problem with the company. By then, SRA was too big for my assets to solve the problem. I could not simply pledge my home and town houses, as I had done in 1978. The payroll was due in ten days. Missing it was out of the question. It would be a breach of faith with the employees and people would leave. Barring approval of a loan, we could either declare bankruptcy or sell the company at a low price.

Bob reminded me of an old business expression: "The best time to get a loan is when you don't need it. Bankers hate to loan money to people who really need it." I told him to arrange an appointment with the president of the bank. I would explain the situation and ask for his help. The meeting was not necessary. A few days later, Bob returned with good news. The loan committee had approved a six-month extension of our line of credit. What a relief! The company was saved.

I thought about our errors and resolved to gain another bank as a source for our loan. I would cultivate a relationship with not only the loan officer, but also the management chain above him. We would develop alternatives in case the bank changed its loan policy or was acquired. Finally, we would be very careful about leveraging; that is, the amount of money we borrowed to expand the business. If something unexpected happened, such as a cancellation of a major contract, there could be a period of months when our income would not be large enough to cover a big loan.

We immediately applied to other banks and received positive responses. We tentatively chose Crestar (now called SunTrust) with the condition that I meet annually with the president, Bill Harris. At the time, SRA business was a tiny fraction of the bank's income, but Bill agreed, and we became good business friends. We shifted all of our business from Bank of Virginia. Over the years, Bill often remarked about our company's progress and how we had become a major customer. Sadly, Bill died a few years ago; but SunTrust managers know us well and have participated in many of our important financial transactions.

By the beginning of 1985, SRA was reaching the end of its first phase of growth. Our talent pool continued to expand and we had hired seven of the twelve people who would stand on the balcony of the New York Stock Exchange seventeen years later as we took the company public. We had achievements to celebrate. We had established a 401(k) retirement savings plan for employees. In 1984 we were named by *Inc.* magazine as the sixtieth fastest growing, privately held company in America. We remained on that list for four years in a row. SRA had found a tenuous balance between gaining new contracts and hiring capable people while we constructed administrative systems to support the firm. We had survived our infancy and created a culture. SRA was heading into a new stage of life.

9

Artificial Intelligence: A Tortuous Path Forward

···⟩ Technological euphoria can lead to
a lot of wasted effort and money.

Many people dream of becoming rich by creating a great idea. The chances of this happening are slim. The U.S. Patent Office is filled with millions of inventions that never went anywhere, often because they were solutions that few people were willing to buy. Creating innovative new technology is difficult, but exploiting it is even harder. Technical euphoria can lead to a lot of wasted effort and money.

From the beginning, I wanted to build a company that provided professional services in computing and communicating and solved problems of large organizations. I also wanted it to use the technology from the services business to produce products. It was a dream that always eluded us.

By 1985, SRA was six years old and had passed through the early survival phase—crawling, walking, and occasionally stumbling. We had built a reputation as a capable analysis firm with an emerging technological base, and a good pipeline of potential work. The coming years would bring more up and down cycles, but SRA was finally a solid business.

We were ready to delve into new applications of technology, and we focused on areas that we knew—our domain expertise. We understood large systems. We knew in great detail the contents of military information systems: inventories of troops, weapons, ships, airplanes, communication systems, mobile hospitals, and supplies. We knew how and why the government struggled to collect, organize, share, and manipulate vast quantities of data but still lacked the knowledge to make the best decisions. We knew the computer systems used: what worked, what did not, and where the greatest needs were.

We also knew that even if information is contained in a database, computers could not always make sense of it. They were often just tabulators. At that time, no software programs were sophisticated enough to infer the intentions of users and help them make decisions.

Sherman Greenstein and I were avidly interested in artificial intelligence (AI). Researchers were trying to understand the processes of human thinking. How do people analyze problems and make decisions? How do they use experience, often with ambiguous or insufficient information, to make decisions? SRA could break new ground if we could find a way to apply artificial intelligence to the military information systems. One approach would be to design software that would enable a computer to read and converse in ordinary English (or any language) and then respond to the questions of humans by manipulating data. Such a program would read newspapers, magazines, trade and scholarly journals, and databases of all types and then determine what is important.

Sherman and I lived near each other and sometimes commuted to the office together. It was a convenient way for us to share ideas and talk about ways to expand the business. This created an early start to the workday, and for several years, my blue 1970 Volkswagen Beetle was the SRA artificial intelligence "think tank."

One day, we were riding home during a thunderstorm. Coming from Southern California, Sherman was a bit unnerved by the lightning, thunder, and torrents of rain that reduced visibility to a car length ahead. Figuring this would be a good opportunity to distract him, I threw out an idea:

"Sherman, do you think we could create an 'expert backseat pilot'?"

Peering straight ahead as the feeble VW windshield wipers struggled against the deluge, Sherman replied, "What?"

"Essentially it would be a computer system that would alert fighter pilots to all sorts of dangers: low fuel, radar signals from enemy air defenses, the location of enemy planes, and other information et cetera."

"Uh-huh," was Sherman's tight-lipped response.

"It could also tell the pilot how to respond."

"Sure," he said, watching the car bumper ahead of us.

"Or, what if we could develop a system that would automatically instruct the aircraft to take corrective actions itself?"

"Interesting," said Sherman.

I should note that Sherman was complicit in this working arrangement and normally enjoyed our AI brainstorming sessions. This was how we did our creative thinking—on our own time. We did not have budgets for exotic research and development.

This kind of shoe-string investing contrasted with the operating model of many commercial product companies. Their budgets provided adequate money for research and development (R&D). Such commercial companies have higher risks than government contractors because there are rarely guarantees that they will end up with a marketable product. But when they succeed, profits can be very high. The profit margins of government contracting firms generally range from 7 to 10 percent; the commercial market often can be two or three times more or even higher. I realized this and concluded that our government services business could spin out technology at a lower cost than the typical commercial firm. SRA could develop proprietary technology and sell it at these high profit margins. This decision created repercussions within the company for more than a decade.

My discussions with Sherman on artificial intelligence continued and often seemed abstract. But I always steered them back to my original goal: Develop an idea using AI to solve a real-world problem. Could we create a smart advisor, ask a computer questions in plain English that it could understand and then answer? The whole system would look like a conversation between two people, but it would actually be a conversation between a person and a computer. Someone would type a question, and an expert would answer it. The expert was a computer.

Sherman thought our system should have an explanatory component so that a user could ask follow-up questions such as "Why?" or say, "Please explain." Answers by themselves may not be persuasive, but answers with explanations could be a winning combination. In what area would we make our system an expert? We needed to define a domain that was broad enough to interest a government client, but constrained so the system could answer the questions without having to understand the universe. The task was formidable.

I suggested that Sherman talk to some functional experts within SRA who knew specific military domains and determine whether any of them met those criteria. One was Bill Crennan, who had left the Air Force and joined SRA in 1983. He knew a lot about command and control and helped determine the requirements for systems that provide data on the readiness of Air Force aircraft.

Over the course of a month or so, Sherman worked with Bill and Stu Rubens during "off hours" learning as much as he could. Finally, he pronounced his conclusion, "I think we can build an artificial intelligence system."

We assembled a team of technical people and functional experts who began to design and code an expert system with the ability to understand natural language, which is conversational speaking. After about six months, we had a basic demonstration. We could type questions into the computer, which would automatically generate an answer in one or two English sentences. If, for example, you wanted to know how many spare engines Bitburg Air Base should maintain in its inventory, the computer might say, "You will need three for the F-4 Phantom fighter, two for the F-15 Eagle, and one for the F-16 Fighting Falcon."

If you asked why it should not have more engines for those aircraft, it would answer, "Within 100 miles, there is a supply facility that contains engines for those models."

Sherman, Stu, and Bill Crennan prepared a briefing for potential clients that outlined artificial intelligence and its major technical challenges, as well as Sherman's work in building natural language processing systems while at UCLA. The briefing included an example of the expert system we were proposing. SRA would combine two systems that would engage with humans conversationally, consider various scenarios, and answer questions. Admittedly its expertise concerning military aircraft was narrow, but we knew of no other system that was as capable. The initial part of my vision to get artificial intelligence technology in SRA was accomplished; we had developed a good idea and were ready to present it to potential clients. Could this lead to new technology, just as the continental air defense system in the 1950s and 1960s gave IBM the basis for commercial computing, and just as the Boeing B-47 and B-52 bombers created the foundation for the 767 commercial airliner? My hopes were high.

It had been four years since Sherman and I began brainstorming in my Volkswagen. We polished his briefing, slide by slide. It was very difficult to estimate the cost of developing an artificial intelligence system; there were many unknowns regarding the intricacies of programming. But we knew it would be expensive. As a general rule, the capability of a well-designed computer system is proportional to the amount invested. Spending $2.4 million would give the user roughly three times more capability than $800,000.

SRA could not afford to divert profits to build such a system at our expense. We needed to convince a potential military client to fund it. So, I scheduled a meeting with an executive at the Department of Defense (DoD) named John Lane, who was intelligent and unassuming. The final slide in Sherman's presentation would show the system cost and how long it would take to build. We had difficulty agreeing on a price. In the end, because we were eager for funding, we decided to lowball it; $800K would be our fund request.

The next day, Sherman, Bill, Stu, and I went to the Pentagon. Sherman delivered the briefing, talking about the advantages of an AI-based system. As the presentation unfolded, he noted that John seemed intrigued. Just before the last slide, on which we had put an $800,000 price tag, Sherman paused. John asked what it would cost. "Two million dollars," Sherman replied.

John did not hesitate. "Okay, I'll see what I can do."

John funded our project under an existing Air Force contract with Martin Marietta; SRA became a subcontractor. Our job was to design and create an expert computer system to help the Air Force assess the capabilities of F-15 and F-16 aircraft in Europe. To accomplish this, we assembled a team of technical people, linguists, and functional experts who began to design and code an expert natural language–understanding system. One of our first new hires for this effort was Hatte Blejer, who had just completed a PhD in linguistics from the University of Texas at Austin. She quickly became a key contributor to this project. We set up an artificial intelligence laboratory on the sixth floor of Arlington Plaza and bought the latest specialized computers and powerful software developmental tools.

After about six months, we had a basic demonstration. A user could type in questions, and the system would generate answers in one or two English sentences. In the case of the F-15 question, for example, we asked, "How many sorties can I get from my F-15s stationed at Bitburg AFB?" (A sortie was one aircraft flight.)

The computer displayed an answer: "In the first seven days, you can fly 400 sorties to a specific battle area from Bitburg." If you asked why more couldn't be flown, it gave an answer such as "You have run out of fuel," or "Your efficiency rate does not permit you to turn around planes more quickly." It could understand and answer more complex questions and infer intent. For example, when someone asks whether you know what time it is, they expect more than a "Yes, I do" response.

We called our creation the Swan, which stood for "System Without a Name." Swan improved weekly. Upon completion, we showed Swan to as many potential government clients as possible. During the next eighteen months, Sherman demonstrated it fifty or more times in Pentagon offices, at Air Force command and control centers, and at conferences in the United States and Europe.

Throughout this time, I reminded Sherman that, besides developing advanced technology, SRA needed work in the intelligence community. I believed that the best entrée was AI because this capability set SRA apart from most other companies trying to get intelligence work. Sherman briefed the National Security Agency and Air Force intelligence organizations, but no potential contracts emerged. Then he went to Omaha, Nebraska, headquarters of the Strategic Air Command, where he demonstrated Swan to about forty officers.

Shortly after returning to Washington, his phone rang. It was from an officer in a new DoD organization, the Joint National Intelligence Development Staff (JNIDS). He saw Sherman's briefing in Nebraska and was working on a classified project. He wanted to send several representatives to SRA to learn more about our work on natural language processing and artificial intelligence. The director, his deputy, and two members of their technical staff came to our new headquarters in Arlington, where Sherman described and demonstrated Swan. About six weeks later, SRA received a classified request for proposal for a system named ALEXIS.

It would be a major analytic tool for the Strategic Air Command 5044th Intelligence Unit, which assessed the Soviet nuclear threat to the United States. Sherman assembled a team that included Hatte to research and write the proposal. Because several people did not have the necessary clearances, we formed "inside" and "outside" teams. Hatte was on the outside team. We hired a former Air Force intelligence officer who had been an analyst with the 5044th and had the appropriate clearances (as Sherman did) to visit the classified JNIDS library. After each visit, they convened at the SCIF that we had installed in our head-quarters.

Two months later, we received a call. SRA had won. The chief technical officer at JNIDS described our proposal as "the best we have ever read." The work was to design and build a natural language processor that would read, understand, and assess intelligence traffic on tactics and capabilities of Soviet weapons and identify and catalog important relevant events.

ALEXIS was our first advanced technology contract with an intelligence organization. It was also the catalyst for a whole new line of work. We began to develop expertise in creating automated tools that could gather huge amounts of data, diagram patterns in them, and create ways to make it easier for human experts to analyze and anticipate events.

SRA won several subsequent contracts to develop advanced technologies supporting the intelligence community's important defense work. Among them were STARFISH, a system that used intelligence traffic to monitor Soviet submarines for the Navy; and PANS, a system that reasoned about events and tried to predict patterns of drug operations in Central America for the Army.

We wanted to continue to make inroads into the intelligence world through our AI work. So in 1987, Ed McGushin hired Kelly Weaver as a consultant. He had a PhD in physics and had worked with the CIA in the Office of Scientific Weapons Research. His job was to help SRA become a CIA contractor. Kelly talked with a lot of our people to understand our capabilities and experience. Over the next two months, Sherman worked with Kelly, Stu Rubens, and a few others to determine how SRA could apply natural language and expert systems to help the CIA understand one of the greatest nuclear threats to national security. They put together what was probably our most complex slide briefing up to that time. It was a set of thirty computer screens that showed how an expert system, using intelligence sources of all kinds, could help analysts understand and predict the movement of Soviet long-range mobile missiles. On one slide, there were four overlays.

Sherman was scheduled to present the briefing to the Office of Scientific Weapons Research; but at the last minute, he developed stage fright. He kept thinking about the slides, the "spontaneous" comments he would make about how the system would reason through intelligence information, the logic it would use, the distinctions between different types of rule searches, and dozens of other details. Nevertheless, Sherman delivered his briefing with polish, and SRA won its first job for the CIA.

While Sherman was the technical driver of much of this work, Hatte Blejer emerged as our visionary, our face to the market. She gave a presentation on our ALEXIS work to representatives of the intelligence community at a technology conference and found a project that would enable us to expand the system we created for the ALEXIS contract.

The project was called Warbuck$ and its details were classified, but the heart of the task was to identify "objects" within long reports and match them to one another, even when they were referenced in different ways. Basically, we were teaching computers how to read. Computers have extraordinary powers of mathematical calculation—difficult for humans—but struggle with the unstructured text found in books, newspapers, and messages. SRA was able to make progress here; computers don't necessarily read with the subtlety of the knowledgeable person, but they can be taught to find and link concepts and build databases around them. These concepts prove to be tremendously valuable. And, of course, computers have good memories and rarely lose their research "notes."

The system could recognize that the "Orioles" and "Baltimore's major league baseball team" are the same. Objects could include proper names of people as well as addresses, post office boxes, restaurants, geographic locations, phone numbers, organizations, groups, gangs, production factories, aircraft, cars, boats, bank accounts, airlines, and various other subjects and descriptions. The contract enabled us to develop expertise in link analysis—an important capability that enables a computer to determine and visualize relationships among any number of things. Warbuck$ pioneered some of the same natural language inferential techniques that, thirty years later, an IBM computer known as Watson used to beat previous champions of a television game called *Jeopardy*.

We followed Warbuck$ with another intelligence agency contract, called Murasaki, that enabled us to create our first multilingual natural language processing system. In this project, which also was classified, we developed ways to process information from newspapers and other sources in Spanish-speaking countries and Japan. It extracted the names of companies, locations, and modifying words and phrases that explained the relationships among them and put it all in a database. The client could then use the information to build a comprehensive but brief picture of events of interest around the world. Eventually, we took a step further and built software that could take such data and apply reason and judgment to better understand events, networks, and individuals. Even today, some of our intelligence work is based on such technologies. It and other efforts were led by Dave Conetsco and Hatte Blejer.

Murasaki had two additional long-term effects on SRA. First; this work became the foundation of a natural language processing product called NetOwl, which performed text analyses and became the core of several SRA commercial products. Second, thanks to Hatte Blejer, we hired Chinatsu Aone, who was completing her PhD in computational linguistics at the University of Texas at Austin. Chinatsu, born and raised in Japan, began leading our natural language projects and continues to this day.

In the early 1990s, nearly ten years after Sherman and I began our artificial intelligence conversations in my VW Beetle, SRA had developed a marketable, proprietary product that was based on technology funded by the government and our internal funds. The Internet technology boom was just starting to heat up, and I wanted SRA to sell our natural language processing and expert system technology in the commercial sector. Bill Albright led the initiative. We used SRA technology to create three subsidiaries. The first, Navisoft, was incorporated in 1993 to provide indexing capabilities for online publishing. Later, Tim Berners-Lee, the inventor of the World Wide Web, described Navisoft as a milestone in its development.

The second company, Picture Network International, was a natural language system that applied computers in the search for photographs by advertisers to convey a specific message. Suppliers of photos created a central file and gave each photo a descriptive caption. Users could search and retrieve high-quality digitized color photos that met their needs.

And the third company was called IsoQuest. It was incorporated in 1996 and used our NetOwl™ software to organize and manage published material based on its content. IsoQuest was an early predecessor of companies like Google.

We were trying to break into new markets, and the initiative did not always go smoothly. Several false starts in the first year included attempts to build business in manufacturing, utilities, and multimedia training. After that, we narrowed our focus to the financial services industry, which was projected to be a leader in IT spending and in the use of advanced technology.

Once again, we sought to hire outstanding people who had capabilities in the market and relationships with potential clients. A small number of organizations had emerged as leaders in the development of natural language processing, and SRA was one of them. The others were General Electric (GE), Carnegie Mellon University, and BBN Corp., which gained fame in the late 1960s by building a Department of Defense (DoD) network that would eventually become the Internet. Both GE and BBN did significant work for the Defense Advanced Research Projects Agency (DARPA), which is the DoD research arm that develops advanced military technologies. DARPA was supporting the development of advanced NLP extraction of information from documents.

Hatte Blejer knew the key people of our competitors. She hired Paul Jacobs, Lisa Rau, and George Krupka from General Electric, thus consolidating two of the most formidable NLP programs in the United States (SRA and GE). They joined Scott Bennett, a young PhD in electrical and computer engineering, who had worked on the PANS Project and was rapidly becoming the SRA guru on a variety of AI projects. Paul and Lisa were an outstanding husband-and-wife team. He earned bachelor's and master's degrees in applied math at Harvard and a PhD in computer science at UCal Berkeley. Lisa earned bachelor's and master's degrees in computer science at Berkeley and a PhD at the University of Exeter. Both would make significant contributions to our technology.

The new unit offered document management systems, corporate knowledge centers, and delivery of IT services. The strategy was to tailor our AI knowledge and technology derived from earlier work to the particular needs of commercial clients. Within a year, we signed our first pivotal account. It was with the National Association of Securities Dealers (NASD), which asked us to develop an Internet surveillance prototype. Its purpose was to identify Internet improprieties among brokers specializing in NASD companies. Some brokers were praising certain stocks in order to gain sales. Our software flagged these messages for further investigation by human analysts. We called the system NetWatch, and senior NASD officials talked about it in glowing terms to the press.

After *Financial Net News* published an article about NetWatch, we received a call from executives in the Securities Industry Association. They were interested in expanding our technology to provide an automated way to monitor email between brokers and retail customers for compliance with SEC rules. That call was followed by one from Dean Witter executives.

This led to our creation of yet another AI-based product, called Assentor™. Securities and Exchange Commission regulations require firms to review all broker communications. Using natural language processing and expert system technologies, we designed Assentor to flag communications that might reveal high-pressure sales tactics, stock hype, and other illegal activities. It quarantined messages that set off our programmed alarms. It was up to the customer to determine what happened next. A suspicious message was sent to a compliance reviewer with an explanation of why it was intercepted. That person could intervene or release the message for delivery as originally intended. Either way, Assentor itself did not delay the communication. The average processing time per message was less than one second.

SRA had achieved the initial part of my vision to provide products from our services work. These early versions of products were based on our natural language processing and expert systems technology. The products did not deliver large profits, nor did they lead to substantial new services work, but it was the late-1990s and the dot-com boom was well underway. Our initial success encouraged us to create commercial companies, but that is another story.

10

Game-Changers and Legacies

⋯⟩ Chance favors the prepared mind.

⋯⟩ Good business development solves many problems.

W hen someone was congratulated on success in a business endeavor, an occasional reply was "Better lucky than good." This humble response often did not reflect the fact that while luck may have been a factor, the person or his organization was well prepared and therefore recognized, and exploited the opportunity. Others less prepared and motivated would have missed it completely. Time and again, this marketing acuity and organizational readiness worked to our advantage.

As a business predominantly focused on government, SRA was heavily influenced by geopolitical events. In 1989 the Berlin Wall between East and West Germany fell, and in 1991 the Soviet Union collapsed. The Cold War had ended, and national priorities were rapidly changing. As a result, our work for the Department of Defense (DoD) and the Federal Emergency Management Agency (FEMA) declined and our growth rate slowed. In 1989 our revenue was $43 million, but by 1991 it had only increased to $49 million. It seemed that we just could not break the $50 million revenue mark. Just when our outlook for the future seemed bleak, new opportunities occurred, and our alertness and preparation paid off. The result was a new round of expansion for SRA.

In 1989 President George H. W. Bush appointed Donald J. Atwood

Major Elmer Volgenau (first on left) shows a rocket
to General Douglas MacArthur (third from left) in
the Pacific during World War II. Rockets helped
suppress enemy fire during amphibious landings.

Ernst at about age ten, just before he took
over management of the small family farm.

Ernst (foreground) as a Naval Academy company commander
in 1955. Three of his officers were roommates (right to left):
William Jerald, Gregory Black, Larry Heisel.

Ernst and Sara shortly after wedding ceremony in 1959.

Ernst outside a centrifuge prior to experiencing 15 times the force of gravity as part of Air Force astronaut training.

Ernst, Sara, and their three daughters (Lisa, Lauren, Jennifer) as Ernst receives the Legion of Merit from Ivan Selin, Acting Assistant Secretary of Defense for Systems Analysis, in the Pentagon 1970 (the "Whiz Kids").

Ernst and Sara at a formal event at Wright Patterson Air Force Base, Dayton, Ohio, in 1973.

Ernst and Bill Brehm on an Air Force 707 that flew them around the world on their review of U.S. Military Headquarters.

Ernst receives the Nuclear Regulatory Commission
Distinguished Service Award from Chairman Hendrie;
former Chairman Rowden is in the background.

*Ernst Volgenau, founder
and facilitator.*

*Ted Legasey, the second SRA employee
and great builder of SRA.*

*SRA first corporate headquarters
in Reston (the Volgenau home).*

Arlington Plaza, the "Crystal Palace."

SRA Penguin, a symbol of greatness.

Zoonar RF/Zoonar/Thinkstock

*Bill Brehm, highly talented
first Chairman of SRA.*

*David Jones, accomplished Air
Force leader and Chairman of
the Joint Chiefs of Staff.*

Stu Rubens, bear skinner.

Gary Nelson, economist extraordinaire.

Barry Landew, our first college new-hire, destined for many contributions.

*Rolland Fisher, an Okie with
a PhD in operations research.*

*Ed McGushin, a creative
and humorous leader.*

*Emerson Thompson and Linda Skelton
discuss a major Army project.*

*Jeff Rydant, an innovative
and hardworking maverick.*

*Lew Hadelman, a demanding
but kind leader.*

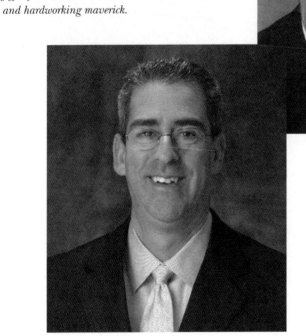

*Mike Fox, highly capable in
marketing and sales.*

*Sue Austin, long time and highly
effective executive assistant.*

Judy Sakowitz, multi-faceted executive.

Sherman Greenstein, a fountain
of originality.

Hatte Blejer, computer linguist
and innovator.

Matthew Black, quantitative economist.

*SRA Officers in 1985 (left to right): Gary Nelson,
Ernst Volgenau, Jerry Yates, Stu Rubens, Bill Albright,
Bill Brehm, Irwin Lebow, Ed McGushin, Bob Russell,
Ted Legasey, Ernest Peixotto.*

Scott Bennett and Chinatsu Aone,
a creative combination.

Jeffrey Westerhoff, the greatest
of all business developers.

Dick Hunter, a creative builder of contracts.

Emerson Thompson, a font of programming knowledge.

to the number two job in the DoD. Atwood had served as vice chairman of General Motors (GM) at a time when overseas competition was pushing the auto giant to the brink of failure. The company's response was to reengineer its corporate information management systems to cut costs. When Atwood arrived at the DoD, the first thing he did was assess its information requirements and capabilities. "If I needed corporate information management (CIM) at GM," he concluded, "I need it in spades at DoD."

Atwood formed a government-industry study group that included as consultants David Hill, the former president of GM, and Paul Strassmann, a former Xerox executive who was the driver and overseer of the GM reengineering effort. The group concluded that the entire defense enterprise needed to integrate and streamline its systems for gathering, storing, processing, and using information.

This was a clear priority, but there was a problem. Atwood concluded that, because of federal contracting rules, the process for hiring contractors was unacceptably long. He turned to another member of the CIM task force, Dr. Mike Mestrovich (Assistant Secretary of Defense for Health Affairs) and asked, "Is there a way around this?" Mestrovich replied that there was. His office was circulating a draft RFP that could be modified to apply to the whole DoD. The new vehicle would eliminate the arduous RFP preparation task and greatly reduce the time required to get contractor support. This approach was a precursor to a new type of contracting that would work to the advantage of nimble companies like SRA. Atwood approved the idea.

SRA was already familiar with the Health Affairs RFP. It was a $40 million, five-year contract for the DoD medical community. We were trying to gain health care work, and this contract seemed like a natural evolution of the expertise we had built since our early mobilization work. During the Nifty Nugget exercise, SRA uncovered two problems that involved military medical service. One was the inability to identify, track, treat, and transport wartime casualties. The second was a cumbersome process to mobilize and deploy active duty, reserve, and National Guard medical personnel to handle heavy casualties in a major conflict.

Dr. Mestrovich was already familiar with the work we had done for his office. We built a prototype medical information system, which was later used in DoD emergency planning exercises. In addition, our experts were working on a five-year contract to help the Army Health Services Command prepare for a major national emergency mobilization.

We were developing qualifications in hopes of competing for this latest health services contract. Suddenly, we found ourselves in the midst of what would become a battle of titans.

This was a single-award contract that looked like an uphill struggle. The changes to the RFP produced considerable turbulence. Sample tasks were eliminated, then restored, and then revised, producing inconsistencies in the RFP. We informally told the contracting officer about them and offered alternatives, which she usually acted upon. In contrast, she said that other companies sent scathing, formal comments, which she then had to distribute to all participating companies. Our suggestions enabled her to send corrections out before receiving the formal letters. She appreciated our cooperative approach toward a government-industry team.

After we finally submitted our proposal, we stood outside the Pentagon entrance counting the big-name contractors entering the building with huge boxes. It was very depressing. For months, we heard nothing further about the contract.

In September, the contracting officer summoned our team, led by Dick Hunter and Barry Landew, to the Pentagon for orals. She led our team into a very small room used as a coffee mess. One evaluator immediately pressed us about our experience with various software tools. Finally, he got to the point: "Why did you propose using Texas Instrument tools, when we have a DoD standard called IDEF?" Barry Landew quickly responded that the RFP required us to bid Texas Instrument tools, so we complied. (A year earlier when the RFP was issued, IDEF was not the DoD standard.) The evaluator asked, "Can you use IDEF?" Barry said yes. He then assured the evaluator that we much preferred IDEF tools and believed in using approved standards whenever possible. (Some other team members said to themselves, "As soon as we learn how to use them.") The statement was indicative of our positive attitude; we believed we could do almost anything.

On September 16, 1991, the contracting officer called and asked us to meet her the next day to sign the $39 million contract, which included $7.8 million for the base year and each of four option years. Ultimately, the contract exceeded $275 million, thanks to the excellent efforts of Dick Hunter, Bernie Cohen, Stu Rubens, and others.

There were so many capable people who contributed to business development and job execution that choosing only a few to discuss is very difficult. Dick Hunter was one of the few. After graduating from the U.S. Naval Academy, he went through the rigorous selection and training process that led to qualification as a fighter pilot on aircraft carriers. Anyone who has witnessed takeoffs and landings from a carrier (particularly at night) recognizes the peril for that type of pilot. Dick flew A-4 fighters on bombing missions over North Vietnam. His plane was hit by ground fire, and he managed to coax the mortally wounded bird out over the ocean. His ejection seat and parachute worked, and Dick was picked up by a Navy destroyer.

In the late 1960s, Dick had an assignment in Washington and was studying at night for a PhD at American University. I was teaching a graduate course in operations research at the time, and Dick was one of my best students, gaining an A in the course. Many years later, he joined SRA and contributed mightily to some of our most important proposal wins. He was a devout Mormon and spent a great deal of time in church and community activities. For years he managed a highly regarded Boy Scouts of America troop. Nevertheless, he put in long hours at SRA.

Dick suffered from apnea and did not sleep well. After returning from an important project late at night, he fell asleep while driving. His car left the highway and rolled over. Dick survived and was confined to a wheelchair but still worked intensively. Once he spent all night working on a proposal while his wife, Lauris (acting as a chauffeur), slept in the van. Without exercise, Dick gained weight. I pleaded with him to slow down, but he persisted. Every week or two I saw him in the wheelchair and wondered guiltily how long he would last. Dick died a few months later. We lost another good friend and great contributor to SRA.

A week after the DoD announced that our firm won the CIM work, we signed another contract, this one worth $48.7 million over fifty-one months. It surpassed CIM to become our largest job up to that time. The work was for the Defense Information Systems Agency and was an extension of our earlier efforts on the Joint Operations Planning and Execution System (JOPES). This time we designed and developed a new computer system.

Lew Hadelman, who had become the director of one of our business units, led the proposal and capture process for the new JOPES Development and Integration project. When we won it, Lew asked Jeff Rydant to join him as deputy project manager. A few months later, Lew recruited Gene Frank, also from GTE, to manage a key task order under the contract. Gene later became project manager for all of JOPES development and integration (D&I).

Lew also needed a domain expert, that is, someone who understood the actual process of mobilization and deployment. He knew Pat Burke as a member of the Joint Chiefs planning group that worked directly on mobilization and preparedness issues. Pat was smart, savvy, and understood the JCS mission, requirements, and policy. While we initially hired Pat because of his expertise in this area, we eventually appreciated his greater value to SRA was not in DoD knowledge, but in an entrepreneurial spirit. In addition to knowing the inner workings of the DoD, he was adept at developing ideas that were appealing to clients.

We needed all of this talent because SRA was stepping into a situation where the incumbent (GTE) had failed to deliver a workable computer system that would automate JOPES processes. As I saw it, GTE (like other large companies, such as Lockheed Martin and TRW) often had functional people write the specifications for the system and then drop them on the desks of the technical people to design and build. This did not work well because a good part of the process of designing a large complex system requires interacting with clients to discern their needs. It is a continuous process of feedback and modification. Knowing this, we hired people who had worked on mobilization planning. Sometimes we assigned them to be surrogates for senior military officers. We put them in a room with domain experts and technical people, and grilled them on how the Joint Chiefs and military would use the system and what it needed to do. Because of the size and scope of this work, we needed to build our capability quickly. For the proposal, we convinced SAIC to be a subcontractor, taking the lead in systems engineering work. SRA would do most of the software development.

To meet the rapidly escalating demand created by the new contracts, we launched a significant recruiting initiative in which we held job fairs, advertised extensively, and hired hundreds of new employees. We brought on twenty-seven consultants. We held a competition for small businesses, small disadvantaged businesses, and small woman-owned businesses. These Small Business Administration designations gave such firms priority in gaining federal contracts. We also hired other large companies (in addition to SAIC) as subcontractors.

We hired fifty software engineers and realized the need to consolidate our technical expertise. Until then, each business unit in the company had technical people and assigned work based on the unit's needs, not necessarily the company's. We found inconsistent hiring practices from one unit to the next. There was little exchange among the people who could have shared information and ideas.

I asked Emerson Thompson to create a new software development group. He stipulated one condition. He would have absolute authority to decide which technology people would work on each job because every project manager wanted the cream of the crop on his or her contract. Someone at a higher level was needed to balance resources in the best interests of SRA as a whole. I agreed to Emerson's condition. He standardized hiring practices, built a database to track the assignments of technical people, and arbitrated requests for anyone. Emerson introduced good management oversight to the internal competition for talent.

By structuring the process in this way, we reinforced one of our most important principles: SRA employees would support rather than compete against one another. At times this meant sacrificing a personal or organizational objective for the greater good. It enabled us to build our expertise quickly. It is interesting to note that one of our competitors (SAIC) had a different approach that was also successful. Their business units often competed with one another under the forceful leadership of their founder, Bob Byster. They were much larger and older than us, but I conclude from this that there are many ways for businesses to succeed.

Emerson set our sights on winning an important certification that would give SRA an advantage in competing for IT work. The software engineering institute at Carnegie Mellon University had created a system that established five levels of capabilities that certify a firm's ability to develop quality software within a budget. Under Emerson's direction, SRA reached Level 2 certification, and created a methodology that the company followed, and eventually Level 3 was achieved as well.

CIM made SRA the contractor of choice for business process reengineering; unfortunately, because of government policies, it precluded us from competing for full-scale system development in related areas of hardware and software. However, the JOPES D&I contract enabled us to begin shifting from analyzing and developing requirements for computer systems to actually designing, building, and operating them. It was an important step in transforming my vision of building an information technology company into reality. It allowed us to hire talented people, who helped us grow in future years. CIM was a precursor to a new type of government contract (known as indefinite delivery/indefinite quantity) that was a perfect fit for our energetic and innovative, young company.

CIM and JOPES D&I significantly helped our growth. For the next eight years (from 1992 to 1999) revenue increases averaged 25 percent per year, and the two contracts made our total business backlog to almost $250 million.

CIM and JOPES were very important but were not the only reasons we did well during the 1990s and beyond. Another factor was a one-man marketing and sales department—Jeffrey Westerhoff. A retired Army helicopter pilot, who flew many combat missions in Vietnam, Jeff joined SRA in 1987. Within a few years, he began to specialize in indefinite delivery/indefinite quantity contracts, and he became adept at winning these umbrella contracts and the task orders that flowed from them. He was excellent in developing rapport with clients. Another reason for his success was hard work. He lived a long way from SRA headquarters and customarily left home around 3 a.m., arriving at the office an hour later, and often remaining until 7 p.m. In the interest of his health, I tried to convince him to adopt shorter hours, but he was incorrigible.

Jeff did not usually perform the work for task orders that he had won, but he followed them carefully to make sure the program team did a good job. When potential clients checked on our previous performance, the references were good. The SRA New Business Development Award is one of the hardest to gain, but Jeff won it three times—in 1992, 1994, and 1997. He continued to exceed his performance from previous years; therefore, I created a new President's Award and presented it to him in 1997.

In 2007, Jeff was diagnosed with terminal cancer, but despite my objections, he continued to work. I wanted to show him how much we appreciated his selfless dedication, but we had already given him our most meaningful awards. Finally after much reflection, we decided on a student scholarship program named in his honor. His name would live long after his death.

We held a brief ceremony for Jeff. After describing the scholarship and Jeff's contributions while in the Army and at SRA, I left the podium, stood in front of him, rendered the military hand salute, and said, "Jeffrey, I salute you and all that you have accomplished."

He stood at attention and returned the salute. This poignant moment was the last time I saw Jeffrey Westerhoff.

11

Innovations in Contracting and Health Care

⋯⟩ **The best ideas win.**

⋯⟩ **Chance favors the prepared mind.**

⋯⟩ **Hire bright, energetic people who will
      bring long-term value to your organization.**

The government procurement process for improving or replacing a computer system can be nearly dysfunctional. Decisions are often made by committee. Rules can be byzantine. As a result, the solicitation and approval processes can be protracted. One of the keys to success in business is learning how things work and how to act effectively within a bureaucracy. Since some of our executives had been in military or civil service, we understood the frustrations of policies and procurement policies. It was not uncommon for a military officer to arrive at a new job, spend months determining what needed to be done, and then learn that it would take another twelve to eighteen months to issue a request for proposal for new work. By this time, he was due for reassignment.

In the early 1990s, the federal government began to change its procedures. To reduce the time and cost involved in buying goods and services and to create a level playing field for firms of all sizes, it introduced a new kind of vehicle called the indefinite delivery/indefinite quantity (ID/IQ) contract. Government agencies described the general type of work they wanted done through an ID/IQ. Contractors competed to prequalify as one of several companies. This limited group then competed again for a variety of smaller jobs, and they actually bid for and began work on task orders within a few weeks. It was a great idea and a vast improvement over the old way of contracting, which often required months or years to make an award.

SRA was among the first group of contractors that detected and exploited this change in government contracting. It became easier for us to compete against large firms such as Electronic Data Systems (EDS), Booz-Allen, SAIC, and Computer Sciences Corporation (CSC). Company size became less important in competing for smaller task orders. CIM was very similar to ID/IQ in this regard. We were the preferred contractor for business process reengineering work emphasized by Deputy Secretary of Defense Donald Atwood, and we won a growing number of task orders. This immediately boosted our revenue and enabled us to build expertise in new areas of government.

Our vision was to help improve government through analysis and computers. Our strategy was to continue to build our military and national security work, while seeking more opportunities to work for civil government agencies, where our domain expertise and technological skills would be assets. Health care was a natural progression of our capabilities. We had developed knowledge of certain aspects of military health care through the CIM contract. We also worked for the Army Surgeon General and the Medical Services Command based at Fort Sam Houston in Texas. Much of this was outgrowth of our earlier work on emergency response exercises. In addition, we helped a DoD health group improve and manage a manpower database. This work introduced us to medical record-keeping and enabled us to hire domain experts (people knowledgeable in a specific area) who would soon help on other new contracts.

Over the course of a year or so, we competed for contracts requiring medical domain expertise, primarily in the Department of Health and Human Services (HHS). Our efforts were largely fruitless. We later learned that some professionals in civil agencies had little regard—and sometimes outright distain—for a contractor in military health care. The proposal reviewers apparently drew a line through our company's name based on our background.

Nevertheless, we exceeded our fairly modest aspirations. Parts of the federal civil agency health community needed our IT systems expertise and our health care knowledge. To expand capabilities and take advantage of emerging networks of computer, civil health agencies faced substantial system modernization challenges. Over the course of about two years, SRA won two large ID/IQ contracts, which gave us the opportunity to compete for the related task orders. As a result, we won six substantial system development contracts from agencies in the Department of Health and Human Services. It was ironic that, after building qualifications in the domain of military health care, we were unable to break into civil government health care; instead, for the first time, our information technology capabilities gave SRA entry to this market.

Almost simultaneously, Cathy McGrane and Rolland Fisher uncovered separate opportunities in other federal health agencies. Cathy found an information technology contract opportunity at the Food and Drug Administration, which wanted to improve its complicated processes for reviewing and approving new drugs and biological products. Moreover, the FDA wanted to improve its basic business process, which was the same type of work we were doing on the CIM contract.

The significance of the FDA goal for its SMART (Submission Management and Review Tracking) system was clear, but we knew little about the federal government approval process for new drugs and therapies, other than that it is complicated and protracted. How could we automate a process that we did not understand? Cathy McGrane, however, was relentless in explaining why this was perfect for SRA.

Most of our senior officers were attending a retreat setting the strategic direction for the company when the SMART RFP surfaced. According to Barry Landew, this was a great opportunity. He and Dick Hunter were in the office reviewing bids. Displaying prescient wisdom (and the usual audacity), they made an executive decision; SRA would bid on the SMART RFP. When the senior executive team returned, Dick and Barry were criticized by some for giving the go-ahead, but they prevailed. They had the best idea, and at SRA, it trumped the alternatives suggested by others.

Months of hard work were required to understand the technical challenges the FDA faced in reviewing applications for new products. The agency receives huge volumes of data with each application. Each was submitted in paper form, making the information particularly difficult to analyze and manage. To ensure safety and effectiveness, FDA reviews of clinical data must be careful and thorough. Historical databases contained information of immense value, but were cumbersome to use. They reflected an underlying problem. Individual organizations within FDA had a history of developing computer applications independently, making it difficult to gain consensus on systems that could serve the entire agency. However, the growing number of networked computers and proprietary software demanded a comprehensive system that could keep track of drug review documents, as they progressed through the review cycle.

SRA won the SMART contract in mid-1994, and working with FDA officials, we helped create a system that improved the timeliness and effectiveness of the new drug review and approval process. We also developed new application software for the Center for Drug Evaluation and Research and the Center for Biologics Evaluation and Research. The software was used by FDA to review requests by companies to study, manufacture, and sell new products.

These experiences led to a standard process that helped us grow our health business over the next decade. We learned from the client, hired people with expertise in that area, and did good work for customers so they would think of us when other opportunities arose.

The National Practitioner Data Bank opportunity came to our attention in this way. A few years earlier, Rolland Fisher was a member of our team supporting FEMA in a civil government emergency exercise in Washington State. An official at the Department of Health and Human Services asked him to quickly provide an automated message system, which he did, making FEMA and our team heroes in the exercise. Years later, one of the HHS people called Rolland and told him SRA should consider bidding an RFP for the National Practitioner Data Bank.

Rolland and Ray Leahy introduced our capabilities to the Health Resources and Services Administration (HRSA), a division within the Department of Health and Human Services. Ray was a retired colonel who had worked for the Army Health Services Command. He led our San Antonio office. Rolland's mission was to convince HRSA that we could build and operate a major database. Ray's job was to persuade them that we knew a lot about health care.

The Healthcare Quality Improvement Act requires hospitals to query a federal database about every health care practitioner before granting clinical privileges, and check the data again every two years. Insurance companies and hospitals report to the database instances of practitioner misconduct, adverse license actions, and malpractice payments. The goal is to protect the public from physicians, nurses, and other practitioners, who have injured patients and then moved to another state, where they might repeat the damage. The existing system was not satisfactory. The database ran on a mainframe computer that regularly produced huge amounts of data (batch-processing). It created a lot of paperwork that was not easily shared.

To win the six-year contract to design, build, and operate the new system, SRA would have to unseat Unisys. With Bill O'Neil as the proposal manager and Sherman Greenstein contributing creative ideas, the development team engineered the data bank operation from the ground up. In addition to online reporting, it included a mail room, a document control facility to handle reports on malpractice and license actions on practitioners, a toll-free help line, a multiple line telephone system, and a computer room. It was a technological leap ahead of the old Amdahl mainframe computer that Unisys was using. Our approach had a database server and backup connected to a network that enabled immediate communication with over twelve thousand health care entities.

In July 1994, we won the National Practitioner Data Bank (NPDB) contract over approximately sixteen bidders, including the incumbent. The customer told us that, in evaluating the proposals, his staff kept referring to the detailed roadmap and flow charts that SRA had produced. We designed, developed, and put the system online ahead of the deadline. The new system reduced the response time from days to less than two hours. The stream of queries increased relentlessly. Starting at 2.6 million per year, it grew at a 20 percent rate to over 3.5 million queries a year by December 1997. We had designed, developed, and operated a major nationwide database system. It was a great achievement for our company. Nearly twenty years later, we were still operating and improving the NPDB.

These two opportunities (SMART and NPDB), and our reputation for acquiring expertise in our clients' domains, began to open more doors. In areas where SRA was previously unknown, facing formidable competition, we began to win contracts that built on our growing analytical and technological skills in the civil government sector.

Our ability to qualify for large ID/IQ contracts was key. We often learned about these contract vehicles before competitors and quickly mastered the art of driving business through them. This was largely because of the tireless efforts of Jeff Westerhoff. Jeff first learned of what was informally known as the "Deadbeat Dad Database" through one of his many contacts.

The Administration for Children and Families maintained the Federal Parent Locator Service database, a federal government system that helped state governments find parents who were not making child support payments. An estimated 50 percent of parents, who were court-ordered to do so, paid nothing; another 25 percent did not pay as ordered. Because the data was often old and not readily available, parents seeking to avoid child support obligations could evade the system simply by changing jobs on a regular basis—and many of them did. As a result, the unsupported families often ended up on welfare. Neither the state child support enforcement workers, who often handled as many as three thousand cases at a time, nor the existing database system corrected this problem.

In 1996 President Clinton signed a welfare reform law that required the development of a better system to give state enforcement agencies information necessary to collect delinquent child support funds from non-custodial parents. The new system would contain up-to-date information on the location of individuals and their assets. It would also be proactive, sending updates to the states whenever new information became available rather than waiting for a case worker to generate a query. The RFP gave bidders one week to prepare a briefing and a five-page white paper on how they would tackle this challenge, and to present both in person.

Within three days, Jeffrey Westerhoff and Mary Lambert, our deputy director of health systems, researched the background and built a team, including two subcontractors with relevant expertise. Mary managed the proposal effort and pitched in wherever necessary. Ellen Moyer took the lead in developing the briefing, and Sherman Greenstein wrote the white paper. The team worked until 4 a.m. the day of our briefing.

After our presentation, we waited, wondering whether the government would actually make a multimillion-dollar award based only on a briefing and five-page white paper. Late in the evening, we received the phone call, and Mike Duffy, director of the health systems group, went downtown to sign the contract. It was 11:30 p.m., the closing minutes of the government fiscal year. The purchase order was for $6.9 million.

Two years later, President Clinton announced that the expanded Federal Parent Locator Service we had helped design and build had found over a million non-custodial parents in its first nine months of operation. The program was selected as one of twenty-five finalists (from over 1,400 applications) for the prestigious Innovations in American Government Award, jointly sponsored by the Harvard Kennedy

School of Government and the Council for Excellence in Government. It was also featured in articles in the *Washington Post*, the *New York Times*, and other publications.

The program demonstrated a level of achievement that is only possible with strong leadership, teamwork, and a focus on mission. Even if it had not received national attention, it would have been a success for the participants. SRA continues to do work on this system, and over the years transformed it from a client-server system into a web-based interface. It offered unique insight into a major problem for our nation, and we took pride in helping to fix it.

Our most scientifically relevant work came from the National Institutes of Health (NIH) through the Center for Information Technology. The Center was seeking firms that could provide technical support for the many institutes within NIH. In 1996, it issued a request for proposal from firms that wanted to be prequalified to win this work. In 1997, SRA and SAIC (a technology giant already deeply embedded in NIH) were the only two firms that qualified. In doing so, we won the opportunity to bid and win (through an expedited process) $164 million of work over the next five years. This became our entrée into some of the most exciting work in the new field of bioinformatics, which is the combination of biology and computer technology into research.

In the late 1990s, biological research was going through a dramatic shift, which was accelerated by a project launched by the NIH and Department of Energy. The challenge was to map the human genome to better understand and develop cures for diseases. By identifying the chemical composition and the location of genes on chromosomes in human cells, it was hoped that researchers could correlate the roles of genes in human health and illness. The stakes were high; success would create unprecedented opportunities for researchers, pharmaceutical companies, and health practitioners. But the effort had become a race to claim ownership of the knowledge produced by this research. This was fueled by the work of a former NIH genome researcher, J. Craig Ventor, who announced his intention to beat the government at mapping the human genome and to sell access to the resulting proprietary databases through a business that he created.

Deeply concerned about the ramifications of privatizing this science, a global consortium of scientists and ethicists issued a statement in 1996 asserting that genomic mapping data was too important to be owned by any one company, research institution, or nation. It encouraged scientists to collaborate and put data in the public domain, where anyone could use it to advance scientific research for the benefit of humanity. NIH leaders shared this view and were working to find technological ways to facilitate this. SRA became part of this effort after winning a task order for the National Cancer Institute. The RFP was vague, in part because researchers often did not reveal much about their work until delivering a paper. In addition, scientific investigators who run NIH research programs hire contractors to perform specific tasks but generally do not view them as substantial intellectual contributors. As a result, contractors are expected to provide capable people who can assist in the work, but not necessarily become creative leaders. Once we gained a better view of the work, we took the opposite approach—helping researchers to put genetic data in forms that could be readily accessed, analyzed, and shared. Lisa Rau, who managed all of our efforts under the NIH ID/IQ contract, recognized this as an opportunity for SRA to exceed expectations.

Rather than simply providing people to fill billets, a practice known in the government consulting world as "body shop work," we began to assemble a team of people who not only knew IT, but were also medical experts and scientists, who understood how data was gathered and used in research. We had a lot of smart people at SRA, many with PhDs, but we needed an expert in molecular biology. Fortunately, through one of our software engineers, Arcel Castillo, we met his wife, Susan, who had a PhD in molecular biology from Virginia Tech and was doing post-doctoral research at NIH on transgenic mice. She understood the problems scientists there were experiencing with IT systems and was able to break down complicated science to the lay person. We persuaded her to join SRA as a leader in our new bioinformatics work. Susan then helped recruit John Greene, a molecular biologist with an IT background and degrees from Harvard and MIT. John had worked at Human Genome Sciences and Gene Logic, both biotech companies, and had a strong background in molecular biology, human genomics, and information technology. He became our on-site project leader at NIH, and quickly demonstrated that SRA people were not typical submissive worker bees.

We created a web database and tools that enabled genetic researchers to collect, access, manipulate, and analyze data collaboratively. It was not aimed at mapping the human genome; our effort tried to identify the expression (or activity) of genes associated with specific diseases, such as breast cancer.

The process of collecting, analyzing, and comparing DNA expressions is called microarray analysis. It is a painstaking and voluminous process, in which the DNA of patients or test subjects is applied to a glass slide, or "chip." Each chip has thousands of small holes, containing genetic material to which cancerous DNA might react. By washing the chip in a dye, the expressive genes are highlighted and can be measured. Data management is a formidable task for one experiment and very difficult for complete research projects. With a microarray of 6,000 gene segments and a sample size of 100 test subjects, scientists have 600,000 data points to analyze in just one study.

This work, which was ultimately patented, was far beyond the scope of conventional spreadsheets and made information technologists the partners of scientists. Our work on this first microarray database for NIH helped pave the road for new discoveries in the treatment of diseases, especially for cancers. Among them was the discovery by National Cancer Institute researcher Louis Staudt that the most common type of non-Hodgkin's lymphoma was two distinctly different forms. One form responded well to traditional treatments; the other did not. This and other evidence helped prompt medical practitioners to consider the genome of each specific patient, not just the cellular characteristics of the tumor apparent under a microscope. Such insights helped revolutionize the concepts behind the treatment of cancer.

That early microarray database work continues to this day, and the analysis of cancers linked to the human genome has evolved. SRA is helping NIH to create a Cancer Genome Atlas. This is an ambitious effort to assemble genomic data for twenty different cancers, including specific forms affecting the brain, breast, colon, blood, and others. As part of this, NIH has a nationwide project underway to gather up to five hundred samples of patients with one of these cancers, as well as healthy genomic data. SRA is responsible for the design, development, and operation of the Data Coordinating Center, which will give researchers worldwide access to the vast amounts of genomic cancer data.

In addition to this work, we standardized and automated Medicaid/Medicare programs in all fifty states for the Health Care Finance Administration, and we designed and engineered a telecommunications infrastructure for the defense department global medical community. Our firm operated a bioinformatics research center to defend the country against bioterrorism. Our role in this work for the National Institute for Allergies and Infectious Disease (NIAID) lasted for five years and focused on pathogens that targeted the digestive system, such as salmonella, shigella, virulent forms of E. coli, as well as the plague. In 2010, SRA also won a contract with the Centers for Disease Control in Atlanta to develop bioinformatics that will help the CDC determine the constituents of annual influenza vaccines.

Currently, health care work is a large part of our business, and we make substantial contributions in technology and expertise for the good of society. It all began because a few of our most talented people recognized that government contracting was changing in an area that happened to be health care. We hired them because of their strategic talents and their minds, which were prepared for innovation in an area where we had an opportunity to succeed.

12

Ethics, Vision, and People

···⟩ **Business success is all about people.**

···⟩ **Be vigilant because, sooner or later,**
a crook will join your firm.

A t an off-site meeting of our senior officers around 1985, someone proposed creating a vision statement for our company. Ted
Legasey and Dick Hunter prepared the first draft and several of
us helped revise it. It contained the following words:

> SRA aspires to be one of the best companies in the world—by
> any measure. A company that: creates real value for its custom-
> ers by providing high quality information technology services and
> solutions; employs the best people, nurtures them, and enables
> them to succeed; and steadfastly commits itself to an ethic of hon-
> esty and service.

This vision statement was unusual in its emphasis on people and
values. Many other corporate statements address financial success and
market dominance. However, as we found out later, our emphasis on
people would lead to business achievement. An old military adage says,
"Take care of your people, and they will take care of you."

It is easy to set lofty goals for corporate behavior, but it is much
more difficult to live by them when business is challenging. In 1981, the
company had two divisions: half of them worked for Stu in the "mush

head" division; the other half reported to Ted in the "wire head" (geek) organization. Ted's division had one contract, which came to an end. We competed for the follow-on work, but lost. We were in a deep hole. We had nearly fifteen people without work. For a company of only thirty people, this was a serious development. We had three choices: We could fire the people. We could assign them to an overhead account, hoping we would find new work soon. Or, we could put them on jobs (direct labor) that were already fully staffed. In the last case, our people could perform the work, but the jobs would soon end, and we would run out of money.

For us, the choice was obvious. Good people are too valuable to lose, and they can contribute a lot to future work. With permission of our customers, we moved everyone from Ted's division to direct labor on jobs in Stu's group. We would exhaust the work and funding on Stu's contracts earlier than planned, but we were betting that we would get new work.

Our bet paid off. We gained new technical work, transferred the "wire heads" to those jobs, and we continued to grow. Our lesson: get good people, treat them well; and they will build the business.

One aspect of our culture involved giving people responsibility and trusting them to perform. We had to take risks, and we recognized that giving people the opportunity to succeed would create the possibility that they might fail. Our operating principles meant that we would not put a person, unprepared, into a no-win situation. We made it clear that it was not considered a sign of weakness to ask for help. If we found a problem on a project, it was our responsibility to solve it. Our clients deserved value for every dollar they paid.

Sherman Greenstein recalls one case in which we hired a project manager who looked wonderful on paper; he had great credentials, experience, and references. But once he got started, it became clear at the first monthly review that there was a problem. "It was a fine opportunity for this person, a wonderful project for a great client, one of the biggest projects we ever had," Sherman says. "But we realized that he was in over his head."

So Sherman and his managers sat down with the employee and gave him their assessment. "We are not going to criticize, but we think this job is too big for you. You don't understand what the client really wants, nor the technology we can bring to bear." Sherman recalls that he agreed with the assessment. We concluded that he was actually relieved to have this problem addressed. Giving frank evaluations to employees may be awkward, but it is the best policy. We replaced the executive with a new project manager and assigned him to a different job, where he was successful.

Perhaps more difficult, but also important, is how a company confronts the realization that an executive is no longer suited for senior positions. We tried to reward people for good performance by advancing them to more challenging roles. Inevitably, some reached positions for which they were unfit. After years of good performance, they stumbled. When this happens in many companies, the initial inclination is to fire the person because he or she is making too much money for any lower assignment. This was not our practice. We usually offered a face-saving but lesser job—a second chance. This was made possible by our compensation structure. Bonus and equity awards were a big part of executive compensation and were directly proportional to their contributions. If an executive did not perform well, those components declined, but salary usually remained the same. If we reassigned a person to a lower position, he lost the ability to earn big bonuses and equity, but he still had a job. And in many cases, he found rewards in new roles.

One of the earlier examples of this came about as a result of our CIM work, which in the early 1990s represented the company's largest effort. It began as a $38 million contract and eventually grew beyond $275 million. But the concept of business process reengineering fell out of favor in the government, and our tasks disappeared. We realized that SRA had not capitalized on the extraordinary access and problem-solving opportunities that work had presented. Stu Rubens, who oversaw that project, had built, with the help of Dick Hunter, Bernie Cohen, and others, an organization that grew from $20 million and a hundred employees to about $100 million and one thousand employees without a single cost overrun. Nevertheless, Stu realized that studies and analysis were becoming a smaller part of our business. Expanding into the design and creation of technology systems was not where his interests were. It was time for a change. He still remained a valued member of our team but in a different capacity.

In 1995, we hired Renny DiPentima as chief information officer. During thirty-three years with the federal government, Renny rose to the position of Deputy Commissioner and Chief Information Officer for the Social Security Administration. He was the most visible IT executive in government and was held in high esteem by his peers. Renny's importance to the company grew rapidly; and within several years, we asked him to lead the government business division. Renny clearly understood client needs, but he faced a steep learning curve in translating that knowledge into business and shaping the company's development. We had to rapidly bring him up to speed on the culture and inner workings of SRA. Stu Rubens understood these factors, as only a founding employee of the company could. Our studies and analysis work was declining, and Stu did not like the business development aspects of it. Therefore, we assigned Stu to be Renny's deputy. The arrangement created a successful transition for both Renny and Stu. Though neither may have realized it at the time, their collaboration smoothed the way for an important leadership shift and helped maintain corporate continuity.

Ed McGushin was another example of someone who excelled as a manager and built a thriving emergency planning practice. However, with the end of the Cold War, that business began to fade and his role diminished. We were unable to find another right position for him, and he retired. I often wondered why we could not find another right fit for such a talented executive.

SRA was never a lifetime employment firm. If someone was lazy or incompetent, we did not hesitate to let that person go. Dishonesty was the offense that worried us the most. As the company grew larger, new employees had little contact with executives who lived by the founding values of SRA. We hired smart, energetic people who were also ambitious. What might happen if an employee in a far-flung office cut a corner or two? With one ethical slip—intentional or otherwise—our hard-won reputation would be damaged, and it would take years to recover. We might even be barred from doing work with the government.

Values are easier to convey when you have a staff of a dozen or fifty. But when a company grows from 500 to 1,500 people, then 5,000 and higher, it's important that values permeate the workplace. By 1993, SRA had grown to nearly nine hundred people. The influx of new employees meant that more than half of our people had been with the company for less than two years. During several staff meetings, executives expressed concern about the dilution, even loss, of our distinctive culture. In response, Ted and I developed a course that we called Culture and Values. It emphasized three vital attributes of the company: honesty and service, high-quality work and customer satisfaction, and an orientation toward people.

When new employees arrive at SRA on their first day, before they receive an assignment and are introduced to coworkers, they attend an orientation session. The people who lead this session share examples of real-world ethical challenges that have occurred at our company and help illustrate what we mean when we say that SRA lives by its values. These sessions are repeated regularly; SRA employees attend periodic refresher courses. Nevertheless, it was inevitable that lapses would occur. In particular, two stand out. In each case, our response was swift and unequivocal, but the company paid a price.

I was blindsided by the first. It was the fifteenth year of our business. I was in Canada celebrating my birthday with Sara, her sister, and my brother-in-law. The trip had been a lot of fun, until I received a phone call.

"The loss could be more than one million dollars," said Jerry Yates, vice president of administration.

An employee, who we will call "Jane," had joined the payables section of our finance and accounting organization about five years earlier. She soon gained a reputation for competence and hard work and received promotions. As was the case for many outstanding employees, I made a point of thanking her for her dedication. However, Jane had come to SRA with the intention to commit larceny, and she was very successful. I sometimes reflect on how she must have felt about our praise for her hard work. Perhaps she secretly laughed at our naivete, or maybe she had no feelings at all. In any case, she gained the confidence of her managers and knowledge of our system for paying suppliers. Then she devised a scheme with her paramour and others.

Our internal processes required two people to approve such claims. Jane was responsible for making payments to vendors. The accounting department then reviewed the paperwork and issued checks. As time passed, Jane found a way to manipulate the system by creating and quickly deleting false records to allow for duplicate payments to legitimate vendors, usually vendors located outside of Virginia. Then she and coconspirators began to cash the duplicate checks prepared as payment for legitimate vendors. She then issued another check to pay the legitimate payee. SRA was growing rapidly and there were many bills from our suppliers. Jane's double payments were buried in the volume. Her scheme was uncovered when the company was reconciling its bank accounts at the end of the year, in conjunction with our independent outside auditor, Arthur Andersen. The scheme had begun in the prior year but was not discovered then because auditors examine the systems and review small, representative samples of invoices and checks. Those double payments issued by Jane evidently escaped the reviews.

Jane could not resist the temptation to continue. Her greed was her downfall, and she was eventually found out. She had conducted a classic tactic for embezzling funds. After we confronted her with the evidence the company had developed proving her theft, she wrote a confession in her own hand and her supervisor walked her next door to the Arlington County Police Station. When she was arrested she even turned over some of the jewelry that she had purchased with the proceeds of her criminal acts.

People who have been robbed sometimes experience frustration with the justice system. The police seem slow to act, too much time elapses before an indictment, more time passes before a trial, and judges sometimes appear too lenient, for example, by setting the amount of bail too low. We felt abused in those ways. Before Jane could be convicted (while released on her own recognizance), she fled to the Philippines, where she had dual citizenship. She had escaped with more than $1 million.

A year or two had passed when Jerry Yates came to my office to tell me that Jane was back in the Arlington County Jail. She had surreptitiously returned to the United States, but then had a falling-out with her common-law husband. A tipster turned her in to SRA and she was arrested and jailed. The prosecutor offered a lesser charge if Jane would make restitution. Otherwise, she would likely spend five years in jail while her young daughter grew up without her. Jane refused. Perhaps she had given it away, or spent it, or secreted it in foreign bank accounts. She went to prison after being sentenced to five 10-year terms to be served concurrently. The whole situation filled me with great frustration, anger, disappointment, and sadness. Our insurance covered most of our losses, but it was the breach of trust that was most disturbing.

The second case is cited often in our Culture and Values courses. It was not a malicious breach of conduct, but nevertheless was deeply troubling and costly. Had we not caught it at the time we did, the results could have been even more corrosive.

A company's documentation of its work is an inviolable record. It should faithfully report how employees spend their time and enumerate that in invoices. Altering time cards is the ultimate sin in government contracting. It amounts to fraud and is grounds for a firm to be barred from doing business with federal entities. We make these rules starkly clear to new employees, and we repeat them regularly to avoid errors, intentional or otherwise. Nevertheless, it happened.

It was the mid-1990s and one of our managers was supervising three separate contracts we were performing for the Army. Two of them were proceeding as planned, and on budget. But the third contract was exceeding our spending allocations, in part because it was requiring more manpower hours than anticipated. The manager rationalized to himself that all three were for the same customer, the kinds of work were generally similar, and so it would not make much difference to shift some of the employee hours among the contracts. He never discussed this with a supervisor, who immediately would have put a stop to it, nor did he tell anyone what he had done. We found out about it because a junior person on one of his teams came to Ann Denison, our director of human resources, and told her that the manager had directed her to change her time card. She remembered from Culture and Values class that nobody in the company can direct an employee to improperly charge her time. This was a principal misdeed.

Immediately, I asked Stu Rubens to investigate. He flew to Texas and interviewed dozens of people over the course of several weeks. He came back and wrote a report. The conclusion: The allegations were true. We had to tell the government. We presented the client with the results of our investigation and returned all of the money on the three contracts. This was one of the few cases in which an employee was fired and escorted from the building that same day.

We wrote off nearly $1 million in expenses against profit for that work and retrained all staff members involved, except for the offending manager, who was discharged. If the young woman had reported the incident directly to the client, SRA would not have had the opportunity to investigate and self-report the improper time charging to our client. We would have been left to wait for the government to complete its independent audit and if the government found the incident was material and not an isolated event we could have faced debarment proceedings that would damage our hard-earned reputation for honesty and potentially suspended us from federal contracting.

Another story occurred during the very early years of SRA, when our survival was not at all assured. We were growing, but also fighting for every job just to meet payroll. We had a good opportunity to win a big Air Force contract in Boston. Then one of our consultants helping with the proposal did something that compromised SRA. He found competitors' bids among discarded documents. From this, he discerned that we were not the lowest bidder. He relayed this information to the proposal team manager who, in turn, informed his boss. We discussed the issue and decided not to change our bid. We removed the consultant and did not share his information with anyone. We lost the bid. No one wanted to win that job more than our proposal manager, but he did the right thing. He was ethical and courageous.

These events demonstrate that having clearly stated values is vital, but it is just the beginning. Constant vigilance and reinforcement are essential. Managers must "walk the talk" by continuously demonstrating high ethics and care for customers and employees. And these humanistic actions must be embedded within a good system of management accounting and control.

13

Investments That Always Pay Off

⋯⟩ **Business success is all about people.**

⋯⟩ **Don't hire your brother-in-law or best friend.**

⋯⟩ **The best ideas win.**

s we entered our twentieth year, SRA had a track record of consecutive growth, a reputation for doing top-quality work, and an
experienced executive team. The average tenure of our forty-
five officers was nearly fifteen years, and we had lost very few to other
companies. But even with all this good news, there was still a disturbing
sign of trouble: severe problems in recruiting and retaining new, talented staff members.

In the late 1990s, the tech world was experiencing an unpreced-
ed boom. This was before the dot-com bubble burst, and unemployment in the Washington, DC, region was low. There were not enough
qualified workers to meet the demand. Younger IT professionals, in
particular, worked for a company only as long as it met their financial
and other goals. It was relatively easy for people with security clearances
and computer science or engineering degrees to contact another technology firm and win a job offer with a 5 to 10 percent salary increase.

The short supply of qualified technical workers impacted SRA as it
did other companies. We began fiscal year 1997 with a staff of 1,139.
During the year, we hired 430 people, but we lost 257. The attrition rate
was unprecedented—more than 15 percent. Companies raided one another. Salaries escalated, putting pressure on profits. We had a choice:

either lower our standards and hire more people, or continue to be selective, and not accept all the work that was available. We chose the latter course and began looking for ways to improve our recruitment and retention programs.

In most good companies, employees are solicited by friends and relatives who would like to join the firm. This was particularly hard for me in the early days and continues to the present. Some people expect preference as part of the friendship or other fidelity. We did not prohibit hiring such people, but we tried to put them through the same selective process as any other candidate.

In competing for capable people, we had an advantage: the SRA reputation for creative risk-taking. We placed good people on challenging projects that engaged them intellectually. If a RFP seemed appealing but the tasks were mundane, we would not bid it. We also told prospects that SRA was an environment that encouraged different approaches in order to innovate. We tried hard to give credit where it was due, not simply to a team leader; and we gave employees bonuses for helping us hire qualified employees.

We often described to candidates how our risk-taking culture had resulted in so many proposal wins. SRA developed a process that was distinct but repeatable. Take a group of smart people, put them in a room, assure them that no idea would be scorned, and encourage them to come up with the most innovative and possibly even outrageous solutions to a problem. Arguing was fine, as long as it did not become personal and was aimed at finding the best solution for a customer. The best idea wins, no matter who suggests it.

In some sense, we began to formalize creativity. This may seem counterintuitive. One can't simply order another *Mona Lisa*—an inspired work that endures throughout the ages—but you can break down the steps required to get there. In preparing a proposal, decide on a capture strategy. Then, in effect, select the colors and canvas, set up an easel, paint, evaluate, and change, adapting new techniques, as necessary. The end result can be, figuratively, a work of art.

Susan Lilly, one of our PhDs, created SRA University, a set of courses taught by volunteers that became popular among employees wishing to further develop their skills. We also launched a seminar program designed to promote knowledge-sharing and help employees build expertise in various disciplines. The work of some of the early proposal writers at SRA, including Barry Landew and Jeff Rydant, formed a basis that would lead to successful proposals. To this day, our proposal training courses, led by Allen Deitz, are popular and important. Another more recent offering consists of classes in business literacy.

The idea for one of our most successful recruiting tools came from an off-site meeting in 1998 at the Boar's Head Inn in Charlottesville, Virginia. Teams of managers were asked to brainstorm about how SRA was spending time and resources and find new ways to leverage our talent and other assets. Recruiting was one important topic. It was clear that we needed to get the word out about what our company offered in addition to a competitive salary—a values-based culture that was more than a slogan.

At a break between sessions, a small group continued talking, and Mike Duffy suggested that SRA try to win a place on the prestigious Fortune 100 List of Best Companies to Work For in America. This would differentiate SRA in an extremely competitive hiring market. Ann Denison, the head of our human resources department, began to develop the idea. She had been recruited to SRA eleven years earlier by Bill Brehm. Ann had technical and program management experience. She also was very good at getting things done.

In 1999 we submitted an application for SRA to be included in the "100 Best" corporate ranking. A significant part of the *Fortune* evaluation is a survey to a random sample of employees at each company seeking a spot on the list. In the first year that SRA applied, 96 percent of our employees responded that they believed their managers trusted them to do a good job. We won a spot on the list in 2000 and remained on it for ten consecutive years—a singular achievement. Our reputation as a people-oriented company was further affirmed when Ann was honored in 2002 at the first Annual Human Resource Leadership Awards of Greater Washington. These kudos reflected our conviction that business success is tied directly to how we treat our people.

SRA holds an annual awards dinner where we honor employees who had particular impact in the company and recognize others who reached annual benchmarks—5, 10, 15, 20 years. In the early years, the ceremonies were modest, but as we grew, so did our ability to offer more elegant settings. We moved from the office conference room to ballrooms of prominent hotels. We still invite employee spouses to the dinner because we want them to see how much we appreciate their husbands or wives. Working here is rarely a forty-hour-a-week proposition, and we know that our people need cooperation at home. All of the awards had meaning, but a few were more coveted than others. The first Leadership Award went to Chuck Perry, a native of Harlem and former army officer. He is still admired and loved by many. Jeffrey Westerhoff won the Business Development Award three times.

Special grants of sick leave are donated to employees in need in honor of an earlier and more colorful manager. Jerry Yates was a retired Army chief warrant officer, who joined SRA in 1983. He knew how to get things done. Jerry's talents made him the obvious choice to take over our company's administrative functions. He managed office facilities, security, and human resources. Ann Denison reported to him.

Jerry was a complex person with a unique set of talents and a volatile personality. He often helped employees in trouble or with special needs. He gave someone who had failed in an assignment another chance and interceded when employees found themselves in legal or financial crises. Jerry's management philosophy was high-minded. He would start by asking, "Have I been fair? Have I given someone the benefit of the doubt? Have I done my best to help this person succeed? Is there anything else I can do to help?" On the other hand, Jerry's temper and old military demeanor occasionally slipped into his work, and some people were caught off guard.

Kevin Graves has ably managed facilities and equipment at SRA for many years. He knew Jerry from their earlier days working in the Secretary of the Army office and was hired by him. Kevin was familiar with Jerry's occasional episodes of thunderous ranting, followed a day later by remorse. Kevin recalls having left SRA six times—five times because Jerry fired him. "Jerry would go home and describe to his wife, Nancy, what happened. She would tell him to go back to the office the next day and apologize. We always worked it out."

Early in 1995, Jerry began experiencing health problems. He suffered severe debilitating headaches. By early summer, he had trouble writing, speaking, and remembering short-term events. In July, Jerry took an extended sick leave to battle what by then had been diagnosed as Parkinson's disease. Relieved from the tension of his job, Jerry seemed to recover somewhat; but three days prior to his expected return, he was struck in the head while playing golf by a ricocheting ball and suffered a severe subdural hematoma. He was confined to a wheelchair, carefully attended by his wife Nancy.

Jerry was depressed by his condition, and the couple moved to the edge of a golf course near his childhood home in Redding, California.

My daughter, Lauren, her husband, Andrew, and four of our grandchildren live not far from where Jerry purchased the home. Sara and I combined a trip to my daughter's home with a visit to Jerry and Nancy. The two ladies tactfully left us on the patio to talk—Jerry in the wheelchair and I sitting beside him. The golf course and a large pond stretched out in front of us and, in the distance, snow-capped Mount Shasta was visible.

"What a beautiful view," I remarked.

"Yes," replied Jerry. "I do not sleep well, and I often rise before dawn and come out here to enjoy the panorama. Once I saw a cougar over there on the edge of the course."

"Really," I replied.

For a few minutes we were lost in thought, but our minds were on the same subject.

Jerry said, "You know, we had something special." I nodded, encouraging him to continue. "I had many wonderful years in the Army, but SRA was the capstone of my career. I made mistakes, but I and you, and all the others, really cared about people."

I did not see Jerry again. His condition deteriorated. One morning he went out onto the golf course behind his patio, put a pistol to his head, and pulled the trigger.

In 1996 we split Jerry's office into two departments, giving Ann Denison the responsibility for running human resources and Kevin Graves the job of asset management. We were at an important point in the growth of the company. Both of those lines of work needed a lot of attention in order to make SRA a better place to work.

An important factor in the inclusion of SRA on the *Fortune* list of 100 Best Places to Work was our employee health program. It was initiated by Kay Curling, whom we hired in 1988 to be the director of training programs. After a couple of years on the job, Kay became pregnant with her third child, who had significant health issues. Jerry Yates supported her through much of this time, often visiting her infant son in the hospital. One day, Jerry told Kay that he had just met a nurse who was interviewing for a position in the company's health business unit. There was not an immediate fit, but Jerry had a good impression of her. Kay asked a reasonable question: "What are we going to do with her?" Jerry responded, "I don't know, but we're going to hire her."

Kay and Ann Denison assigned the nurse to review the company's health insurance claims. She audited large hospital bills for SRA employees, and researched questions about procedures, costs, and treatments. Within the first six months, we found enough anomalies to save SRA three times more than a nurse's part-time salary. It also became clear that managing health care issues was a significant issue for many SRA employees and that providing assistance would be a useful benefit. Recognizing the need for truly personal support, Kay hired a full-time nurse, Karen Amato, who created an on-site clinic. Karen provided assistance to employees facing health crises and launched other initiatives: offering smoking cessation, weight loss, allergy shots, blood pressure checks, and fitness and other programs at the office.

Karen worked with employees who had been diagnosed with life threatening illnesses. She helped them understand their medical circumstances and options. She intervened with our insurer to get the best medical care for employees and their families, and helped determine the best services for them, as was the case with the family of an employee who was in a coma for four months.

In Fall 2002, I was diagnosed with a serious case of melanoma on my right arm. The next step for me was a second operation that would penetrate nearly to the bone, combined with the removal of lymph nodes under my arm. Karen Amato heard of my condition and came to my office to offer support. She explained in clear, direct terms what I was facing. "The surgery that you'll have is similar to a procedure that some women experience in a mastectomy. The biopsies determine the next stage of treatment. If the infection has reached the lymph nodes, the prognosis is not good."

I knew this. My niece had just died from melanoma. Karen described the details of the surgery and various treatments. In an attempt to offer encouragement, she said, "I had breast cancer surgery a few years ago and thought I might die. But today I seem to be quite healthy."

After our meeting, I reflected on what Karen must have gone through and how it may have positively shaped her life. She has a sense of compassion that, year after year and even today, provides hope for employees suffering from serious illness. I have concluded from her experience, mine, and many other friends and relatives, that when facing a life-threatening event or some other serious challenge, the result is less important than how you approach the challenge mentally, and what you learn from it. In some sense, much of life is about playing the game well.

Regrettably, as SRA grew we had to discontinue the walk-in clinic. Although employees appreciated being able to see a nurse practitioner at the office to get allergy shots, prescriptions or address other health issues, we could not afford to offer such clinics at the many locations, nationally and internationally, where thousands of SRA people work. We continue to have nurse care managers who are available to assist all employees by phone, and we added an advocate to help with disability, maternity, and other leave issues. Karen Amato has continued to develop our health programs and provide wellness coordinators. Nevertheless, our need to close the popular clinic provided a difficult lesson: A great program designed for five hundred employees is not necessarily scalable to a much larger company. Adaptation is an essential part of corporate growth.

While there is always more a company can do to invest in its people, our efforts to attract new employees and treat them decently continued to pay off. Three years after Ann Denison took over human resources, SRA was recognized for having one of the most innovative programs in the Washington metropolitan area. We were highlighted frequently in the press for our successful recruiting techniques. Our public advertising and our employee magazine (*In Depth*) won awards. And we created a new salary planning structure and designed a system of learning tracks to support the development of our people. We did all of this because it was the right thing to do. But we continued to search for investments that would yield even greater returns for our people.

The long-range impact of such initiatives may be impossible to measure. Most of the SRA founding members retired or moved to other ventures. But their values are woven into the fabric of the company. Now, a new generation of corporate leaders must carry this culture forward.

14

Commercial—A New Course for a While

⋯⟩ Technological euphoria can be expensive.

⋯⟩ If you provide services, forget products.

⋯⟩ If you are a government contractor,
forget commercial work.

Becoming a government contractor was an easy decision. Through many years in military, higher education, and the government, I tried to solve challenging problems. I had good contacts in parts of the military community and, with the help of others, was adding ethical, talented people to SRA. However, even as the company became increasingly successful in the government market, there were times when I felt that to truly be an entrepreneur, we should develop products and services for both the government and commercial markets.

During the dot-com bubble of the mid and late 1990s, the business appeal of firms like ours paled in comparison to young technology firms. Yet SRA had developed information technology innovations that seemed to be as advanced as those of commercial firms that were experiencing huge stock price growth. Wall Street investors were enamored with them, though many had never posted a single dollar of profit. Federal Reserve Chairman Alan Greenspan lamented the irrational exuberance associated with Internet stocks. At the same time, it was unclear where the federal contracting market was heading during the Clinton administration. The Soviet Union had collapsed a few years before Clinton was elected, and the Cold War was over. It was difficult to predict how long the period of tight government budgets would last.

For more than a decade, we had debated about the degree that SRA should delve into commercial business. I and several others believed that we would be a more exciting company, if we could be successful in commercial markets. We would have higher profits and greater interest from public investors. Others argued that our firm was not built to assume the up-front costs of developing new commercial technologies, and we could not afford to divert profits produced by government work to speculate in the public market. On the other hand, in 1994 SRA had passed $100 million, and our federal contracts could provide the necessary stability for a commercial practice. Excitement about the Internet was growing, and I wanted to exploit opportunities provided by our technology.

There was precedent for this kind of strategy, particularly in defense technology. For example, Boeing's early role in building the B-47 and B-52 bombers gave the company a big advantage in creating its 707 commercial passenger jet in the 1950s. And our country gained a large lead in the development of commercial computers because of the Air Force work on transistors and integrated circuits for weapon systems. There were many other cases in which government-sponsored technology spawned entirely new markets.

Ten years after Sherman Greenstein and I began our artificial intelligence conversations, SRA had successfully developed a number of natural language products for government clients. With the Internet growing, perhaps we could adapt them to the commercial world. Our strategy for new commercial ventures was simple. Solve a business problem using our software and technical expertise, find a partner in a specific market, and convince investors to provide start-up capital.

One day, Gary Nelson suggested that we meet with John White, his friend at Kodak, to see if we could get commercial consulting work. Kodak Legal Systems, a division of Eastman Kodak International, Inc., had purchased a company that had a contract to develop a document management system for a major law firm in Chicago. The job was going poorly. John asked us to evaluate the situation and try to develop a solution. We agreed, but our assessment was not optimistic. Their team did not have the necessary experience, and their approach was problematic.

I requested a meeting with the chief information officer of the law firm, accompanied by Bill Albright, who had joined SRA a decade earlier. Bill was a key member of Gary Nelson's business development team and was leading our efforts to identify and pursue new commercial ventures. The law firm's CIO invited us to their office in Manhattan for cocktails and dinner. As we entered an elaborate conference room on the top floor of a skyscraper, instead of cocktail glasses and dinner plates, we found six places, each with a long yellow legal pad and pen. Our host had not yet arrived. I turned to Bill and whispered, "They're having *us* for dinner!"

Our goal was to end the project tactfully, and with as little damage as possible to Kodak. John wanted SRA as a corporate partner, providing technical expertise and sharing equity in the firm, but it was clear that without customers and a good technology, the small firm would surely fail. We advised John to shut it down, which he did. Nevertheless, we maintained our relationship with John, who was honest, intelligent, and personable.

After a few months, Bill Albright came across another commercial opportunity. *National Geographic* photographer, Nathan Benn, and his business partner, Jeff Weiss, suggested an Internet company through which stock photographs could be sold online. This was long before the application of the World Wide Web for online selling. SRA provided the technical expertise, Kodak supplied image storage technology, and the Tribune Company of Chicago contributed $10 million. The result was Picture Network International (PNI).

The new company was launched three years before the creation of similar firms (Getty Images and Corbis) and introduced users to a new type of photographic commerce using our natural language processing software. Using the PNI Internet site, advertisers, corporate brochure editors, and others could, with descriptions in plain English, find just the right picture from thousands of candidates. They could view the results of their searches and make purchases online. Although PNI was innovative for the time, it burned through the investment capital and was sold at a loss several years after it was funded. We had a lot to learn about the complexities of commercial online companies.

This baptism under fire did not deter us; we proceeded with several other new ventures.

Bill had, for several years, carried on a business dialogue with David Cole, a venture capitalist who ran a fund that specialized in early stage start-ups. His partner was Miles Gilburne, who joined our board many years later. David and Miles were instrumental in our next spin-off which included Linda Dozier, a creative systems engineer in our company. Browsers, which allowed users to interface with documents on the Internet, were still in the early phases of development. Netscape was months away from being released. David and Miles wanted to invest in an Internet navigation company. Linda's idea was to develop a tool that would enable users to read and edit content simultaneously. It would be an online publishing company. The innovation propelled users beyond the "read only" function that had existed until that point. We incorporated Navisoft in 1993. Linda became its chief technology officer. Tim Berners-Lee, the creator of the World Wide Web, later called Navisoft a milestone in the development of the web.

Not all of our commercial initiatives were directed toward new companies. Karl Wilhelm joined SRA in the early 1980s and worked on our missile contracts. One of his later jobs was to create a business plan for a legal services practice. The plan targeted firms of several hundred attorneys and offered local and wide area networks, desktop software, and document management. Most law firms of this size during the early 1990s had modest computer capabilities.

It was tough going at first. We bid a lot of jobs in eighteen months with little success. When we finally won one, the client knew we bid the job thin and picked up the check for the victory celebration. Our business prospered for several years, until virtually all law firms of this size had finished their capital investments in these systems.

The financial world was also a target of opportunity, because it was projected to be a leader in information technology spending. Two of our most promising commercial services spin-offs grew from a contract that SRA won in 1996 with the National Association of Securities Dealers. One of our clients was Mary Shapiro, who later became Chairman of the Securities and Exchange Commission (SEC), but at the time was head of the National Association of Securities Dealers, a self-regulatory industry group. She was a good customer, discerning but fair, and I was impressed with her. I remember sitting in her office well after working hours and seeing a screensaver flashing, in multicolored words, "Mom, come home!" I have always marveled at women who are able to succeed in highly demanding jobs *and* as mothers. And I very much admire those, like my wife and daughters, who are full-time moms and raise wonderful children.

At this time, new government regulations required brokerage firms to create systems that could identify fraudulent trades. Emerson Thompson led this project. His team developed data-mining software that could uncover irregular and potentially illegal activity in the hundreds of thousands of trades executed each day. We called this data mining software Mantas, and we customized and sold it to Wall Street brokerage firms, including Fidelity Investments, Merrill Lynch, and Schwab.

Financial institutions also had to monitor email between brokers and customers for indications of insider trading, misleading sales practices, and other illegal activities. When email was still relatively new, brokerage firms would manually scan a small subset of all the messages. As that traffic grew, they needed a less labor-intensive, more effective method of doing this. Our solution was called Assentor. It used sophisticated natural language processing to recognize and quarantine questionable messages. At its peak, Assentor technology read 75 percent of all email traffic on Wall Street.

In 1996, we incorporated a business, called IsoQuest, which used SRA software to organize and manage published material based on textual content. We spun it out, but IsoQuest did not last long.

Then another opportunity arose. Former Postmaster General, Paul Carlin, and his business partner, Gene Johnson, approached SRA about collaborating on the development of a new company that they had recently started called Mail2000. It was little more than a concept when they brought it to us, but the ambition of the firm was grand: to revolutionize mass mailing by printing correspondence close to where it would be delivered, saving time and money.

Richard Spires and Gary Nelson sponsored the idea, and we agreed to invest cash and, more importantly, to create a demonstration that would stimulate sales. John Young and his technical team transformed the vision into reality. In less than a year, SRA designed, developed, and deployed a pilot system. Within a few years, it became our most profitable new venture. Our partners later sold it, and *Washington Technology* named it a deal of the year.

Health and telecommunications were two other areas in which we sought commercial business. Again, much of our experience was based on work we had done for the government. In the early 1980s, we won a contract to analyze the telecommunications needs of the Department of Treasury. This enabled us to hire new people. Among them were David Garbin, a talented MIT graduate who became an expert in modeling wide area telecommunications networks. Ron Sherwin was an electrical engineer with satellite communications experience, and

Richard Spires was a young EE graduate of the University of Cincinnati. Ten years later, their efforts helped launch our commercial telecommunications practice, which offered network design services to clients such as MCI Corporation, Boeing, AT&T, DuPont, Sprint International, and Bell South.

Another area that offered promise was based on work that Susan Castillo, John Greene, and others had done to help create a database for scientists involved in genomic research. Dr. Edison Liu, the deputy director of the National Cancer Institute, oversaw much of the research and was impressed by our team's innovative suggestions. Later, when Dr. Liu left the Institute to create similar research projects in Singapore and the Netherlands, he asked us to create customized systems for them as well. Eventually, we provided that technology to the Centers for Disease Control, and started to incubate a spin-off that would look for ways to apply our systems capabilities to commercial markets. We called this prospective venture Tapestry, but it never gained traction, and we abandoned it.

By the middle of 1995, our new products and technology unit had delivered $3 million in commercial revenue, about $700,000 of which was in financial services. In contrast, the core federal business was annually bidding more than a billion dollars in major new opportunities. Overall revenue had reached $157 million, and that year we won nearly $500 million in new, mainly federal, contracts. SRA was moving beyond adolescence into adulthood and we needed to make room for some of our young stand-outs to grow. I also wanted to centralize and professionalize our commercial efforts. So I elevated Ted Legasey to chief operating officer and together we reorganized the work under two business sectors: federal, which was run by Renny DiPentima, and commercial, for which there were no obvious in-house candidates.

We engaged a search firm to find someone to lead our commercial group. Among several candidates, one seemed particularly promising. Errol was an executive, who had played a role in building a commercial sector within Computer Science Corporation (CSC). His capabilities were attractive to us because CSC was one of the few government contracting firms that had been successful in the private sector. In interviews with SRA executives, Errol came across as confident, personable, and knowledgeable. Reference checks were positive, and we hired him.

Errol seemed to give us a firsthand look at the differences between the way commercial companies and government contracting firms do business. Because he was going to market clients different from the typical SRA customer, Errol wanted his team to present an image different from that of a government contracting firm. He hired about five people and leased space for forty employees on Park Avenue in Manhattan, and he elaborately refurbished office space in Fairfax. When people from our commercial and federal sectors traveled together, the commercial team sat in first class, while federal members flew coach. Despite—or perhaps because of—such measures, commercial sales did not grow. Errol had strategic perspective and a good track record with a big company, but he was a poor fit for SRA in terms of both business and culture. It seemed, as the saying goes, that Errol "was all hat and no cattle." Within several months, we quietly parted ways.

We took several lessons from this episode. SRA is a business that deliberately built itself on a particular set of values. Our people were intelligent, entrepreneurial, and sometimes idiosyncratic—more interested in creating their own way to greatness than in following someone else. The work itself was always more important than the accoutrements; it was contrary to SRA culture to spend on appearance rather than substance. The cohesion of our management team and our principle of "the best idea wins" meant that we had to choose people who would prosper in that culture.

After Errol's departure, we decided to select someone from within SRA to lead our commercial business. Richard Spires was technically capable, polished, and experienced; I saw in him a potential next-generation corporate officer. I asked him to develop the commercial group and Emerson Thompson to oversee operations.

On the federal side, Barry Landew had become a versatile and valuable team member, capable of taking on many projects and performing them with excellence. He needed new challenges to grow. I promoted Barry to lead business development, succeeding Gary Nelson, whom I asked to serve as vice chairman of the board, where he assumed a leadership role in evaluating and helping to guide new technologies. Jeff Rydant was upgrading our internal finance, accounting, human resource, and other back office systems, and he eventually moved up to lead the commercial group after Richard left the company.

Through trial and error, we learned that business success depends on a lot more than good technology. There were occasions when we knew that our commercial offerings were better than those of competitors, and yet we could not sell our services or products as effectively.

Market knowledge and presence are far more important factors. It also was clear that commercial business operated on a model that was completely different from the federal sector. Federal contractors strived to keep overhead as low as possible and competed fiercely for work. Contract profits were low, but the government always paid its bills, and the contracts often went on for years. The commercial business was sometimes erratic. Some customers did not pay or canceled a contract without warning or cause. In one instance, a telecommunications giant told our project manager on Friday that the one hundred or so SRA people working on the project should not return to work the following Monday. The client simply assigned the work to another firm.

We debated the costs and benefits of our commercial efforts. Executives in the federal business resented the profits of their work being spent on frills to attract commercial clients. They also argued that the resources SRA was diverting to create new companies could have been used to further expand our federal business. On the other hand, proponents of creating new spin-offs were frustrated that SRA could never invest enough to make them successful. Our Mantas technology was a good example of the conundrum.

By the summer of 2000, it seemed that success of our Mantas products on Wall Street boded well for the creation of a company based on that technology. I asked Richard Spires, who by then was leading our financial services business, how much money it would cost to achieve this, and he suggested $2–3 million. We could not afford to make that kind of commitment, so I found an investor who was willing to provide capital for technology companies that SRA incubated. Philadelphia-based Safeguard Scientific would retain a partial equity interest in each new firm. This partnership helped advance our ambitions of creating valuable spin-off, but it was increasingly obvious to me that the debate over whether SRA should continue to pursue its commercial ambitions would have to be settled at some point. What I could not see, at the time, were the national and global markets at work that ultimately would make the decision clear.

In the late 1980s, people began asking me when SRA would become a public company. They had seen articles about executives becoming wealthy during public offerings. This became a perennial question, and my answer would invariably fail to satisfy: "Not yet, conditions are not right." We needed revenue of several hundred million dollars, good profitability, and prospects for continued growth. Equally important, the stock market had to value companies like SRA. Over the years, I consulted with investment bankers to assess how SRA would be received by the market if we were to go public. By 1997, SRA had posted eighteen years of steady growth, all of which was organic; we were profitable, and had developed a reputation for performing excellent work. But the stock market was not favorable. Wall Street was inordinately focused on new Internet companies. The potential stock price quoted by investment bankers did not adequately reflect the value of our company.

But the world was about to change, and with it the future of SRA. In 2000, the dot-com bubble burst. It was still rapidly declining on September 11, 2001, when terrorists attacked the World Trade Center and the Pentagon. The Bush administration signaled its intention to ramp up defense spending. Suddenly investors became interested in government contractors. I began to receive calls from investment bankers who wanted to take SRA public, or whose clients wanted to buy the company. It seemed likely that we could finally get a decent price for SRA stock on a public exchange. After some deliberation, we chose a Citigroup team led by Ed Wehle as our investment banker to explore alternatives.

The Citigroup team looked at our company's financial projections and strongly advised us to divest our commercial products and ventures and become a pure play government contractor. They pointed out that investors specialize in specific markets and some would focus on the government contracting sector. They knew nothing about the commercial markets of our new ventures and, therefore, would regard these initiatives as risky. They would think that it was not a good way to use the money that they would invest in SRA.

The logic of the Citigroup advisors was compelling, and they knew a lot more about the investment community than we did. When we sold Navisoft to America Online eight years earlier, it produced a good profit; Mantas and Assentor were promising, but the others had not paid their way, except for Mail2000, which produced more than $10 million in profit. Overall, we could not continue to invest the substantial capital required to build all commercial lines of business into successful concerns. Reluctantly, we abandoned the idea of developing our genome research technology into a new company.

Many SRA people had worked hard on the companies that we did launch, and we lost some talented staff when we sold them. Richard Spires and Dan Ilisevich were two of the key contributors to our earlier telecommunications work, and they left when we spun out a subsidiary.

That company continued for several years and was ultimately sold to Oracle. Richard left to become chief information officer of the IRS and then of the Department of Homeland Security. We sold Assentor for $5 million to iLumin Software Services, Inc., a private equity backed firm. Emerson Thompson left with it and remained at iLumin until it was sold to Computer Associates in 2005. Gary Nelson, who had been deeply involved in the new ventures, retired.

We learned a lot from these new ventures. We were proud of our technology and the fact that SRA could compete in commercial markets as well as the government arena. However in retrospect, we probably could have had more success if we had concentrated solely on professional technical services for the federal government and avoided the commercial sector. Furthermore, developing and selling products required expertise and capital that we did not have. It was difficult to see so much talent and so many capabilities fall away, but SRA was now on a course that would change the company's future.

15

Going Public

···⟩ Get money when it is available;
don't wait until you really need it.

···⟩ Values are vital; capable people want
to be part of something great.

W hen I first began to think about forming a company in 1970, I imagined that one day it would be listed on a public exchange. I got the idea from Ross Perot, who at that time had the most successful initial public offering (IPO) for an IT company. His success caused *Fortune* magazine to label Perot "the fastest rich Texan ever." I had met him many years before then, in June 1954, on a Navy destroyer, the USS *Sigourney*. I led a group of midshipmen from the Naval Academy and civilian universities that were on a summer cruise to Europe, learning firsthand about shipboard life. As the midshipmen officer in charge, I had the opportunity to stand watch with Perot, who was a highly regarded ensign. He had graduated from the academy in 1953.

A Navy ship operates around the clock, and a captain's responsibilities are formidable, but even he needs time to sleep. The captain, therefore, delegates to the officer-of-the-watch the responsibility to guide the ship. During our first few watches together, Ensign Perot described what he was doing, gave me tips on his job, and small tasks to perform such as changing ship speed through commands to the engine room. The midwatch (midnight to 4:00 a.m.) was an excellent time for me to learn. We were steaming in a convoy with larger ships inside and the destroyers (manned by about three hundred people each) in a circle around them. This is a classic formation designed to protect the larger ships from torpedo attack, although our nation was not at war and there was no threat.

At that time of night, the bridge (located in the upper part of the ship's super structure) is dark to give officers outward visibility. Even the various indicators are dimmed. The ship rolls back and forth slowly. Sailors are expected not only to stand watch at night but also to perform a full work day. It is easy to get sleepy—but not Ensign Perot. An energetic, voluble man, he provided opinions in a twangy, Texas accent filled with aphorisms on subjects ranging from geopolitics to military life. I listened, occasionally inserting a brief question during his rare pauses. His guidance and leadership example, together with that of many others during my military career, would serve me well in building a business.

The night before the end of the cruise, I asked him a final question, "Mr. Perot, would you briefly give me one guideline on how to be a good officer?"

Without hesitating, he replied, "Do what you have been taught at the Naval Academy. Be honest, work hard, take care of your men, and they will take care of you."

Although devoted to the Navy, Perot was too impatient to endure the slow promotion process. After a few years, he resigned his commission and joined IBM selling computers. He exceeded his quota well before the end of the first year. He had many ideas for improving business, but his managers were slow to act on them. So in 1962, he left IBM and formed Electronic Data Systems (EDS), which processed Medicare forms for the government. Only six years later, the initial public offering for EDS created a great deal of excitement in the media. I was still in military service at the time but saved the articles about Ross Perot, reasoning that I could learn from his example.

At the time that I formed SRA, EDS was a giant in computer services and often hired former military officers. We admired their élan, which included recruiting ads containing the phrase "Eagles Do Not Flock."

Perot and his company made big headlines again in 1979. The Shah of Iran had been overthrown, and the new revolutionary government refused to make the final payment on an EDS contract to develop a computer system. Therefore, EDS did not deliver the final product. In response, the government jailed two EDS employees, who had been stationed in Iran. Perot turned to former military commandos, who worked at EDS, to form a rescue team, which he led into Iran. The team located the EDS people in jail, created a riot outside that freed them, and, in a harrowing trip north into Turkey, everyone got out.

In 1984, Ross Perot sold EDS to General Motors (GM), which intended to use its information technology expertise internally and continue to sell its services. As part of the deal, Perot became the biggest shareholder in GM and a member of the board of directors. However, he soon became embroiled in conflicts with Roger Smith (the chairman and CEO of GM) and resigned from the GM board. A few years later Perot formed a new company with his son called Perot Systems. During the last twenty years, SRA has competed often for government contracts against EDS and Perot Systems.

In 2009, Perot and I were guests at a small luncheon at the U.S. Naval Academy honoring the tenth year of the Stockdale Center for Ethical Leadership. Perot had run for president in 1992, and James B. Stockdale was his vice presidential running mate. Stockdale was a naval aviator and Congressional Medal of Honor winner. Perot and I were recognized for fostering ethics at the Academy. I, together with Bill Brehm, supported an ethics chair for several years and had recommended the creation of the center more than ten years before then. I reminded Perot of our conversations while standing watch aboard the USS *Sigourney* back in 1954 and told him that he had been an inspiration for me. He was polite, but I suspected that he did not recall the dialogue. We, in leadership positions, are sometimes unaware of our influence (good or bad) on young people. In any case, Perot's successful public offering years before occasionally entered my mind as SRA grew and the market became more receptive to firms like ours.

The primary objective of an IPO is to raise money so that the company can grow faster. A secondary reason is that employees and other shareholders can sell some of their stock at a higher price than would be offered in a limited, private market. In the early 1980s, we adopted an incentive stock option program to help us recruit and retain good people. Our logic was that if an executive performed well, he or she would have stock options granted at a low price. Someday, when the company went public, the price would be much higher and the employee with equity could benefit.

The decision to go public was not easy. Our executive team and the board of directors debated the issue. An offering would deliver funds for a more aggressive acquisition program, and under the right conditions, could steadily increase the price for our stock. On the other hand, we could borrow money to make acquisitions and therefore would not need an IPO. Finally, a lot of expense is associated with being a public company. Government and exchange regulations require many more reports and organizational oversight. This adds costs for accounting, legal, and investor relations. Charles Rossotti, the founder and chairman of American Management Systems (AMS), once remarked to me that while he did not like many of these requirements, he felt that public companies were generally held to a higher standard of accountability than private firms. After spending considerable time in these discussions, I recommended to the board that we proceed with the initial public offering.

In May 2002, Ted Legasey, Steve Hughes (our chief financial officer), and I set out on a cross-country tour called "The Road Show," to educate and entice investors. With the help of Citigroup, we assembled a package of documents that described SRA and the market we served. Every word had to be checked for accuracy. If we said that we fulfilled a $100 million contract, we had to verify the exact amount. If it was $100.6 million, we corrected the number—no guesses, no estimates. We polished and timed our presentation; twenty minutes to show charts that told the SRA story, forty minutes for questions.

We had to meet with many investors across the country in approximately two weeks. Flying commercially would make it difficult for us to visit enough of them on a tight schedule. Therefore, Citigroup chartered a small executive jet. Our road show began at a terminal in Dulles Airport reserved for private aviation. Compared to commercial travel, the accommodations were plush. The pilot and co-pilot insisted on carrying our bags to and from the plane. We could order meals before the flight. A driver met us at each stop, delivered us to the meetings, and returned us to the airport afterward. We had never experienced such luxury. But there was little time to enjoy it; we spent all our time in the air and cars preparing for a meeting, reviewing the results of the last one, and refining our presentation.

During the late 1990s, at the height of the dot-com boom, I attended a conference in which several of the older speakers seemed to want to impress the rest of us with their flexibility and market savvy. They explained that within a few years, technology was going to rapidly change our shopping and entertainment habits. A new, young group of computer entrepreneurs was going to mold the way we live; they were the teachers and we, the students. I disagreed, believing that the impact of technology was exaggerated and that, a few years after the turn of the century, we would not be shopping solely from home. Malls and supermarkets would still exist. No one agreed with me. I was just a curmudgeon resisting change. They did not know that we had initiated several dot-com companies and had learned some of the bitter lessons of new ventures.

These thoughts went through my mind during the road show. The investors and analysts knew a lot more about investments than we; however, they were specialists and narrow in their own right. They knew about certain financial markets and types of companies, but little about professional technical services or the government market. It was our job to convey this message in a way that was not condescending.

After the first few meetings, we began to relax, and I tried to find humor in our situation. Early in one meeting, I noticed a successful young fund manager wearing a Casio watch (retail price $29.99). Others were wearing watches perhaps a hundred times more expensive. I held my arm next to his and said, "Hey! We're brothers." After that, our team was more relaxed. We presented to seventy-one different groups of investors in two weeks. At times, we lost track of what city we were in.

I looked for other ways to relieve the intensity of the trip. Steve Hughes had maintained an A average in accounting at James Madison University, where he was also a member of a rock band. I never enjoyed that genre of music, even when I was young in the days of Elvis Presley. Occasionally I teased Steve saying, "You should have focused on classical music in college. Acid rock and hip hop have burned out neurons in your brain, and you have decayed from the status of savant to mere genius. You should reform and start by watching good musicals."

Steve took my comment in good humor. When we were landing in Kansas City, I began to sing the words, "Everything's up to date in Kansas City" from the musical "Oklahoma." Steve did not recognize the song, and there was probably a good reason. I studied trombone for a few years in high school but never learned to sing. Every fifth note was flat. After that, I made a point of introducing a new song at each stop.

Throughout the trip, we sometimes discussed what the price for SRA stock should be when it was first listed on the New York Stock Exchange (NYSE). If the price was too high, investors would not buy our stock. If too low, the new buyers, rather than our company and our shareholders, would benefit from the subsequent increase in the price. The decision was as much art as science. After intense discussion with our bankers, we agreed that the initial share price would be in the $16–18 range. We received comments on this at the end of each day of our trip. Specialists at Citigroup surveyed prospective investors and asked for reaction to our presentation. If the investors liked it they might say, "We may buy 300,000 shares for $18." Investors were pegging their price at the top of our range, and demand was greater than we had expected. Citigroup estimated that before a single share went on the market, we could have oversold our initial stock offering twenty-two times, at $18 a share.

Since 1903, each day's trading on the New York Stock Exchange has usually begun with the ringing of a large brass bell on a platform overlooking a vast floor, which is crowded with stock traders screaming requests and responses at one another. The honor of ringing the bell is generally given either to the CEO of the company that will be newly listed or to a prominent national figure. The first public SRA stock was scheduled to be offered on the NYSE on Friday, May 24, 2002. But at the last minute, executives in the exchange realized there was a problem. General Richard Myers, Chairman of the Joint Chiefs of Staff, had been invited to ring the bell the following Monday. But someone had forgotten that day was Memorial Day, and the Exchange was closed. When they realized the error, they asked the general to ring the bell instead on Friday—the day of our initial public offering. We were invited to attend, but would have to return on Tuesday for our official ceremony. In the end, it all worked out well.

I stood on the platform next to General Myers and the other members of the Joint Chiefs of Staff that Friday before the Memorial Day weekend as he rang the bell. On the following Tuesday, the leaders of our company and their spouses returned to the exchange for our official bell-ringing ceremony. Ted Legasey, Renny DiPentima, Steve Hughes, Barry Landew, Kathy Adams, David Kriegman, Stu Rubens, Tony Valetta, Matthew Black, Ann Denison, and Mike Duffy were there with me to witness the trading of the first SRX stock on the New York Stock Exchange.

We had set the minimum opening price at $18 a share and increased the offering from 4.4 million shares to 5 million. Then we watched the market respond. SRX stock opened at $22.25 a share. It closed, at the end of the day, at $22.98. It turned out to be the sixth most successful offering on the New York Stock Exchange that year. The public launch of our company had exceeded our expectations. It was a wonderful moment for all of us.

With the IPO an unqualified success, celebrations were in order. Although a small number of us had enjoyed the bell ringing at the New York Stock Exchange, we later scheduled a dinner in Northern Virginia in order to thank the larger number of people who had contributed to our performance. Cocktails and hors d'oeuvres preceded the dinner. Sara and I were a little late to the celebration. As we walked through the doors into the party room, everyone turned in our direction and began to clap. Without thinking, I began to clap as well. The applause was not for me, but for the entire executive team. The brief moment was poignant reminder of a strong kinship in our united success.

Our challenge now was to continue to grow profit and revenue; except that now, we had a responsibility to a new set of shareholders. And we had requirements to report our progress publicly. By the end of March 2003, SRA had gone through four financial quarters as a public company. The Securities and Exchange Commission requires public companies to issue quarterly revenue and earnings-per-share results and projections for the next quarter. Analysts use these projections, known as guidance, to create a consensus on how a company will perform in the future, and their results are published regularly. In each quarter of our first year, we exceeded our projections as well as those of the analysts. The results were apparent in the SRA stock price that, by the end of May 2003, hovered around $28. Our profit margin improvement was even more impressive. During the road show before the IPO, we promised to increase operating profit (sometimes called earnings before interest and taxes, or EBIT) from 7 percent to 9 percent in three to five years. We achieved that in less than a year. We also had $85 million in the bank, nearly as much as we had immediately after the IPO.

The world was continuing to change and we needed to stay ahead. SRA was a high-flyer in a series of successful public offerings by government information technology firms. We were competing at the time with companies such as Veridian, Anteon, CACI, ManTech, and PEC Solutions in providing IT services, mainly to the federal government. (These companies ranged in size from $300 million to $1 billion.)

SRA ran near the front of the pack in financial performance, and our reputation was stellar. Although Wall Street liked our sector, which was doing well, we all felt the repercussions when even one of the competitors stumbled. In February 2003 our stock price declined from about $28 to $22 simply because a comparable company missed its earnings and revenue estimates. This is an example of an old fact in business, politics, and many other aspects of life: perception sometimes trumps the facts.

We were watching our cash carefully, out of concern that we could use it up and then be inhibited if the equity and debt markets tightened. Our strategy for future growth was to acquire companies that would expand our capabilities or bring us new business, and to compete for larger contracts. To do these things, we would need even more money, although not immediately. Nevertheless, I remember the advice of seasoned business people: "Get money when it is available; it may not be there when you really need it."

At the time we were considering what to do, interest rates were at a low 1.5 percent. Borrowing seemed less expensive than issuing more stock. But investor perception is also important. If a company has an initial public offering and its stock price rises continuously after the offering as ours did, this indicates a consistent demand for shares. Investors who wanted to buy substantial blocks of shares would likely drive up the price. Therefore, they hesitated. A secondary offering could provide investors the opportunity to buy a lot of SRA stock at an average price that is lower than would otherwise be the case. A well-planned offering might raise the share price modestly and could be a better alternative than borrowing money.

We filed the prospectus with the Securities and Exchange Commission on May 29, 2003. The listing price was $28.84. Preparing it was not nearly as difficult as in the case of the IPO, which had occurred a year earlier. Nevertheless, Steve Hughes, Chuck Crotty, Wayne Grubbs, Stuart Davis, and other members of the finance and accounting team devoted long hours to the prospectus.

We made a change to our investor presentation that I believe was significant. In the IPO road show, our conclusion referred to the SRA ethic of "Honesty and Service." But this time, I decided that phrase should be our opening statement. We explained that honesty requires highly ethical behavior; service demands quality work and customer satisfaction, great people fulfilled in their work, and serving our country and communities. "Honesty and Service" had helped SRA recruit and retain outstanding people who did the rest. This, rather than financial performance, became the first and primary point we made to investors.

Fund managers, analysts, and other professional investors have often been criticized for their materialistic outlook. We wondered how this new emphasis would be received. During each investor meeting we developed the habit of watching body English. Was the audience looking through the prospectus instead of listening to the presentation? Were their eyes glazed, while they just pretended to hear us? We were pleasantly surprised. Almost all of the investors seemed to be genuinely interested in the SRA ethic and culture. Neil Gagnon of Gagnon Securities wrote, "We are convinced that you are really a stealth Tier 1 company and the class act of the group, so our clients . . . will benefit from the extraordinary effort of you and your team." (Tier 1 firms are multi-billion-dollar government-focused information technology companies such as Computer Sciences Corporation, Lockheed Martin, Northrup Grumman, Accenture, and SAIC.) Capable investors are like other talented people; they want to be part of something special.

This road show, although intense, was a week shorter than the fifteen-day tour for the original IPO. Ted, Steve, and I gave the initial presentation in New York on June 9, then followed that with investor meetings in Philadelphia, Wilmington, Baltimore, San Diego, Pasadena, San Francisco, Houston, and Denver. In California we were joined by others. Renny DiPentima and Stuart Davis drove to Pasadena while Steve and I continued in San Diego. Then it was back to New York for seven appointments, eight in Boston, a flight to Milwaukee, and three meetings in Minneapolis.

An unusual phenomenon occurred during the road show; the SRA stock price went up. Normally when a follow-on offering is announced, the stock price declines by 10 or 20 percent, a result of the diluting effect of issuing more shares. Everyone had a different theory about why that did not happen, but no one seemed to have a convincing explanation. One probable factor was the purchase of the Veridian Corporation by General Dynamics at a price of roughly 1.3 times revenue. Our investment bankers described strong, positive reception by investors and analysts to SRA. Our previous year's performance as a public company was a factor. These were positive signs.

Several weeks before we held the follow-on offering, most of our executive team had been willing to agree to an issue price as low as $25.

Our investment bankers had recommended setting the share price at $30. We sold 527,000 shares on June 18, 2003, closing at a share price of $31.71. Ultimately, the offer raised $71 million for the company. The SRA secondary offering was a success. Now we needed to determine how to use the money effectively while still making the numbers for revenue and earnings-per-share.

16

Growth through Acquisitions

⋯⋗ Acquisitions are a double-edged sword;
they can lead to new opportunities,
but most do not live up to expectations.

⋯⋗ Cultural incompatibility can cause
businesses to suffer.

C ompanies buy other firms for a variety of reasons: to gain new business capabilities and customers, to grow in size and market influence, and sometimes to hide deficiencies in the current business. This latter tactic may work for several years but usually becomes evident over time. Most acquisitions probably do not live up to expectations. However, actual statistics are difficult to obtain because the results of the acquisitions are usually buried within the combination of the two firms.

For the first twenty years of business, we focused on winning contracts and building them into larger, more challenging work. This approach served us well. We developed strong relationships with hundreds of federal government clients, and this expanded our expertise and built a track record, enabling us to branch into new areas of technology. Looking ahead, we planned to continue expanding organically—but we also began to consider acquiring firms that would expand our markets and bring us new capabilities. We wanted to complement existing lines of work and develop opportunities in new areas. At the same time, we were concerned that any acquisition would dilute our culture. SRA was the gold standard among federal contractors because of our bedrock principle of honesty and service. Clients recognized that value in our work. We had to be careful about acquisitions.

Our first acquisition was a business that we had known for years. It had a value system similar to ours. Ted Legasey met Amy Marasco in 1990 at a meeting of environmental service firms. The setting was a public hearing for a new Environmental Protection Agency (EPA) rule barring any company that did policy consulting from then performing the work. The intent of the rule was to prevent conflicts of interest, for example, a policy recommendation that helped the same company perform engineering services. Amy was working for a company that did consulting work for the EPA, and recalls wondering in the meeting how her work would be impacted by this new rule. She stood and asked a lot of questions. After relentless grilling, the speaker finally put his hand over the microphone and said, "Yes, Amy, you are going to lose your job."

Ted approached Amy afterward and said, "I don't know what that was all about, but you seem to have a good understanding of this industry." He asked Amy if she would like to work for SRA, helping to build its environmental portfolio. "Actually, we're going to start our own company," Amy replied.

For the next several months, Ted served as a sounding board as Amy and her partner and husband, Dave Newton, began to build their environmental consulting business. Many years before then, American Management Systems (AMS) had helped our fledgling company, and both firms had benefited from the experience. Realizing this, we offered the new Marasco Newton Group (MNG) rent-free space at our headquarters to help them get started. Our people often dropped in to see how things were going. They served as an informal advisory council for Amy, Dave, and their team. Amy said later that the support from SRA people was greatly appreciated and accelerated their entrepreneurial learning curve.

"We joked that the day SRA gave me a bill me for paper that I had used, we would move out."

MNG grew to a $31 million company and 350 employees. Their strength was in environmental services rather than information technology, and they were mediators for high visibility projects, such as the Hudson River cleanup and debris recovery after the space shuttle Challenger exploded. MNG developed a reputation for excellent work.

Then the Environmental Protection Agency changed another set of rules that dictated which firms could compete for work. It required any company seeking a prime contract to have completed three projects of similar scope. MNG wanted to bid on an important job defining a new EPA computer system to track the cleanup of hazardous waste. It would be an ambitious undertaking, but well within the company's expertise. Yet suddenly they were shut out for lack of comparable experience. SRA had done many contracts of that size and complexity, but did not have the necessary relationship with EPA to understand how it operated and what it needed. Therefore, Amy and Dave proposed that Marasco-Newton join forces with SRA to bid on the job. If we won, they would have the opportunity to fulfill a contract larger than anything they had done, while we would expand our expertise.

MNG got the job and SRA was its subcontractor. The project was more than $50 million and could lead to even greater things for both companies. Unfortunately, their next step was precipitated by Dave Newton's health; he had cancer. Amy and Dave reevaluated their plans. They decided to discreetly put their company on the market, inviting a few companies to bid. They received several offers. Ultimately, similarities in values of SRA and MNG played a big part in the decision for both firms.

We purchased Marasco-Newton on January 1, 2002. Despite our similar values, we discovered significant differences in employee demographics and workplace habits. Our 2,100 employees were generally older—in their mid-forties with children in school and aging parents. The average age of Marasco-Newton people was nearly two decades younger. They cared about entirely different things. To our employees, pension and retirement issues, health care, and life insurance were important. On the other hand, Marasco-Newton employees enjoyed a higher profit-sharing plan and wanted flexible work hours.

Other differences arose because we were merging a smaller, more nimble company into a larger firm with a stronger and more structured quality assurance program. At the time, SRA was working diligently to become qualified to win larger, more complex jobs. This meant that we were instituting new systems and procedures that struck some of the Marasco-Newton employees as bureaucratic. Other issues were institutional, such as executive titles. Should the young MNG vice presidents have the same status as the older, more experienced SRA VPs?

We realized how different we were in one of the earliest meetings between MNG managers who worked on environmental problems and SRA people who supported the Department of Defense. Peter Trick had worked for sixteen years at SAIC and then created and managed a successful division at Marasco-Newton, where he was senior vice president. Peter explained to his new SRA colleagues what his division was all about: "I named our group EOS, which stood for Environment and Organizational Services." He pointed out that EOS was also the name of the Greek goddess of dawn. Tongue in cheek, one of the SRA executives said, "Oh, we like dawn; it's a good time to bomb!"

To help smooth the merging of two corporate cultures, Renny DiPentima (president of SRA federal business) created a transition management team consisting of Amy, Dave, and himself. Each had a vote on important management issues that arose. They held weekly calls to discuss the integration. It took some time to resolve differences, and everyone worked hard to ensure that our clients did not bear the brunt of this process. Our acquisition of Marasco-Newton was a lesson that none of us had expected. Even when two companies have similar values and believe themselves to be a good fit, integrating cultures is never a simple process. Nevertheless, we paid $15 million for Marasco-Newton, and within a year or two together, we gained $100 million in new business.

Our next acquisition occurred a year later, eight months after our IPO. It and all subsequent acquisitions were strongly influenced by the fact that we were now a publicly listed company. When a public company announces that it will acquire another firm, all of the analysts covering that firm provide views on the implications for the combined corporation. If the combination can increase earnings per share (for example, by reducing costs), the outcome is likely to be viewed favorably by investors, and the stock price will probably increase. However, the executive team must manage the acquired company well and retain and motivate its key executives. We were not always successful at retaining executives in firms that we acquired and, in some cases, we did not have the expertise to properly manage the company. On the other hand, some of our acquisitions were reasonably successful, and executives from them have prominent roles in SRA today.

We acquired Adroit Systems, Inc., in January 2003. It was very different from Marasco-Newton in its type of work and the personalities of its leaders. The Adroit acquisition occurred only sixteen months after the terrorist attacks on the World Trade Center and the Pentagon, and we knew that national security would continue to be an important part of the nation's future. We, therefore, wanted to build our defense and intelligence business. Since going public, we had reviewed more than 150 firms as possible acquisitions, but Adroit was clearly superior. The Alexandria firm had a long history of profitable organic growth and was a leading provider of surveillance and reconnaissance services to the Department of Defense and intelligence agencies.

"Adroit was at the top of our list," Renny DiPentima recalled. "Tony Valletta and Pat Burke knew the company and its people and said they were outstanding. Our interest in them was immediate because we imagined a deal where everyone could benefit."

All we needed to do was to convince the Adroit executives. Terry Ryan (president and CEO) had been inundated with acquisition offers; nevertheless, Barry Landew called him.

"The purpose of the call was to explore the possibility of a future meeting, but we ended up talking for over an hour," Barry recalled. "It was clear from the beginning that SRA and Adroit were a good match."

Although no deal is ever perfect, Adroit had advantages, including good customers, shareholders, and employees. At the time, Anna Hogan was chief operating officer for Adroit. She liked the idea but, as a prerequisite, insisted on the support of the company's employees.

"In my view, the ability to provide long-term employment and challenges to our employees was paramount," said Anna, who is now a SRA vice president. Terry Ryan felt that the cultures had to complement one another for the merger to be successful.

We bought Adroit Systems, Inc., in 2002 for $40 million. Its client base complemented ours, and its record of delivering value to customers, strong growth and profitability, and its focus on employees, made us comfortable with the deal.

Anna Hogan managed the integration of the two companies. We decided to keep the Adroit team together (about 330 employees and $43 million) and add to it about $14 million of SRA intelligence business. The process moved smoothly. Adroit was twenty years old and had an employee base demographically similar to that of SRA—engineers, mathematicians, former military people. The primary challenges Anna recalled were "just the overwhelming number of processes and procedures that Adroit people needed to learn." This ranged from the significant (adapting to new financial reporting requirements, which were different in a publicly held company) to the mundane (adjusting to the new SRA travel agency and coffee vendor). Adroit had subsidized its staff's soft drink habit (a can was just 25 cents in their vending machines) but SRA did not. This might seem like an insignificant issue, but it was something Anna recalled having to negotiate with the delicacy of an international treaty. "For a little while SRA let us keep it, but ultimately we knew that it was something we had to let go because other SRA employees didn't have it."

We also introduced Adroit employees to our proposal tanks. Shortly after the acquisition, the augmented Adroit group had the opportunity to bid on a $50 million contract to develop a joint tactical radio system. Everyone worked long days and weekends to develop the proposal. "I don't think we would have won without SRA," Anna said. "It was larger than anything we had ever competed for at Adroit." Our bid was successful and so was the Adroit acquisition; however, we eventually lost some of their key executives, including Terry Ryan. Cultural differences may have been a factor.

The next acquisition aimed to expand our ability to directly support the functions of certain organizations—so called mission-critical work. Orion Scientific Systems specialized in counterterrorism, counterintelligence, and law enforcement services and products. Orion was a small company but was considered an industry leader in solving certain types of information processing problems; its size limited its ability to compete for larger contracts. Barry called Orion co-founder and chief operating officer Jim McClave, who agreed to a lunch meeting. Jim recalled giving Barry his standard response to acquisition inquiries: "Absolutely not." Undaunted, Barry continued talking.

"It became apparent that SRA was different," Jim said. "There were a lot of common themes—goals for the business and our employees." The words and images Barry used to describe SRA work, employees, and vision were strikingly similar to Orion's.

After three months of negotiation, we presented an offer to Orion. The sale was completed in January 2004; we bought the firm for $34.5 million. Because Orion had more cyber security work than we did, we wrapped our business into theirs and called it the Orion Center for Homeland Security. Their work also opened new doors to the area of law enforcement. Combined, our new unit had $40 million in contracts. The ultimate result was our homeland security division, which by 2010, had about $200 million in business.

Within two years of going public, we had spent $90 million to buy three companies and had immediately expanded our footprint in the government market. Our combined teams often did quite well in gaining new business, despite cultural differences. Each transaction taught us new lessons about melding corporate cultures and personalities. Our next acquisition provided a different opportunity to learn how to merge the new company into SRA.

We already knew the firm from having worked with its people on an earlier project for homeland security. Touchstone was a small, boutique firm that specialized in high-end strategic consulting for federal executives. One of its contracts was to help the first chief information officer of the newly created Department of Homeland Security merge the missions and personnel of twenty-two technology offices into one cohesive unit.

Touchstone expertise was not technology, but in a specialty known as organizational dynamics or organizational psychology. The company helped government executives set priorities and align people and positions. We believed that it could help us find new types of business and fulfill existing contracts in different ways. We bought the firm for $27 million in April 2005.

The work and professional backgrounds of Touchstone employees was quite different from SRA people. Many were behavior experts and management consultants, not information technologists. We decided to wait a year before making any decision about restructuring or integrating Touchstone. One of our goals was for Touchstone to contribute to work SRA was already doing. But after familiarizing themselves with those contracts, Touchstone employees found just one that suited their capabilities. Greater emphasis on federal regulations related to potential organizational conflicts of interest caused us to maintain an information firewall between SRA and Touchstone, a consulting firm whose work sometimes gave it insider knowledge of the government's top offices. This complication meant the synergies we saw between SRA and Touchstone could not be leveraged in the way that we had hoped.

Our experience with Touchstone taught us that achieving synergy with a firm unlike ours is more difficult than acquiring a similar business. Touchstone was an example of cultural incompatibility in the type of business services that each company provided.

We took a different approach with the next acquisition. We bought Galaxy Scientific Corporation in July 2005 for $98.7 million. Galaxy was a small firm that did engineering work for the Department of Defense and civil government agencies. We thought that it would bring us new types of federal contracts. Galaxy had worked with the Federal Aviation Administration (FAA) to help consolidate and support its air traffic control laboratories. It developed a test facility for the FAA, where researchers analyzed airstrip pavements, the flammability of materials, fire safety, and weight limitations. In addition, Galaxy provided airport security training and created and managed a database of potential threats. Their researchers bought mundane items from retail stores, such as a Walmart, made mock improvised explosive devices, and embedded them in toys or other household objects. Then they put them through screening machines to assess their detectability. Images of those devices were added to the FAA security library.

We assigned Galaxy functions and more than 450 employees to appropriate business sectors of SRA. We moved their FAA work into our civil sector, defense work into our defense sector, and other parts into our C3I operations. We still hold FAA contracts that contribute to the nation's aviation safety.

In November 2005 we acquired Spectrum Solutions Group for $16.7 million. It gave us expertise in a fast-growing segment of the contracting market where we had little presence or knowledge. Their specialty was applying Oracle software to manage logistics, financial, human resource, and other processes used by very large, complex organizations. This enterprise resource planning (ERP) capability became a good business segment. It helped lead to the largest contract win in SRA history. In 2010 we won Midas, a system for the U.S. Department of Agriculture (USDA) to track grants and loans and manage the financial processes associated with them. The potential value of the work was $500 million over seven years. We also won a $125 million contract to provide the USDA with a web-based system to manage the supply chain of its school-lunch programs. Much of this was based on capabilities we acquired with Spectrum.

We bought RABA Technologies, which catered to the government intelligence community (including the National Security Agency). This acquisition helped us create a new business group specializing in intelligence. That work subsequently grew, but there were challenges in retaining employees who apparently preferred working for a much smaller business and whose primary loyalty was to the government client missions they supported, not to any one employer. At the same time, the talented employees had critical skills that were very much in demand; we lost people.

By the end of 2006, we had made seven acquisitions. Most of them probably did not live up to initial predictions of likely growth. Executives, who have decided to sell a company, portray it in a favorable light in order to get the highest price possible. We discounted these projections, but despite substantial investigation, we could never learn as much about the company as the sellers. We were also sometimes disappointed when some of the key executives in the acquired firms left SRA. On the other hand, we were pleasantly surprised by joint successes when we gained new customers. On balance, the acquisitions through 2006 were probably worth their cost and effort, despite delivering mixed results. However, they masked the decline of organic growth in 2006–2007. Revenue was increasing, but we were not winning enough jobs to sustain our excellent performance up to that time. Then two subsequent acquisitions made the situation much worse. One was partially successful but the other would cost the company a lot of money and cause me a great deal of personal and professional angst.

In 2007 we purchased Constella, which had health care services work that complemented SRA contracts. However, we did not want to acquire two parts of the company. One involved the administration of contracts supporting the U.S. Agency for International Development (USAID). The other potential incompatibility was the work supporting drug companies in clinical trials. These two parts of Constella were a poor fit from a business standpoint. They were culturally incompatible with our current work. We knew it at the time, but the owner would not sell us just the part of Constella that we wanted. We had to pay for the other parts too, and we knew that we would eventually sell them. The central part of Constella (the business that we wanted) worked out reasonably well, but the combination of business losses and low subsequent sale price for the other two components proved to be expensive.

A few months after buying Constella, we purchased Era, which was based in the Czech Republic and provided air traffic control products and related services to airports around the world. It also had latent capabilities in military defense, but no significant business base. The purchase turned out to be the worst decision in our corporate history. The basic acquisition strategy was flawed. We had no experience with its type of products and services, and we did not know how to sell to the market. We did have contracts with the Federal Aviation Administration, and our CEO at the time had managed somewhat similar groups, but he was far too busy to provide personal attention when the acquisition began to fail. Era was, therefore, another example of cultural incompatibility in a business sense. By the time Era was divested in 2011, it had cost our company nearly $150 million.

The problems with both companies were compounded at the outset because of poor due diligence. Companies are often put on the market because of some shortcoming. The stated reason for listing a firm is sometimes different from the actual latent deficiencies. The listing statement is phrased to attract buyers; for example, "We want to be acquired by a large firm in order to grow more rapidly." When a company decides to seek acquisitions, the executives in the acquiring firm should insist on thorough due diligence aimed at disclosing deficiencies, and a tight purchase contract with a substantial escrow fund in case deficiencies become evident in the first year or two. If we had done a better job of due diligence for Era, we probably would have recognized that gaining customers would be a challenge, and we likely would have paid a lower price and required more conditions on the sale, such as a higher escrow for contingencies.

Acquisitions are usually not isolated transactions. Rather, they are imbedded in many other complex factors such as the personalities of the people involved and the state of the business. Our decisions concerning the Era and Constella acquisitions are another story that involved many complexities.

17

Big Bids, Big Wins

···⊱ Good business development is essential
to the culture of a successful company.

···⊱ Chance favors the prepared mind.

W hen our shares began trading on the New York Stock Exchange in 2002, we told analysts and investors that SRA would
probably grow at least 20 percent a year; of that amount, 15
percent would be organic and 5 percent would be through acquisitions.
We exceeded those estimates because our employees were imbued with
the importance of expanding the business by finding new ways to create
value. Clients liked our work and added new tasks; meanwhile our business development and proposal teams steadily improved while bidding
one project after another. We did not realize it at the time, but the federal government procurement processes were becoming much more
sophisticated and even subtle. The evolving system rewarded our company because its creative, energetic people responded to those changes.

In 2001, we learned about a RFP that the National Guard Bureau
issued for a project called GuardNet XXI. The task was to manage and
evolve a computer network linking Guard offices in all fifty states and
four territories with high-speed data and video communications. Ultimately, the network needed to reach National Guard armories in 3,000
communities. The existing system to activate Guard resources and communicate with other agencies was inadequate, although the incumbent
contractor (EDS) had struggled to make it all work.

GuardNet XXI was not a large project, about $30 million a year, but we were happy to win it. Our team leaders went to the National Guard network operations facility in Arlington, Virginia, on a Tuesday morning to get badges and meet with the outgoing contractor. Allen Deitz (who had led the proposal effort) recalled that they were preparing to leave when someone called out, "Wait a minute, and come look at this." He and the other SRA people—Anita Stanton, Rob Gentili, and Mike Yocom—gathered around several television screens and watched images of a jet flying into one of the Twin Towers, then a second. When a third plane hit the Pentagon, the National Guard network operations center went into lockdown mode. Guard executives turned to Allen and asked, "What can you do to get your people here faster?" Allen called Renny DiPentima (head of our federal business) who said, "Give them whatever they need." Suddenly, the network project became urgent, and we began pulling people off other work to join the GuardNet team.

The facility, in the National Guard Headquarters, was inadequate to manage the network. It was overcrowded, lacked physical security, and did not have room for expansion. The terrorist attack on September 11, 2001, exacerbated this situation. The National Guard needed an entirely new operations center that would be fully operational within three months.

There was another issue. The Guard wanted the contractor to provide the facility, rather than house the network on one of its properties. We had committed to doing the work at a fixed price. Under the contract terms, the National Guard Bureau would pay SRA for the first year and decide whether to continue beyond that. Building a communications center required a significant initial capital investment of about $10 million; this effort involved a variety of complex technologies from advanced video teleconferencing to network security. We agreed to these requirements, knowing that we would not recoup our initial expenses unless we successfully transitioned the GuardNet operations to the new facility and operated it for several years.

Our team met the deadline, and the Guard told us that SRA exceeded its expectations. Not only did we recoup our investment, but suddenly SRA was positioned to compete for a much larger piece of work for that client.

In late 2002, the National Guard Bureau issued an RFP to manage a wide range of its advanced information technology services, a project known as the Advanced Information Technology Services (AITS). The incumbent (SAIC) had held the contract for a several years; concurrently, SRA supported the Guard project manager, providing oversight of the program (cost, schedule, and reviews of technical quality). We knew the client's needs. "We had a very good understanding of what the National Guard was trying to accomplish in a big picture way," recalls John Luongo, a member of the team that assembled our proposal. "We knew that the operations could be streamlined to be more efficient in delivering software and other technical solutions."

Jeff Rydant pushed our proposal team to be innovative. The incumbent had focused on making continuous piecemeal adjustments to sustain the existing IT systems. Our team took a bold route and suggested that a fundamentally different technical approach was in order—grouping "families" of projects to which we deployed multi-disciplinary teams that could produce integrated, rather than isolated, solutions. The Guard issued the RFP in November 2002. On Christmas Eve, with snow falling, our team worked late to meet the government end-of-year deadline. The "proposal tank" was littered with half-empty cups of coffee, soda cans, bags of chips, barrels of pretzels, and empty pizza boxes.

"Some customers are sensitive to contractor holiday schedules and some are not," said Allen Deitz, who remembers working nearly continuously for thirty-six hours to meet deadlines. He drove to Pittsburgh to be with family on Christmas Eve and then turned around to get back to our Fair Lakes headquarters that night so he could be in the proposal tank in the morning. "Every day wasn't like that, but when a proposal deadline came up, you dropped everything. It's too intense and too short a time to worry about sleep."

Ultimately, fifty-two SRA people contributed to the National Guard proposal (AITS). When we won the contract, their efforts helped put our company on the same playing field as large systems integrators. It was one of our largest contract wins. Don Edwards, a retired major general with a thirty-eight-year career in the Army, served as project manager.

Many who crafted the SRA proposal—a cadre of talented people in their twenties and thirties led by JR—eventually evolved into a new generation of leaders at SRA. Brian Michl led software development for the National Guard project, then became a vice president and chief information officer and moved on to increasing responsibilities. John Luongo and Eric Kurzhals are also vice presidents and hold important positions. Allen Deitz is a vice president and directs the proposal development group that handles the company's largest bids.

Brian, John, and Allen were hired directly from college through a program that Barry, Ted, and JR led at various points. Eric came to SRA as a young engineer with two years' experience. All of them became involved in proposal writing early in their careers, and eventually formed a "tiger team" of technical performers who also had the ability to interact with customers and develop solutions. This concept continues today.

The amount of work that goes into a proposal is about the same, regardless of whether it is a $50 million or $500 million bid, so we decided to pursue larger contracts. We focused on large indefinite delivery/indefinite quantity (ID/IQ) contracts, often called task order contracts. Some were in specific agencies and others served multiple organizations, so called government-wide acquisition contracts (GWACs).

These vehicles were a major change in government contracting introduced in the late 1990s. Until that time, many large procurements were ponderous. Because the stakes were high, the process was slow and expensive. It took months, sometimes years, for a government agency to prepare a draft RFP and gather comments from contractors. More time and effort were required to make changes and issue the final RFP. Even more months passed as contractors went through the expensive process of preparing large proposals. Then a source selection committee required several months to evaluate them. Meanwhile, information technology was changing rapidly, and the original requirements frequently became obsolete.

GWACs and other new task order contracts vastly improved the process. Many contractors submitted proposals, but usually only a few were selected and became eligible to compete for smaller task orders. These vendors, who won a prime contractor designation, could bid on future RFPs without having to compete against many other companies. This process enabled an agency to issue a job procurement within days or weeks. It also leveled the playing fields for smaller firms like SRA in competition with large companies, such as Lockheed Martin, SAIC, CSC, and Booz Allen Hamilton.

This trend presented an extraordinary opportunity for growth, and we anticipated and prepared for it ahead of most of our competitors. One of the most important wins in SRA history was the government-wide contract vehicle called Millennia, which focused on large system integration and development projects. Government evaluators rated

SRA first technically and first overall (including cost) among twenty-one firms that bid for Millennia. I still proudly display in my office a framed table prepared by Dick Hunter that shows how, in April 1999, we outbid CSC, Booz Allen Hamilton, Lockheed Martin, SAIC, Raytheon, Unisys, and others. Millennia gave us a significant advantage over many competitors.

By the end of 2000, SRA had become a contractor on four of the five largest information technology government-wide acquisitions contracts. By 2004, we were managing large service contract vehicles for the General Services Administration and large blanket purchase agreements for the Department of Defense. Led by Jeffrey Westerhoff, who worked tirelessly to cultivate them, qualifying for GWACs had become a specialty. We won a significant piece of work, for the National Guard, under one of these GWAC vehicles; it was called ITOP II.

Even so, when we learned that the U.S. Agency for International Development (USAID) was considering a re-compete on a contract to control its entire information technology infrastructure. It was not immediately clear that we should pursue this RFP because we had no experience in this area. USAID was established in 1962, by President John F. Kennedy, and is the State Department's strategic partner in implementing our foreign policy around the world. It extends assistance to countries recovering from disaster, trying to escape poverty, and engaging in democratic reforms.

A former employee brought the opportunity to our attention. In late 2002, Steve Flannery was working at a firm with ties to another USAID project. He knew the agency's IT needs and, perhaps more importantly, had a strong desire to return to SRA. He had worked for us from 1997 to 2000 before trying his hand in the dot-com boom. "I kept in contact with a lot of people at SRA and really wanted to come back," Flannery recalls. "When I heard about the opportunity with USAID, it was a no-brainer."

A great deal of persuasion was required to bid such a challenging project. Several members of our senior team thought we should let this pass because it would be very difficult to convince the government that SRA could run the USAID network better than top-tier firms, such as CSC and Northrop Grumman. David Kriegman looked at the opportunity and said, "This is exactly the kind of work SRA should bid in order to get to where we want to go." David showed his sincerity by volunteering to give up his higher position as head of the Defense Systems business unit in order to manage the project, if we won it.

This effort resulted in the largest and most strategically complex proposal our firm presented up to that time. It helped that the process happened to be structured in such a way that we were able to demonstrate a technical solution that differentiated SRA from other firms. The RFP was issued under the Millennia government-wide acquisition contract (GWAC). John Streufert, who was then deputy chief information officer of USAID and head of the bid process, wanted to maximize engagement between the government officials overseeing the work and contractors who would provide solutions. He invited prospective contractors to the agency to meet with senior people in his organization and ask questions. Our team participated in at least a half dozen of these meetings, in order to understand the USAID people and gain a clear picture of their problems. This was a valuable foundation from which we could build our solution.

We needed the right team to deliver a good effort. Barry had written significant parts of many large SRA proposals; while JR was a master at leveraging our resources and leading project strategy, pricing, and review. Barry and JR were known for delivering unvarnished and discerning reviews of proposals. Brian Cross recalled JR's assessment of his work in the early 1990s, not long after Brian joined our company: "On my first proposal ever, JR described my initial draft as 'prosaic' and 'insipid.' Needless to say, we immediately became good friends." Brian also clearly recalls JR's terse but inimitable critique of his rather mechanistic description of the SRA maintenance support technicians: "What are they, mindless automatons?!"

Nevertheless, JR recruited Brian to work on the USAID proposal, a grueling process that ended with a day-long internal review of the final draft. At one point, Brian remembers the review team called a section of the proposal "a train wreck." Confident that the proposal team was on the right track, JR (the proposal manager) ignored the comment.

Allen Deitz also worked on the USAID proposal and recalled that it helped that JR "believed in keeping things light." JR encouraged diversions to soften the stress of the proposal tank. The environment generally consisted of a utilitarian conference room with walls of whiteboards, stocked with tables of junk food, and populated by group of bleary-eyed team members working to be as creative as possible under intense deadline pressure. A Nerf bazooka was furnished and used to shoot down toy motorized helicopters. A few of the company's mascots were always lying around, ready for the impromptu penguin toss contest. During one session in "the tank," JR, Allen Dietz, and Eric Kurzhals made pickled cucumbers in a giant-sized pretzel tub and discovered that adding asparagus to the concoction produced rather unappetizing results.

Although that recipe has not been repeated, the proposal process has not changed much since the early days. "The work is great, if you like criticism and you are not afraid to fail," says Deitz. "Pressure is intense; hours are long; weekend duty is common, and the environment is often chaotic. Yet it's an experience that leaves an impression. I can relate my kids and my marriage to what I was working on at the time at SRA. Many of us grew up here. That's the kind of place this was, and we really wanted it that way."

With only sixty days to submit the USAID bid, our proposal team rapidly defined the strategy. Before the bid submission deadline, they summarized the approach making clear that we understood the client's needs: establish, refresh, add. It meant that SRA would establish USAID as a world-class IT services provider; and refresh its IT capabilities. These became the tagline for our proposal. Our team bought a machine to make buttons and printed a slogan summarizing the points. We wanted to inspire ourselves and the client. And we succeeded. When we won the contract, Mike Fox, who was head of marketing and sales, credited the comprehensive, cohesive work of the proposal team with making a strong first impression and positioning SRA for more work in the future. Mike recalls, "USAID was talking to us about everything from their accounting and procurement system to merging their infrastructure with the State Department. It shows that we had insight when we put this team together, and it paid huge dividends."

USAID was our first and largest international contract. More options were exercised and it quickly grew into a more than $100-million-a-year business. Not only did it give us the credibility to win other international work, but it validated our strategy of reaching for much larger jobs.

This became even clearer after a client encouraged SRA to bid for a contract that would grow by multiples over the coming years. It was a $341 million task order to provide a range of IT infrastructure support services to the Federal Deposit Insurance Corporation (FDIC), the agency that oversees the American banking system. The work was being awarded under the familiar Millennia vehicle. We had not spoken to anyone at FDIC before this time, much less worked for the agency. But our credibility was growing, thanks to the National Guard and USAID contracts. The job was to consolidate thirty-six existing IT vehicles into one five-year performance-based contract. If our bid was successful, this would be the largest single prime contract awarded to SRA up to that time.

Investigating the FDIC information technology RFP immediately illuminated several management and coordination challenges. The contract winner would have to integrate workers under nine labor contracts, ranging from data center operations to asset management and security. There were twenty-seven non-labor contracts, including telecommunications services and hardware and software maintenance. "They wanted to get away from managing many vendors, and we gave them the right solution," recalls John Luongo, who helped write the bid. With so many contractors handling pieces of disparate technologies and systems, there were often disagreements over the rollout of new hardware and software, scheduling maintenance outages, and other basic day-to-day functions. Clearly frustrated, FDIC employees later confided that they had referred to the help desk as "the helpless desk," said Bryan Polk. "One of our initial challenges was to establish a credible help desk where people could get their problems solved."

Our team defined a disciplined engineering process for adapting and upgrading IT for the FDIC. In the past, when someone wanted to implement a new software product they just muscled their way through the bureaucratic process, installing the tool often without warning and with disruptive results. Or a contractor would shut down an operating system over the weekend but not be able to get it running when business opened Monday morning. Under our proposal, SRA would create a change review board, offer training, consolidate equipment and software upgrades, and bring predictability and order to IT operations. We would provide client and help-desk support, program management support, telecommunications hardware and software maintenance, data and video operations, and overall data center operations.

We hired Kathy Adams from the Social Security Administration (SSA) several years earlier. She was our first senior female executive to run a business sector and was overseeing all of our civil government work. It was an important area of business; however, Kathy recognized immediately that the IT overhaul FDIC needed was exactly the kind of work she had managed several years earlier for the SSA.

Kathy was not a technical person; she held a Bachelor of Arts in English from the University of Maryland (Phi Beta Kappa). But she had worked her way up from being a management intern at the Social Security Administration to overseeing all of the information technology people. Because she had worked in many different areas of the agency, she understood thoroughly what was needed in order to do its job better. And she was an excellent communicator. Kathy was familiar with the way IT development often happened in agencies—the technical people built systems and handed them over to users, with little engagement or explanation. The results were often inadequate. Over the years at SSA, she slowly changed that dynamic by serving as a translator between IT people and users. As she rose through the ranks, Kathy helped streamline and reshape technology so that it no longer thwarted users, but improved operations.

So Kathy jumped into the FDIC bid effort and Tim Atkin, her deputy, stepped up to manage the day-to-day operations of our civil business. She recalls walking into the proposal tank on the first day. JR was running the effort and began to make assignments, writing them on a whiteboard at the front of the room, along with deadlines. Slide presentations would have to be done quickly.

Knowing JR well enough to realize that he would not suffer fumbling or incompetence, she turned to Steve Tolbert who sat next to her and whispered, "I don't know how to do PowerPoint!" She remembers thinking, "I'd always had seven assistants. It wasn't the best use of my time."

Steve whispered back to her, "Do you know what to put on the slides?"

"Of course," Kathy said.

"Then no problem," he reassured her. "You tell me what to put on them and I'll add my ideas."

The team intentionally proposed a solution that might make the FDIC uncomfortable because of its scope and comprehensiveness. "We would win the contract only if they were serious about reforming their IT environment." The FDIC proposal team included some of our more seasoned people: Bernie Cohen, Tim Cooke, Allen Deitz, Anne Donohue, Frank Durso, Mike Fox, Gene Frank, David Kriegman, John Luongo, Peter Trick, and Jeffrey Westerhoff.

SRA was awarded the contract in September 2004. "This win says we're here to stay," Tolbert remarked, and he was right. Kathy Adams ran the project, with Steve as her deputy; therefore Tim Atkin succeeded Kathy as director of our civil work. Our good performance on the FDIC job led to additional tasks, and the work grew beyond the initial proposal amount to $100 million a year. Such large contract wins solidified SRA operations in civil agencies, giving our firm a more diversified government portfolio.

Meanwhile, other competent managers in the national security area were quietly expanding their contracts. One good example was Chuck Perry, a retired Army colonel who had an excellent career at SRA. Chuck won our first leadership award in 1992. He and many others demonstrated often the importance of organic growth by doing good work for customers who then asked for more effort by SRA. However, as the years passed, we gradually began to lose this super motivation to exceed customer expectations and propel SRA ahead of its competitors.

In 2005, *BusinessWeek* named SRA to its list of "Hot Growth" companies, and we once again made *Fortune* magazine's list of "100 Best Companies to Work For." There would be more contract wins to come, but aiming higher meant taking greater risks. We were moving into a period in which our strategy, capabilities, and focus would be tested and found wanting.

18

A Time of Troubles

····⟩ When the founders retire, watch out for problems.

····⟩ Cultural incompatibility can cause businesses to suffer.

····⟩ A management team without focus invites chaos.

····⟩ Acquisitions are a double-edged sword;
        they can lead to new opportunities but most
        do not live up to expectations.

I never felt threatened by talented people and had always cultivated potential successors to lead the company by delegating substantial authority and responsibility. I very much wanted the SRA name, values, and culture to succeed me and knew that would require strong continuing leadership. For a number of years, the logical contenders were Ted Legasey and Gary Nelson. However, as we entered the new millennium in the year 2000, Gary decided to retire and Renny DiPentima began to emerge as a possible successor. There were five of us on the senior leadership team. Ted and Renny were ten to twelve years younger than I, and Barry Landew and Steve Hughes were ten to twelve years younger than Ted and Renny. I felt we had a strong pipeline of potential successors, perhaps two generations. But things would change significantly over the next seven years, and leadership succession would become a major problem.

Not long after SRA went public, our early corporate mentor, American Management Systems (AMS), provided a cautionary case study in bad succession planning. For nearly thirty years, AMS enjoyed a stellar reputation for integrity and high-quality work; and it reached $1.2 billion in revenue. Charles Rossotti, whom I knew from the Office of

Systems Analysis, had founded AMS with several former "Whiz Kid" colleagues and served as CEO from the mid-1980s until 1992, when he became chairman. He and his partners built a strong executive structure and capable teams to perform the firm's work. As mentioned earlier, SRA benefited from the excellent market position of AMS. Ted Legasey and Bill Purdy (a member of Rossotti's executive team) were creative partners in developing new business for both of our firms. The AMS executives were intelligent, energetic, and highly principled.

When Rossotti became chairman, Paul Brands and Phil Giumti co-led the company for one year, until Brands became CEO in 1993, a position he held for seven years. Paul had worked for me in the Pentagon and was quite capable. Rossotti left AMS to become Commissioner of the Internal Revenue Service in 1997, and the firm began to stumble.

In 1999, the government of Mississippi terminated an $11.2 million contract with AMS to modernize the state's tax system and sued the company for $985 million in damages. In August 2000, a jury awarded the state $474.5 million in actual and punitive damages, causing a drop in stock price from $44 to $14. Brands announced that he was stepping down, and Bill Purdy was named Interim CEO for the next fourteen months. The company subsequently settled the suit for $185 million. That same year another AMS customer, the Federal Retirement Thrift Board, canceled a contract for a system that was intended to make Thrift Saving Plan data available online. The subsequent lawsuit was settled for $5 million in June 2003.

Apparently frustrated by these public failings, the AMS board decided that it needed a "professional CEO" from a larger commercial public company. They hired the new CEO in December 2001. His background was in the telecommunications industry, and he apparently had little experience in professional services work for the federal government. Although the troubles leading to lawsuits started under Brands, the decision to choose as his successor a person who did not understand the underlying business and the people-centric culture of AMS signaled more problems ahead. Years later, we would experience similar problems and make many of the same mistakes.

The new CEO reportedly had a mandate to grow AMS from $1 billion to $3 billion with a goal of a "big bang merger of equals." This brought about cultural changes that had far-reaching effects. Where a core group of dynamic leaders had once led the company, the new

CEO imposed significant staff reductions and introduced new managers and systems that were perceived as bureaucratic and arbitrary. The early collaborative environment that helped make AMS great was largely eliminated. The new mandate failed, and by 2004, AMS no longer existed. It was split apart and sold piecemeal. The Canadian firm CGI bought its commercial and non-defense government business, and CACI purchased its defense and intelligence business.

I feared that without good planning and cultivation of future leaders who carried the company's cultural DNA, SRA could suffer a similar fate. So, after the successful secondary offering in June 2003 in which SRA raised additional capital based on its prime market position, I began to engage the senior leadership team and the board regarding my successor as CEO. I had extensive discussions with Ted and Renny, both individually and together, since I felt either of them could lead the company.

I had worked closely with Ted for nearly thirty years, and there was a natural rhythm in our relationship. We had complementary skills and we shared a common approach to the business. Ted had deep knowledge of what made SRA successful. He was an excellent problem solver, an inspirational leader, and was respected throughout the company. On the other hand, Renny had much more experience working with our key customers. He had served roughly three decades in the federal government and had eight years of progressively increasing responsibility with SRA. He had a magnetic personality and was highly regarded throughout government and our industry. He was an excellent candidate to be the external face of the company.

Ted and Renny worked well together, and they respected one another. We even talked about them serving as co-CEOs, but the board did not like that idea. I was not sure what to do. In the end, Ted took the decision out of my hands. He came to me in the fall of 2003 and said that, after all the discussion, he simply did not have the burning desire to be the CEO of SRA as a public company, particularly if it meant he would be committing to stay seven more years until he was sixty-five. He said that he was going to retire, but that he would work part time to aid in the transition. I could not believe he was serious, but in December 2003, he stepped down as chief operating officer (COO), became a part-time employee, and moved to a beautiful oceanfront home he had designed in South Carolina. Years later, I learned that the primary motivator for his decision was that he did not feel that the SRA board was leading the company in the right direction, and that as CEO he would have been in constant conflict with them.

In January 2004, Bill Brehm gave up the board chairmanship, and I became chairman and CEO. Renny was named president and COO. He served in that position for a year until I decided to step down as CEO, and the board appointed him to succeed me. As president and CEO, Renny's portfolio of responsibilities was quite broad. He carried all of his duties as the head of our government business, plus many of Ted's COO responsibilities, although some were assigned to Steve Hughes who had become senior vice president for finance and administration. Unfortunately, a number of key operational activities that Ted had naturally done as a longtime leader at SRA simply fell through the cracks. Eventually, this gap led to problems in the operation of the company.

In retrospect, despite my focus on succession planning, I did not get it right. Indeed, I found in Renny a successor who could lead the company around the same values and culture that had served it well for many years. But I failed to establish a complete leadership team to replace the complementary skills that the departing team had performed so well. As I reflect on this, it is now obvious that Ted played his role as a complement not only to me but also to Renny. Working together, the three of us, supported by Barry and Steve, were a complete and unified team. When Ted retired, we were missing some key pieces, but we did not realize it. Even though we prepared Renny to take over as CEO, we failed to cultivate someone to replace him as COO and to fill in more missing pieces. When Renny became CEO, we named David Kriegman, a highly successful twenty-two-year SRA business executive to be COO. David would not be successful in that role because we had done nothing to prepare him for it.

During 2005 it gradually became clear that David, despite his many other talents and accomplishments, was not a good fit for the demanding job of COO. His strengths and interests were in driving business results and not in managing the internal operations of a company that was now growing primarily by acquisition. He became bogged down by the details of SRA internal operations and could not make decisions quickly enough. Regrettably, he decided to leave the company.

The principal job of the COO was to focus on the overall health of the business. The CEO is very busy with other activities, for example, external relations involving investors and customers. I had, in fact, two people focused on the health of the business: Ted as COO and Renny as head of the government business. After his first year as CEO, Renny had no one in the COO role and the company began to lose its focus on such things as quality work and customer satisfaction, business development, and overall infrastructure. As we were to learn again later under a new CEO, no single person can perform all of these functions in a company like SRA, which requires continuous cultivation of its senior executives. Without a COO, SRA lost some focus. Despite these emerging problems, when Renny retired in March 2007, SRA growth was slowing, but we were still in relatively good shape. However, we were about to begin a new chapter in the company's leadership succession that would prove to be very difficult.

Succession planning is not just about choosing the next CEO; it also means ensuring that the entire leadership team can carry out the responsibilities effectively. Unfortunately, I learned this lesson again when it came time to select Renny's successor.

The board did not immediately replace David because it could not reach consensus on the next two logical candidates: Steve Hughes (chief financial officer) or Barry Landew (head of corporate development). The board discussed whether to do a COO search, possibly broad enough to identify a CEO candidate. Renny was sixty-five and willing to remain as CEO for a year or two, but he was not a long-term solution. The board, therefore, decided to recruit a CEO from outside the company and reasoned that, since a new CEO would want to participate in the recruitment of the COO, the decision on the latter could be deferred.

This was, in retrospect, a significant error. For the first time in our history, we had no logical successor to the current CEO and no viable candidates in training. More importantly, we had no one performing the vital functions of COO. The dilemma haunted SRA for three years, as weaknesses began to creep into our management systems.

Times of corporate prosperity are precisely when executives should be most wary. The company is growing rapidly, new jobs and people are added, and confidence is high. The natural tendencies are to embark on even more ambitious growth programs or to relax and enjoy the euphoria. During fiscal year (FY) 2005, which included the first six months with me as CEO and Renny as COO, and the second six months with Renny as CEO, revenue grew 43 percent. By the end of FY 2006, with Renny as CEO for the full year, growth was also 34 percent. But in

FY 2007, Renny had served as CEO for nine months and a new CEO for three months; revenue growth had declined to 8 percent.

There was another important indicator of problems ahead. When a company is acquired, its revenue and profit become part of the financial records of the acquiring company. The result is growth in the overall revenue and profit, which can serve to mask the organic performance of the primary company (that is, growth and profitability without the acquisition). If organic growth is slowing, then it is often a sign that the basic business may be ailing. In FY 2005, organic growth was 38 percent; in FY 2006, it was still a respectable 17 percent; but in FY 2007 it was only 3 percent.

A key problem affecting organic growth was business development, which had historically been one of the strengths of SRA. Building new business begins in the customer-facing organizations; our goal is to exceed client expectations on all contract engagements. There is some evidence that focus on excellent work for the customer began to slip during this period as the company was working to absorb and integrate its acquisitions. However, most of the problem was in the central marketing and sales (M&S) organization, which provided the real leadership for the largest and most important bids. SRA had grown a great deal, but M&S had not expanded in proportion to the rest of the company. The same small band of heroes (Jeff Rydant, John Luongo, Allen Deitz, and others) was supporting a much larger capture burden. Mike Fox (head of M&S) had performed very well in many other capacities, but argued that he could not deal with the problem because of lack of authority.

A third problem involved our overall structure for assuring quality work and customer satisfaction, which, like business development, had not kept up with the growth of the company.

This issue did not become evident until early fall of 2007, when a large project got into serious problems and another job began to lose customer support.

During the latter half of 2006, I interviewed several candidates for CEO and checked references. The most promising was Stanton Sloane, who headed a system integration group in Lockheed Martin. This was just the type of work that I had always hoped SRA would get. I wanted our firm to have real engineering jobs, in addition to our information technology and consulting practices. Stan seemed to meet our needs.

The group he headed was about three times the size of SRA, and Lockheed was a public company. Therefore, he was familiar with those additional responsibilities. The headhunter and I checked many other references for Stan, and the results were good. However, I did note one or two comments to the effect that he was somewhat remote. I broached this and other potential issues with Stan during five long meetings, spread several weeks apart. Often I mentioned "Honesty and Service" and its implications: high ethics, caring for our customers and employees, and serving society.

I came to understand that part of Stan's perceived aloofness was his natural personality; another component may have been the corporate culture in which he had been steeped. One of the questions I asked him concerned whether he intended to bring in his own team to replace our most senior executives. Stan said that he would not do this because SRA was not broken. He responded quite positively to all of my questions. He was open and communicative, had a sense of humor, and expressed confidence in his ability to break into the engineering system integration market. He was confident that he could expand our footprint in new markets and boost our revenue quickly.

After becoming convinced that he was a good candidate, I suggested that each board member meet with him individually or in small groups. The directors did this and agreed with my assessment; however, late in the process, Ted gave me a reference check that raised questions about Stan's leadership style. I decided that this one reference was not reason to change our course. I invited Stan to meet with several of our senior executives, and their assessments were generally positive. The board weighed the information from all of this effort and voted unanimously to select him as our next CEO. Ironically, it would turn out that despite my knowledge and care, we seemed irrevocably destined to repeat the mistakes of AMS, although that thought did not occur to me until many years later.

Stan assumed the job in April 2007. His senior executive team consisted of Steve Hughes as chief financial officer, and Barry Landew as diIt soon became clear that he intended to act decisively. He revised the incentive compensation system that had worked well for over ten years and began to build corporate staff organizations, intending to bring more formal processes to the company. Within three months, he recommended to the board that we buy a health care IT company (Constella) that had substantial work for the federal government. Stan's request was somewhat surprising because based on our due diligence the board had voted against an earlier proposal by Renny DiPentima to buy the same firm, less than a year before.

From one point of view, the acquisition made sense because Constella's work complemented existing SRA contracts in this area; but as previously mentioned, there were two parts of Constella that did not fit into our business. The board decided to approve the acquisition, reasoning that the new CEO should be given the opportunity to carry out his program.

After a few more months, Stan made another surprising recommendation. He suggested that we purchase Era, a company based in the Czech Republic that provided air traffic control products around the world. This work was alien to anything we had ever done, but Stan expressed confidence that this would be a good strategic move for the company. There was no question about his knowledge of certain aspects of aviation. He earned a pilot license at age fifteen and had flown ever since. He owned an acrobatic biplane and a small executive jet. He described similar work he had done at Lockheed Martin and said that he intended to hire people qualified in this area. After reviewing the Era business and based on the judgment of technical experts, the board once again agreed with Stan's recommendation. In retrospect, buying Era was one of the worst decisions in our history; I and the board should have been far more circumspect.

One of Stan's first publicly stated objectives was to increase SRA revenue from $1.5 billion to $5 billion and to gain a 10 percent profit margin within five years. I agreed with this objective. We had always set ambitious objectives for the future. We called them stretch goals. But in this case, the goals were unrealistic and they may have caused us to make unwise decisions.

The Constella and Era acquisitions proved to be major distractions. Perhaps because of preoccupation with the acquisitions and also the fact that there was no chief operating officer, problems began to emerge on several important SRA contracts but were undetected by the senior management team until it was too late to fix them. Early in 2008 we had to announce that we had lost the re-compete of one of our largest contracts. It was by some measures the worst loss in our history. As the months passed, work for two other large contracts declined, and we were unable to replace it with new contracts. Our growth slowed substantially.

The management team of Stan, Steve Hughes, and Barry Landew did not have much good news to report during the quarterly conference call with investors in October 2008. To make matters worse, two weeks after the conference call they concluded that our formal guidance given to stock analysts regarding likely company performance was not achievable. We had to publicly revise downward the estimate for the fiscal year. Our stock price plummeted. In the eighteen months since we hired Stan, the stock initially climbed from $25 per share but then fell to $11 per share. Not all of this was his fault. Some business indicators had begun to decline before he arrived, but there was no question in my mind that most of the problems had emerged during his first year and a half as CEO.

I was extremely frustrated and called a special meeting of the board. We debated for two hours. Following our usual custom, I left near the end of the meeting. The objective was to encourage open dialogue without me (as chairman and chief shareholder) present. Michael Klein, our lead director, informed me that the board would ultimately support my decision on the issue.

I thought about the issue for several hours. I was concerned about a split board. Stan had made mistakes, but he was intelligent, experienced, honest, and hardworking. He also had inherited two projects that were beginning to encounter problems. In our history, we had similar cases with talented executives and usually gave them a second chance. I decided to do this. At Michael's suggestion, we created an Executive Office of the Chairman consisting of Stan, Tim Atkin (whom Stan had previously appointed as COO), and me. We met every Tuesday morning and at other times when necessary. I made it clear that we would get back to the basics.

By this time, it was evident that the senior executive team consisting of Stan, Steve Hughes, and Barry Landew was not working. And Stan was not using Tim Atkin well as COO. Barry complained about the decline in SRA culture. Steve was frustrated as well.

For several years, I believed that Steve could be a good CEO candidate but that he should demonstrate his ability for growth by taking over one of our major sectors. Such a position was lower in our hierarchy, and Steve declined. Meanwhile, several directors thought that Steve was too narrow (a numbers guy) and cited dissatisfaction with his performance. I felt the criticism was unfair.

Stan apparently had also decided that Steve was not inclined to help

Susan Castillo and John Green,
innovators at the NIH.

Barry Landew, exploiter of new
contracting and procedures.

Ethical and cultural leaders (left to right): Barry Landew,
Renny DiPentima, Ted Legasey, Steve Hughes.

Stu Rubens, versatile, flexible executive discusses issues with Bill Albright.

Susan Recame and Karen Amato, our caring nurses.

Jerry Yates, forcefully compas-
sionate and mercurial leader.

Kevin Graves,
able administrator.

Kay Curling, innovator
of HR initiatives.

Ann Denison, a compassionate HR director.

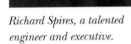

Richard Spires, a talented engineer and executive.

Dan Ilisevich, a facilitator of business initiatives.

Ringing the bell on the NYSE (left to right):
Ann Denison, Tony Valletta, Stu Rubens, Barry
Landew, NYSE representative, Mike Duffy, Ernst,
Renny DiPentima, Ted Legasey, Steve Hughes,
Kathy Adams, David Kriegman, Matthew Black.

Executive jet—Steve Hughes, Stuart Davis,
Ted Legasey, and Ernst (back to camera)
confer with Citigroup representative.

Anna Hogan and Terry Ryan,
leaders of Adroit.

Amy Marasco, co-founder
of Marasco-Newton.

Renny DiPentima,
the second SRA CEO.

John Luongo, Brian Michl, Allen Deitz,
superb performers over many years.

SRA Fair Lakes, location of our
fourth headquarters.

Kathy Adams, successful government and commercial executive.

Chuck Perry, an excellent leader.

Steve Hughes, able CFO for many years.

Stan Sloane, the third SRA CEO.

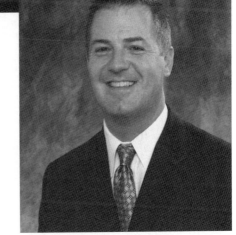

Tim Atkin, versatile executive.

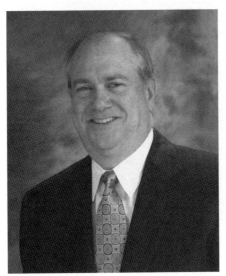

Rick Nadeau, accounting depth and business acumen.

*The first SRA Board
(Bill Brehm, Ernst, Sara).*

*SRA Board in 2000 (left to right)
front row: Bill Brehm, Ernst, Gary Nelson;
back row: David Crockett, Delbert Staley, David Jones.*

Michael Klein, talented lawyer and businessman.

Miles Gilburne, entrepreneur and philanthropist.

John Barter, seasoned business executive.

Bob Day, the SRA Everyman, and wife Barbara,
a former SRA executive assistant.

Bill Ballhaus, living up to a family of CEOs.

Julie Richardson, sage businesswoman with Midwestern pragmatism.

Chris Ragona, multifaceted business analyst.

Charles Gottdiener, experienced corporate strategist.

The new executive team (left to right)
front row: Anne Donohue, Bill Ballhaus, Tim Atkin;
back row: John Reing, David Keffer, Paul Nedzbala,
Pat Burke, George Batsakis, Tom Nixon.

him to accomplish the company's goals, so Steve was the first to go. Stan negotiated a generous separation package. I hated to see Steve leave SRA. He joined us in 1981 and had made large contributions over many years. Melissa Burgum took over as Acting CFO in April 2009. She did a good job, and was ably supported by accounting experts such as Chuck Crotty and Sue Caravelli. But Melissa was due to have a baby in July.

Although board chairs are not expected to participate in quarterly conference calls with analysts and investors, I joined Stan, Tim Atkin, and Melissa Burgum in February 2009—the first time in nearly four years. At the end of the call, my message was that SRA was returning to the basics, focusing on our customers, employees, marketing and sales. In view of our problems with Constella and Era, there would be no more acquisitions for the foreseeable future. In my initial meeting with Stan and Tim Atkin, after we had created the Executive Office of the Chairman, I told Stan that I did not intend to micromanage or undermine his authority; however, I did want to discuss with him all major decisions before he made them. I also reminded him of a prerogative that I had exercised since the founding of SRA—the right to talk to anyone in the company about any business subject. However, I would not give those people direction and would avoid issues that might inadvertently cause conflict.

Barry was the next to go. He was extremely bright, but sometimes came across as outspoken. These characteristics were useful when red-teaming a proposal or debating with a peer on an important decision, but could be divisive for those who did not know him well. His contributions to SRA over the years were huge. He was loyal, honest, and highly competent; but there was concern about the impact of his occasional sharp-edged communications.

I tried to find other ways to compensate for the loss of Barry's skills. He had decided to form a company. After substantial effort we reached an agreement where Barry's company would help SRA win new work; however, we never regained the value that he once contributed.

Stan began the recruiting process for a new CFO. Bob Grafton (one of our board members) mentioned Rick Nadeau to me. I had a high opinion of Rick, who was our principal auditor from Arthur Andersen during the 1990s. His current job was CFO of Sunrise Senior Living. Sunrise had experienced substantial financial difficulties and was decreasing in size and consolidating, but not because of Rick. He accepted our offer and joined SRA in June 2009. He soon became a useful member of the management team. The next three years would require all of Rick's talent and experience.

My relationship with Stan during 2009, when I was more actively involved in the management process, was good. He may not have enjoyed my greater involvement, but he understood and respected my authority as chairman and majority shareholder in SRA. Stan had, after all, come from a rigidly hierarchical environment, first at General Electric (GE) and later at Lockheed. General Electric is often admired for consistent business success and became known for the executives that it cultivated who went on to successfully lead other large companies. However, the GE culture lacked the humanistic approach that we pursued at SRA. Jack Welch, the GE chairman and CEO, left no room for emotionalism in business. Units that had contributed significantly in the past to the great history of GE were treated the same as new arrivals. He had fired so many people that many GE office buildings stood vacant, and the media began to call him "Neutron Jack," an allusion to a bomb, which emitted high-speed neutrons that did not damage structures but were lethal to humans.

General Electric raises an interesting issue concerning the nature of corporate succession. GE certainly produced capable executives. However, they tended to be individual supernovas—strong-willed people who dominated their organizations but did not necessarily tolerate dissent. They were not the type of leaders who cultivated junior people and built strong management teams. Instead, their primary criteria for promotion seemed to be business success, not inspirational leadership. Some critics said that at GE, people seemed to be regarded as machines. They were not necessarily abused, but if they did not perform well, they were readily replaced. GE offered adequate benefit programs and good training, but proactive caring for employees did not seem to exist to the same degree as our company.

In retrospect, the cultural incompatibility between Stan and SRA was substantial. Stan's background was with large aerospace engineering firms where process and discipline are often more important than in companies our size. Moreover, he was a sole manager, more comfortable dealing with key executives on a one-to-one basis than collectively. SRA, on the other hand, had a collegial culture under the concept that the best ideas win. Disagreement with the CEO and other senior executives was the habit rather than the exception. Stan may have interpreted some of the counterarguments to his proposals as lack of loyalty. And, he seemed unable to inspire team unity, probably because his culture and that of our longtime executives were so different.

When an executive team lacks cohesion and individual members are not inspired, the people working for them detect it, morale suffers, and executives begin to leave. The SRA attrition rate remained slightly below the average for similar companies, but we were losing some of our best performers, who in turn recruited their friends to other companies. The number of those departing was not excessive, but the effective loss of human capital was troubling.

The result was predictable. Our growth rate remained near zero, and we were afflicted by two acquisitions that had been imposed on a staff intimidated by the CEO (and the board in its acquiescence).

In the first eighteen months after Stan had taken over as CEO, the two top executives on his leadership team (each of whom had over twenty-five years of experience at SRA) and many other key people had left our company, and the stock had declined by more than 50 percent. During the next two years, the situation became somewhat worse. There were three primary reasons for this state of affairs: the tumult caused by change in leadership (succession), lack of focus because of distractions (particularly acquisitions), and incompatibility between the CEO and the company that he was leading. One major investor asked, "Where was the board?" As chairman of the board and therefore its principal representative, I did not have a good answer.

19

The Board Faces Challenges

⋯⟫ Hire a capable board that provides more than fiduciary oversight.

⋯⟫ Cultural incompatibility can cause businesses to suffer.

During the early years, the SRA board of directors consisted of Bill Brehm as chairman, my wife (Sara), and me. I knew that Bill would serve our company well. He is very talented. An accomplished engineer, businessman, and government official, his hobbies are also impressive. Bill's photographs of landscapes and towns hung in SRA hallways and received comments on their beauty.

Bill is also a creative musician. He led a dance band in college and became a proficient pianist and began to compose music. Later he wrote pieces that were played by the Army Band. He composed and published sacred music, which was performed in the United States and Europe. He and his wife, Dee, founded a center for performing arts at the Fuller Theological Seminary. Concurrently, they sponsored cooperative medical research initiatives within several universities and research institutions.

Over many years, I have known only a few people who have the ability to reach consensus among leaders at the highest levels of the government, military, and business. One of them is Bill Brehm; the other is Norman Augustine. Norm facilitated the merger of Lockheed and Martin Marietta corporations. He is a well-regarded author and successful leader of important studies for the President and Secretary of Defense.

In 1995, we created a Board of Advisors that would provide diversified business experience and also become candidates for a more formal board. They would be outside directors (non-employees) and would add credibility to the company. Bill Brehm and I chose people who had been eminently successful in business, government, or the military. Among them were Delbert Staley, the retired chairman and CEO of NYNEX (New York New England Exchange); General David C. Jones, Air Force (retired); and Hewlett-Packard executive E. David Crockett. Each brought a wealth of business experience, understanding of people, and knowledge of management that we thought would help SRA grow and diversify. Without Bill's excellent reputation in government and business, we never would have recruited them.

Delbert (Bud) Staley provided invaluable insights into how to manage and motivate people. He had learned this by starting at the bottom and working his way to the top. During World War II, Bud enlisted in the Army and was trained as a signal corps technician. One of his jobs was to climb telephone poles in combat zones and string wire. When the war ended, he found a job with American Telephone and Telegraph Company (AT&T). Bud possessed only a high school education, but, through hard work and intelligence, moved up through the AT&T hierarchy. In 1985 a legal decision broke up AT&T and Bud soon headed one of the new companies, New York New England Telephone Company (NYNEX). He served SRA from 1992 to 2007, when he suffered a stroke. He is still a loyal friend.

David Jones brought to the board a broad view of the military services. He grew up in North Dakota, enlisted in the Air Force, was commissioned a second lieutenant near the end of World War II, and flew B-29 bombers during the Korean War. Later, he graduated from the National War College, the military equivalent of graduate school, was selected to head the Air Force and became Chairman of the Joint Chiefs of Staff (JCS), the most senior military position in our country.

Presidents and defense secretaries had tried unsuccessfully to introduce constructive changes to the outmoded joint structure for managing the military services. It took the courage of a sitting chairman—General Jones—to push for reforms. SRA was only three months old at the time, but Bill Brehm (then an executive in another company) enlisted our help in an assessment and a report, "The Organization and

Functions of the JCS." General Jones, Bill Brehm, and others helped to produce landmark legislation in 1986, known as the Goldwater-Nichols Act, which significantly improved the military command structure. Its biggest effect was to foster joint action by the military services, which, until that time, had each reported independently to the President. General Jones considers this one of his greatest accomplishments. A few years after he retired, Bill Brehm convinced him to join the SRA board in 1991, where he provided excellent advice in a variety of areas for many years.

There are many reasons why a company needs a board of directors. The board is supposed to hold the management team accountable, ensuring compliance with the letter and spirit of laws and providing business success. This includes hiring and, if necessary, firing the CEO and approving compensation structure for senior executives. The board sets strategic goals and monitors the company's progress on them, although the executive management team maintains control over day-to-day operations. Ultimately, it is the board's responsibility to make major financial decisions that would impact the firm's performance such as buying other companies and being acquired.

The board ensures that the company follows the practices of good financial governance, in part by reviewing an annual audit by an independent outside company. In 1985, as a privately held firm, we hired an independent accountant to audit our financial records. Later, we augmented that by creating a small internal audit organization, as well as a hotline where employees could report problems without fear of retribution.

New laws, such as Sarbanes Oxley, made audit and compensation one of a board's most important functions. After the fall of Enron, WorldCom, and Tyco in 2001, there was an outcry for more government intervention to decrease corporate risk and limit the compensation of greedy executives. The boards of the companies affected were presumed to have failed in their oversight responsibilities, and the New York Stock Exchange (NYSE) and other independent bodies imposed additional checks on public company boards. Bowing to this pressure, corporations added safeguards, which greatly benefited law firms and other groups that provide a plethora of advice on these subjects.

During this era, SRA decreased the number of directors who were current or former executives. All but two of our ten directors were independent; that is, they came from outside the company. This was considered to be a good governance practice; internal directors were perceived as having conflicts of interest regarding their desires and those of the company. We created a lead outside director who, at the end of board meetings, convened meetings without the chairman or CEO present, both of whom were insiders.

Michael Klein joined the board of directors in 1999 and became the longest-serving member of the board. His contributions were countless. Michael was SRA lead outside director and chaired the governance committee for many years. He was a pivotal influence in the 2002 decision to go public and played a key role in selling the company nine years later. He brought to the board a keen legal and business mind, having been a partner in the law firm Wilmer, Cutler, and Pickering, and having founded and run several successful companies. Michael also created the Sunlight Foundation, which tracks political contributions by special interest groups to lawmakers and draws lines to legislation benefiting the contributors.

John Barter joined our board in 2003. He had been chief financial officer of AlliedSignal, later part of Honeywell International. Prior to retirement, he was named Executive Vice President, and President of AlliedSignal Automotive. John headed our audit and finance committee for many years. It is one of the most important positions on any board. Despite other demands on his time, he remained on our board until SRA was purchased by Providence Equity in July 2011.

As some of the earlier directors retired from the board, I thought more about the criteria for the selection of board members. My theory was that outside directors would bring new ideas and fresh perspectives, offering encouragement and challenges to do even better. A few months prior to our initial public offering (IPO) in 2002, investors from General Atlantic Partners persuaded me to sell 10 percent of our stock to them. Their argument seemed convincing. We knew nothing about being a public company. With General Atlantic's investment, its CEO, Steve Denning, would join our board, providing the financial sophistication and experience of a private equity investor. I felt that a well-regarded firm like General Atlantic would add cachet to our stock. Once on the board, Steve began urging us to do more. He believed that we were thinking too narrowly about our future and saw SRA as a multibillion-dollar company masquerading as a $400 million firm.

Steve and the rest of the board never got into the details of how we could quickly become a multibillion-dollar company, but the most realistic way of doing this would have been by initiating an aggressive program of acquisitions. There were private companies that might be candidates, but those big enough to make a difference in our revenue either demanded a premium price or were on a path toward an IPO themselves. There were many other smaller private firms, and during that time period, we acquired two: Adroit Systems (revenue $43 million) and Orion Scientific Systems (revenue $30 million). However, to achieve Steve Denning's goal would have meant acquiring ten of those companies in a short period.

Tiring of Steve's arguments, I asked one of our most talented and experienced directors, David Langstaff, to take a new look at our growth strategy. David had built a company called Veridian to more than $1 billion in revenue, taken it public, and sold it to General Dynamics. He spent several months preparing a paper that described strategic alternatives. The recommendations in his report were useful, but the management team resisted his suggestions, and I was unconvinced that we should change the strategy. Steve and David may have been right; the company could have pushed harder to grow more quickly or differently. But for several years after the IPO, SRA organic growth (that is, without acquisitions) regularly exceeded 20 percent per year and our stock price steadily rose. We seemed to have our hands full simply dealing with current growth.

Business was going well, and we enjoyed the challenge of beating the estimates that we had set for quarterly and annual earnings. Our management team was working well together, and the company was headed in the right direction. Therefore, near the end of 2004, I told the board that I wanted to step down as CEO but continue to serve as chairman. The board accepted my decision. However, near the end of the meeting, I was surprised by a comment from one of our directors.

I had known Miles Gilburne for ten years. He was an investor entrepreneur who was a partner in our initiative called NaviSoft, which we eventually sold to America Online (AOL). As part of that transaction, Miles also went to AOL, where he orchestrated all of its mergers, including Netscape and Time Warner. Ultimately he was elected to the board of directors of AOL–Time Warner. Miles was very busy, but on several occasions I asked him to join our board. He politely declined. I persisted, and after leaving AOL–Time Warner, he joined our board in 2004.

After my announcement about stepping aside as CEO, Miles suggested that we should consider selling the company while SRA was at the top of the pack, and the stock was approaching an all-time high of $30 per share. It was unrealistic to assume that the price would increase at the same rate in the future. He suggested that it would be good for the shareholders, and for me, to sell SRA.

I was shocked but tried to hide my disappointment. For years I had tried to convey to the board the hope and idealism of our values and culture as a standard for corporate America. These attributes also (unintentionally) gave us a market edge. Capable people were attracted to the firm and remained with it. Our reputation among customers was stellar, and our company flourished. I had reasons to be optimistic. Our organic growth rate (growth not counting acquisitions) for that fiscal year (FY 2005) would be nearly 38 percent. However, Miles and some of the other directors seemed to discount all of this and spoke only in terms of financial and stock performance.

My emotions were high, but I tried to reply rationally and calmly. "Miles, I cannot agree with your statement. We are just beginning to hit our stride. There is so much more to be done. We are demonstrating that a company can stand for something and yet still be a business success."

I left the meeting feeling discouraged and almost betrayed. The directors did not seem to understand the true value of SRA, which was far more than its profits. I felt a keen responsibility to all the shareholders, and some of our key employees held substantial equity in the form of options or stock. As I reflected on the conversation, I realized that Miles was trying to provide advice that was in the best interest of the shareholders and me. We simply had different viewpoints.

Subsequent events would prove that Miles was right, and I was wrong. One of the board's primary responsibilities is to represent the interests of shareholders when making decisions about the operations of a public company. I disagreed with Miles, but he was simply doing his job as a director.

When a company is doing well, the role of a board is mainly to offer suggestions for improvement and to avoid future difficulties. However, as problems began to develop, there were times when I became frustrated by what I viewed as the limitations of some board members. All of our directors were ethical, intelligent, and accomplished in various areas, but they were busy with responsibilities aside from SRA. Attending board meetings four times a year and additional committee meetings intermittently did not provide adequate time for directors to provide substantial contributions.

My thinking shifted about how to build a board. Recruiting intelligent, accomplished people was not enough. A corporate board should also include people who know the business of the company. Few of our directors had been line managers and moved up through the ranks to oversee thousands of people, and they did not comprehend the fundamentals of information technology services. More importantly, they did not appreciate the role that values and culture had in the success of SRA. For about half of the board, it was a classic case of cultural incompatibility. Those directors did not understand the business or the culture of SRA.

When we had leadership problems in 2008–2009, they did not know how to diagnose the problems and make appropriate corrections. Some directors understood the issues, but others did not. Therefore we could not reach a consensus on what to do. On the other hand, years later the board was outstanding when it came to financial leadership, such as in the sale of the company.

In retrospect, I had unrealistically high expectations for our board. I took for granted that SRA would be well managed and, therefore, the board would provide a unified strategic vision that company executives might not develop because they would be preoccupied with daily activities. But this did not happen. And when trouble arose, the board was ill-equipped to provide much assistance and it could not articulate a long-term leadership strategy for the company. I do not necessarily blame the board. I led the recruiting effort for the directors as well as the CEO. But it was clear that those who were most responsive to our growing crisis understood our business or had enough management experience to recognize there was a problem. My early theory about hiring for general intelligence and creativity was not sufficient when constituting a board.

As the company's troubles grew, one of my challenges was to try to hold the board together in consensus. I worried that if a director became frustrated, he or she could resign, signaling to the stock market even deeper problems within the company. Nobody resigned, or even threatened to, but I could have done a better job, and the board could have made better decisions along the way.

SRA limped along like this for another two years. After the board decided to retreat from our acquisition strategy and return to basic business fundamentals, the economy had shifted. Amid fears of a global recession, the federal government began to review contracting budgets and it was unclear what programs might be cut.

Profitability had declined, and within the board room, SRA directors debated the next step. Once again, the subject of selling the company was broached. I did not like the idea any better than when Miles Gilburne first raised it five years earlier. But this time, I began to listen to prospective buyers.

20

The Big Decision

⋯⋗ Values are vital; capable people want to be part of something great.

I stood on a cold, windy hill in Arlington National Cemetery in early March of 2011 as six soldiers in Army dress blue uniforms lifted a casket, draped with the American flag, from a hearse to a caisson. The funeral was for Colonel Robert Day, U.S. Army (retired), one of the longest serving SRA employees who, until his death, still worked part time. Bob was a great guy, quiet and selfless, and highly competent in his specialty, which was the use of computers to solve logistical problems. When Bob's team accomplished something significant, he always gave credit to the people who worked for him.

A ramrod stiff major with the chiseled face of a Spartan warrior and a chest radiating colored metals commanded, "Present arms!" A small platoon of about thirty men raised their rifles vertically in front of their chests and stared straight ahead, while those of us who were former or current military officers saluted.

The pallbearers lifted the casket onto the caisson and formed a line on both sides. The major gave another command and the platoon marched off toward the gravesite, followed by a small band that softly and slowly played "God Bless America." The caisson began to roll, drawn by six large horses. Behind it, a soldier led a riderless horse with boots reversed in the saddle straps, the symbol of a fallen leader.

As Ted Legasey and I walked behind Bob's widow, Barbara, and other family members, I thought back to an email message Bob had sent me several months before. It was dated Wednesday, December 1, 2010. Bob, who never complained, was concerned that yet another key, longtime SRA executive was leaving. National Security, one of our largest and most important sectors, had been struggling; part of the problem was the executive in charge. He had worked for Stan Sloane at Lockheed Martin, and his leadership style was consistent with a much larger, more authoritarian environment. I had suggested to Stan that he assess and mentor the executive, whose response to slow growth had been to browbeat his people. The result was predictable: the sector continued to decline and more people left the company.

A few hours after sending the email, Bob suffered a heart attack and never regained consciousness. The advice from a dying friend was the last straw. I called Stan and told him that I feared that the sector director would reflect poorly on our company. I did not ask Stan to fire him, only to remove him from the position and put him in a job that he could perform. A few days later, however, a company announcement stated that the executive had resigned to attend to family business. We assigned Jeff Rydant to run the national security sector. He assessed its state to be in even worse shape than had been suspected. Its declining sales, together with attrition of talent, would lead to a poor fiscal year.

I had already been weighing the company's future, but remained reluctant to fully embrace the idea of selling the company. Earlier in the year, one of our longtime directors, Michael Klein, raised points similar to those Miles Gilburne had made in 2004. Michael understood that I was devoted to seeing SRA remain successful and suggested that I consider the company's future while I was still its controlling shareholder and chairman.

Michael was a shrewd investor, and active in several successful companies. Moreover, he had gained the respect of our board and was elected by his colleagues as lead outside director. Like Miles, I knew he was trying to do the right thing for the shareholders and for me.

The decision was difficult. Virtually every year since our founding, I had been approached by the CEO of a company that wanted to buy SRA. Most overtures were quite similar. A firm much larger than ours was embarked upon a strategy of acquisitive growth. The CEO described how our companies together could create much more value than individually. When I said that I wanted to retain the SRA name, values, and culture, the CEO noted that his firm also had high values. While I don't think any of those CEOs and companies were unethical, I did not believe they could compare with SRA. I began to refer to them with a few close friends as "sausage factories" that would grind up SRA and homogenize us into their system. Our name, values, and culture would be lost forever. Many of those companies were quite successful, but I did not want SRA to become an Oscar Meyer wiener. In thinking about a potential sale of the company, I was afraid that the buyer would be a large company that would break SRA up into pieces and digest it. So in each case I declined, explaining that we were on a mission to create one of the world's great companies—a business and ethical success.

However, the problems of 2008–2009 convinced me that Miles and Michael were right, and I needed to listen more carefully to the overtures. It was not a case of me trying to hang on to control of the company or my influence in it. I had happily given up the CEO position more than five years before and had avoided trying to overrule Stan's decisions, even when I felt some of them were unwise. I knew I had to do something but wanted to protect, if at all possible, the name, values, and culture of SRA. Early in 2010, I was contacted by a private equity company that suggested an option for SRA that appealed to me. Private equity firms raise money from investors (such as big retirement funds) to buy companies, improve their management or make other changes, and then sell or take them public. The firm suggested it would be interested in exploring a possible transaction in which it would invest money in SRA and augment it with a large bank loan in a so-called leveraged buy-out (LBO). This would allow us to preserve the name, values, and culture of SRA, and they would ask me to be chairman of a small board that would oversee the launch of a refurbished, privately held firm. The shareholders would be asked to approve the LBO at a price that would be substantially higher than the roughly $20 our shares were selling for on the New York Stock Exchange.

This alternative seemed promising. SRA would once again be private. In theory, I might chair a small board without all of the regulatory procedures associated with running a public company. Working part time, I potentially could help restore the company's luster and see it safely on its new voyage, at least for a few years.

I asked David Langstaff (an SRA director who had led a publicly listed company and then sold it) to educate me on how such a transaction would work. He explained that the first step would be for the board to create a special committee that would evaluate a range of options and solicit proposals from prospective buyers. The committee would include directors disinterested in the transaction and independent from any interested party, for example me, and would be independent of the full board of directors. I would be unable to influence the process in any way, and could not participate in the deliberations, and would have little information about what was happening during the process.

David said that the committee would likely solicit bids from other parties interested in buying SRA, not just private equity firms but also large competitor companies that might want to integrate SRA into their business, rather than keep it as a stand-alone company. He suggested that if all of SRA shares were sold to an investor, the stock price would likely rise substantially higher than the public market. He said ultimately, the special committee would recommend the alternative that offered the greatest benefit to shareholders.

I spoke to other executives, who confirmed his view of what would happen if I indicated a willingness to sell. I also learned from these colleagues that any transaction would very likely attract a lawsuit claiming that the shareholders other than me were shortchanged in the deal. Such lawsuits rarely go to the merits, and the lawyers filing the suit—characterized by my colleagues as "parasites" and "scumbags"—instead hope to extract some monetary settlement from the buyers and sellers who would rather avoid the expense and distraction of a trial. It was my colleagues' opinion that these lawsuits were factored into the price buyers would be willing to pay, and so ultimately would come out of the pockets of SRA shareholders.

I was initially uncomfortable with the notion of a committee on which I could not serve. Colleagues had reminded me that as the controlling shareholder, I could veto the recommendations of the special committee, due the ten-to-one voting power of my shares, created back in the 1980s at the time SRA went public in order to prevent hostile takeovers. But I knew that my veto of a transaction recommended by the special committee would be seen as my vote on a transaction simply to foster my ideology and to preserve the SRA name, and I also was uncomfortable with going into the process with that kind of mind-set.

Some seasoned business people also suggested that, in return for surrendering my majority voting power, I could demand a premium for my shares. Almost all my stock was going to charity and this would have provided more money for good causes, but I knew it would be regarded as a greedy act on my part and I rejected it.

I considered the options carefully. On the one hand the private equity firm's proposal, with my continued involvement in a lean and focused SRA, was attractive to me. On the other hand, I had no strong desire to hang on as chairman or CEO. I wanted to build our family foundation and fulfill my obligations as Rector (chairman) of the Board of Visitors (board of trustees) of George Mason University.

Because I wanted to be sure to go into any decision with the most information available, I suggested, and the board approved, formation of a study committee to assess all options for the future. Possible scenarios were for SRA to continue current operations, merge with a similar company, sell to a larger firm, or allow an investor to take the company private.

In the summer of 2010, we had learned that Lockheed Martin was selling one of its divisions. The division had reported to Stan when he was at Lockheed and he was intimately familiar with its work and its market. Therefore, he recommended to the board that we try to buy it. In view of our problems with Era and Constella, the board and I were wary. The business was estimated by a number of bankers to sell at a price near $1 billion. This would be a much bigger acquisition than SRA had ever made, and the risks were significant. But the business performed the type of system engineering work that I had always craved for SRA. After substantial discussion, the board approved a sequence of gradually increasing bids. But we lost the competition to a private equity firm.

The loss of the Lockheed Martin acquisition put me back in the same position I was in before formation of the study committee: I had to make a decision on whether to support the board taking steps, independent of me, to explore a possible sale of SRA. I weighed the options carefully, made my decision, and told the board in a special meeting at the fall of 2010. My preference was that SRA would not be for sale in a formal auction; the name, values, and culture of the company would be preserved; the shareholders would receive a fair price; and the management team would support the process. I knew that the committee might not accept my suggestions, but I thought that this might be the way to rebuild SRA and preserve its ideals.

The board immediately formed the special committee and chose Michael Klein as chairman. He arranged a meeting including himself, the committee's counsel (George Stamas of Kirkland & Ellis), me, and my attorney (Steve Glover of Gibson Dunn & Crutcher). I expressed the hope that if there was a transaction, the deal be completed quickly in order to minimize disruption of the company.

Michael agreed that the committee should act as quickly as possible, and assured me that he would do what was right for the shareholders of SRA. He paused and then said, "How about a hug?"

Michael Klein, a longtime tough and highly competent business attorney and entrepreneur, was just as humanistic as the rest of us. It was comforting to know that he was leading the special committee. However, one event led to another and the process dragged on. At the time of Bob Day's funeral at Arlington National Cemetery on March 7, 2011, it was not clear that there would be a deal.

The soldiers, band, caisson, riderless horse, and mourners for the funeral wound their way down the small knoll to the gravesite. As we walked behind the family in the cortege, I thought about Bob and the events leading up to and since his email message expressing concern about the company losing its people, and its way. He was utterly devoted to his family, country, and SRA. The only two jobs he had held were as a soldier and a SRA employee. His wife, Barbara, told me that he was buried wearing a white shirt with the SRA company logo, and I knew that this devotion was inspired, not by me, but by the ideals of our company. He was the SRA Everyman.

A large green carpet had been rolled out before Bob's grave to provide dry footing for his family, seated in folding chairs. The rest of us stood behind them while the major called the platoon to present arms. A military chaplain read a few passages from the Bible and spoke briefly about Bob. On a hill about thirty yards away, three soldiers stood with rifles ready. A corporal gave a command and they pointed their rifles at 45-degrees to the sky, and fired three shots. Then another soldier standing nearby played taps, slowly and mournfully. Afterward, the honor guard, major, and chaplain performed the solemn ritual of presenting the carefully folded flag to Barbara.

At that point, I renewed my vow to myself to do everything possible to conclude a deal at a fair price for the shareholders. The actual price meant less to me, except for the charitable good I could do with it. If a large company were to express interest in SRA, I would try to negotiate terms that helped retain our name, values, and culture, but I would support the decision of the board.

21

The Grind

⋯⋗ **Hire a capable board that provides
more than fiduciary oversight.**

T he special committee included Michael Klein (chairman), Miles Gilburne, John Barter, Bob Grafton, and Larry Ellis. One of the committee's responsibilities was to ensure that no one could corrupt the objectivity of the process. The committee's decisions and actions were disclosed to other board members, the management team, and me only when our knowledge of a subject was necessary to perform a specific function. Michael had served as legal counsel or board member in numerous merger and acquisition (M&A) transactions, including Time-Warner and Unocal. Other members of the committee also had substantial M&A experience. All of them understood my concerns about values and culture. Although I would have little knowledge of the committee's work, I knew the members would present the best possible options.

The primary advisors in this process were investment bankers and attorneys, who command substantial fees to ensure that the work is conducted properly. They create documents that present the company's current state and outlook for the future and then support negotiations. Hiring $1,000-an-hour attorneys and paying banking commissions that are five to ten times higher than actual labor costs run contrary to my customary frugality. It seems logical to question whether the value derived from their effort merits these high expenses. Invariably, other attorneys file lawsuits alleging improprieties between buyer and seller. Attorneys make even more money helping to defend from these suits. The wonder of it all is that any transactions are executed in view of the complexity and cost of lawyers and bankers, not to mention the occasional greed of major stockholders and company executives. But these are the financial and legal mores in this country, and their roles in deal making are inexorable.

The committee hired Kirkland & Ellis LLP to provide legal counsel, and engaged the investment banking firm Houlihan Lokey to help the management team develop a company prospectus and perform other functions. As this work progressed, Anita Antenucci, the lead investment banker for us from Houlihan, developed a long list of potential buyers. She knew my desire to preserve the values and culture of SRA, if possible, but her primary objective was to provide the best price for shareholders. The preferences of mine or the management team would not necessarily be a component of the deal. She and George Stamas, our lead counsel at Kirkland & Ellis, prepared our CEO, chief financial officer, and other key executives to make presentations to prospective bidders. Under the committee's established process, the lowest offers would be eliminated. Buyers would always have an out, in case they later discovered potential problems. The committee, with the help of the investment banker and attorneys, would conduct detailed negotiations and develop purchase contracts with the remaining potential buyers. Ideally, there would be at least two bidding against one another. The special committee would then select the best offer and present it to the board for approval.

Before the process ended, we followed all of these steps. But when the special committee was created, we did not know how many interested buyers there would be. Providence Equity Partners had expressed an interest. Providence was a company with nearly $25 billion under management and an excellent reputation. However, their experience was primarily in media, communications, and entertainment. Julie Richardson, a managing director at Providence, convinced me that SRA could have a new beginning as a private company, preserving its name, values, and culture, and perhaps moving to new heights of business success. I appreciated Julie's honesty, work ethic, and Midwestern sensibility, which she attributed to her schooling at the University of Wisconsin–Madison. Once dubbed a "private equity superstar" by *Time* magazine, Julie observed that while finance people who grew up in the Northeast know a lot about Wall Street, it takes tenacity and a more proactive approach of a Midwesterner to truly understand the business system and find ways to contribute.

Providence submitted a proposal near the end of 2010. The committee believed that other companies would express interest in SRA and, therefore, took no action on the bid. Instead, the committee directed the management team to compile detailed financial information in a virtual data room that prospective buyers could access via computer once they signed a confidentiality agreement. David Mutryn, a young SRA executive who managed the company's investor relations, oversaw creation of the data room and many others contributed to the effort.

Various companies accessed the data room. When a firm expressed an interest in bidding, the committee arranged for Stan Sloane, Rick Nadeau, and others to provide detailed briefings. I was not present at these meetings. Anita Antenucci introduced the prospective buyer and asked its team to talk about their firm. Stan, Rick, and other supporting managers were well prepared for these meetings in part because Anita had hired an expert in due diligence to play the role of prospective buyer. In those practice sessions, the consultant reviewed the SRA business briefing with our management team, helping them polish the presentation and prepare for the kinds of questions prospective buyers would be expected to ask. Stan, Rick, and others, particularly in our finance and accounting and legal groups, were busy with the usual company business, but through long hours of work, did a good job of performing these additional functions.

The committee responded to inquiries from other private equity firms besides Providence and from strategic investors (large government contracting firms). Providence and at least one other firm requested that we conduct negotiations exclusively with them. However, it would have been counterproductive to end the competitive process too early. So on several occasions, the committee declined. At the time that we began holding serious discussions about selling, SRA stock was trading at about $20. Based on projections of future business growth and an analysis of comparable acquisitions in recent years, the special committee had in mind a selling price in the $30 range. Over time, as a result of the committee's aggressive and diligent negotiations with bidders, the proposed price for SRA rose and the bidders were winnowed down to those able and willing to pay more for the company.

Even so, the process seemed to drag on and on. There was always another delay. One reason was that the bidding process was complicated. While high price was the primary criterion, other conditions of a proposed contract were also important. One company might submit a price that initially appeared higher than the others but included so many conditions that the result was, in fact, a lower bid.

Another complexity in the process occurred because many of the bidders needed bank financing for the purchase. In order to get the banks to tentatively approve loans, each bidder had to describe the essentials of the transaction. This increased the number of documents that contained details of our business and bidder proposals. It also expanded the pool of people who had access to this information. While all involved signed confidentiality agreements, leaks may have occurred, and the results were not constructive. In one of the more troubling instances, a reporter wrote that a large company submitted a bid of more than $2 billion. The company had, in fact, sent a preliminary letter indicating interest, but the price quoted was substantially below that figure. Apparently, equity analysts who covered the bidding company began asking questions. As a result, the firm withdrew its bid, perhaps because it feared negative analyst evaluations.

Then the previously interested company issued a public statement that it was not involved in any discussions with SRA regarding an acquisition. This created several issues of concern for us. Amidst media speculation about what was going on, the SRA stock price had risen. We were concerned potential bidders might drop out because they thought SRA already had a buyer in mind. If we decided against selling, our stock price might fall precipitously, which would not be good for business.

Other companies submitted expressions of interest and engaged with us over a period of time, and several of them withdrew for various reasons. The special committee had anticipated this, and took steps to ensure SRA would receive the best offer. At one point, there were only financial bidders at the table. Though initially I had expressed concern about selling SRA to a strategic bidder that might break up the company, the committee decided it was in the best interest of shareholders to solicit bids from all potentially interested buyers—both strategic and financial—in order to get the highest possible price for the company.

Michael informed me of the special committee's decision, and five prospective strategic bidders suggested various prices; some of them were above $30 per share.

By early March 2011, the process seemed to be approaching a conclusion, and the special committee asked me to meet with four finalists. Two were private equity firms and two were large companies that had business similar to ours. I tried to visualize the best way to deal with each contestant. An important element of business success is in planning ahead, which extends to preparing for each business meeting. Most of us are not good at quick decisions in the intensity of a specific gathering. Proper preparation ahead often pays off.

The meetings went well, and I was pleasantly surprised when executives from even the large companies said that our name, values, and culture were important in the market; if successful, they did not intend to homogenize SRA into their organizations. I had been wrong about the sausage factories, at least for some of the strategic investors. I left the meetings feeling that I could agree to any of the four and would have no regrets about the final choice of the special committee. Price, after all, would be the determining factor, and I had committed to supporting the decision of the board.

The dramatic finale came on the last two days of March 2011. A meeting of the special committee was set for the evening of Wednesday, March 30, at the law office of Kirkland & Ellis in Washington. The full board of directors would convene afterward to consider the recommendations of the special committee. All of the strategic buyers had dropped out of the process as the auction price for SRA rose. There were two finalists, Providence and another private equity firm. Apparently, the special committee was going to recommend one of them to the board.

I did not know what went on leading up to these final meetings, but apparently Michael Klein had negotiated to a basic price level that he had been seeking. Providence offered a bid of $30 a share and indicated that was the highest it would go. Then the other bidder offered $31.

That evening Michael Klein told me that the committee had a new offer from Providence that required me to take on some additional risk in order for Providence to raise its price in what had become a bidding war between the two private equity firms. He reminded me that SRA was in the process of selling two subsidiaries, Global Clinical Development and Era. Providence could raise its offer to $31 a share by adding in the anticipated proceeds from those sales. The problem was, until they were sold, it was unknown whether the subsidiaries would yield the amounts SRA had projected. This is where my assistance came in.

Providence was proposing that I personally guarantee a loan based on the sale of the two subsidiaries. My loan would guarantee that the total price of Era and Global Clinical Development would be at least $30 million. If SRA sold them for more than that amount, the company would keep the money; if less, I would have to pay the difference. Put differently, there was no upside to the loan and instead there was only downside risk.

Initially, I was incredulous. Making such a loan seemed foolish. On the other hand, SRA had invested a great deal of time and money over the previous year exploring the company's options and proceeding down a path that the board believed was the best way forward for our company. Furthermore, if Providence stayed in the game, there would still be two bidders, which was good for the shareholders. But why should I shoulder that burden? The estimated value of the two subsidiaries was more than $30 million, but Era had been a terrible acquisition. SRA had written off more than $100 million, and Era was still losing $750,000 per month. There was a good possibility that I would lose money if I agreed to Providence's proposal.

I continued to mentally debate these issues while driving toward Washington in rainy evening rush hour traffic. When I arrived at the Kirkland & Ellis law office, the special committee was still meeting. A few minutes passed, and I was invited into the special committee meeting. I still didn't know what my answer would be—would I go with logic or emotion?

Once in the room, I told the committee, "I shall agree to the loan." I knew this sounded unwise, but keeping two bidders in the auction would be better for shareholders.

After I left the committee meeting, Michael Klein and his team contacted the other private equity bidder and reported that the competition had increased its bid to $31. Upon hearing this, the firm raised its bid to $31.25. It also requested a period of exclusivity to negotiate the remaining terms of the transaction.

The board of directors convened about one-half hour later. The committee's recommendation was in favor of selecting the other private equity firm and giving that company an exclusive arrangement until 3 p.m. on the following day, during which time the final conditions of the contract would be negotiated. I recused myself from the meeting, and the board voted for this plan.

It was nearly midnight by the time I reached home, and I had to rise early to approve and sign some of the final contractual conditions. The lawyers worked most of night, undoubtedly tired but comforted by the fact that their every hour would be billed. Mark Schultz, Anne Donohue, Cathy Steger, and others in the SRA legal department also worked most of the night but without additional compensation.

Thursday began with a review of draft documents prepared by the attorneys. At 9 a.m., Providence representatives called Houlihan Lokey inquiring about the status of the firm's proposal. They were told that we were in an exclusive negotiating period with another bidder. But shortly after 3 p.m., when the exclusivity period ended, Providence responded, matching the price of the other bidder. Evidently neither offer was higher than $31.25, but the contract terms were different. Around 4 p.m. I received a call from the CEO of the other private equity firm, who said that, regrettably, he was dropping out of the competition. In my meeting with him several weeks before, we developed good rapport. I felt bad about the time, effort, and cost that his firm had invested in the transaction.

I immediately called Michael Klein. He had already heard the news. All of the paperwork had to be revised as soon as possible. The objective was to sign a contract with Providence in time to make a public announcement before the stock market opened on the following day. Word of the negotiations might leak out and jeopardize the deal. On Thursday, March 31, 2011, I signed several complex documents that indicated the intent to sell SRA to Providence Equity Partners for $31.25 per share at a total valuation of $1.88 billion.

I cannot explain my relative equanimity in the face of such life-changing events. Perhaps it was exposure to frightening events during my military career and later bouts with melanoma and thyroid cancers. I noticed that many people do most of their worrying at night. I resolved not to do this. If I woke at night, I usually got up, stretched, and then began thinking about difficult problems in mathematics. Those challenges usually put me to sleep.

When I stepped aside as CEO of SRA in 2005, I reduced my time in the office to three days a week, although I often took work home. But in late March 2011, many of my responsibilities had increased when negotiations with the final bidders for SRA were approaching a climax. Concurrently, we were recruiting an executive director for our family foundation, and the longtime highly capable president of George Mason University (Alan Merten) announced his retirement. This meant that in my capacity as Rector (chairman) of the Board of Visitors (trustees), I had to organize the process for selecting a new president. It was a lot of activity for a seventy-seven-year-old man; however, I did not feel the tension of my younger years. I entered each meeting relaxed and usually well prepared. My healthy diet and exercise routine did not change.

A lot of work by many people made possible the public announcement on Friday, April 1, 2011, followed by my letter to employees and a teleconference with senior executives. We wanted to tell the employees as much as possible, while not divulging information contained in confidentiality agreements.

A decision had been made. I and most of our senior people were relieved that the period of uncertainty was over. However, there was still much to be done before a shareholder vote could be held and, assuming approval, the transaction could be consummated.

After the announcement of a prospective purchase, another process begins that is as long as the effort required to sign a merger agreement—about four months. It can take longer if an issue is encountered. The first step was a thirty-day "go-shop" period in which the special committee notified other companies of the proposed transaction and, in effect, asked if they would like to submit a higher bid. The phase was optional but it provided extra assurance that an open and fair competition was performed and would ensure that the highest possible price for SRA was obtained.

During the go-shop period, a proxy is prepared and sent to the Securities and Exchange Commission (SEC) for approval. The proxy describes the deal so that shareholders can decide whether to vote for the merger. The SEC can take a month, or longer, if the transaction is complex or contains an issue that requires detailed investigation.

This caused me to reflect on the entire process for selling a company. For hundreds of years in this country, corporate executives have used their positions in ways which, by modern standards, would be considered illegal, or at least unfair. One of the most common methods is through executive compensation. Some chief executives reason that they are worth a lot of money because their leadership has the potential to bring in a significant profit. They hire executive compensation firms to demonstrate that their rewards are comparable to other firms of similar size and type. Other insiders, such as founders and large shareholders, use various methods to enrich themselves. When a new particularly egregious technique emerges, Congress passes additional laws to close loopholes and provide more government oversight. Federal regulatory agencies respond, often adding embellishments. Over the years, the process becomes inefficient because of a hodgepodge of laws and regulations. It is expensive to taxpayers and investors.

All these laws and regulations meant that even though we had signed a contract to sell the company, there were now many more documents to prepare. Our proxy was filled with detail, including a chronology of negotiations, and consisted of 111 pages and five appendices, comprising another 76 pages. As for the people who would actually vote on the proxy, there may have been a few institutional investors who read every word. Perhaps others skimmed it, but, I doubt that it was actually read closely by average shareholders, whom the law is designed to protect.

Even after the contractual documents had been signed, there was always a lingering doubt concerning whether or not the transaction would take place. Would some economic trauma cause the lending banks to withdraw? Would the majority of the minority shareholders approve the deal? This was a requirement added by the special committee to demonstrate that, even with my ten-to-one voting stock, I would not overrule all the other shareholders.

Within a few days of the announcement on April 1 that SRA would be acquired by Providence Equity Partners, two lawsuits were filed (one in Delaware and the other in Virginia) alleging that there were improprieties and our shareholders had been somehow cheated. This was despite the fact that the sale price was one of the highest at the time. It was "the scumbags" about whom a friend in another company had warned. The lawsuits were wasteful and needless distractions that benefited primarily attorneys.

Since SRA is incorporated in Delaware, any trial would likely take place in that state; the Virginia lawsuit was stayed and the suit brought by a law firm on behalf of the Southeastern Pennsylvania Transit Authority (SEPTA) against SRA International, individually named members of the board, and Providence Equity Partners continued in Delaware court. The abbreviated title for this case was SEPTA vs. Volgenau, et al.

Various lawyers told us that a small number of law firms file suits in 95 percent of the cases in which a publicly listed company is purchased. These complaints are filed by firms that make a livelihood of class action suits and therefore cultivate groups of investors to participate with them. The investors (often pension funds) have nothing to lose since the costs of the suit are borne by the law firm, even if the complaint is dismissed. On the other hand, if the suit is won by the plaintiffs, then the investors gain part of the award and the law firm receives a significant percentage of it.

In Delaware, the case is tried by a chancellor (a judge) and there is no jury. Most of the plaintiff's cases are settled out of court before a trial occurs. The law firms hope to at least recover their costs, and if they can show merit to some of their points, gain a profit. They are betting that a business will engage an expensive well-known law firm to protect itself and that the costs of preparing for trial will be disproportional for the business (and its insurance company) compared to their costs. That is, the cost and distraction of the lawsuit will be large enough so that most companies will settle out of court. The suit was certainly costly and time consuming for us. It lasted for more than three years after the initial filing by the plaintiff on April 7, 2011.

There were many follow-on filings and legal actions by our lawyers and theirs. One of the most time consuming and therefore expensive processes was discovery in which, at our expense, all corporate documents having any conceivable relationship to the transaction were laboriously gathered and copied by paralegals under the supervision of attorneys from both sides.

Gathering my records alone was a big effort that was multiplied several times by similar records from the CEO, CFO, other board members, and staff. The plaintiffs were entitled to my records, either at the office or home, that had any relationship to the sale of SRA. This included all email, letters, meeting notes, personal information papers, and so on. It did not matter where the data was stored: on my computer, in SRA central files, in my desk and credenzas, or in similar storage of my executive assistant. The search required a substantial amount of my time simply to ensure nothing was missed.

The process reminded me of countless warnings I had received from lawyers who said that virtually everything you say or do in business is recorded and may be used against you. Emails are one of the biggest sources of legal evidence, and I continue to be amazed by the lack of discretion on the part of some executives with regard to their correspondence. Some people naively assume that a destroyed email or word processed document is eliminated; however, that is not the case. Such data is routinely archived and retained for years. The primary reason is that computers occasionally fail and primary storage is destroyed; therefore a secondary source is needed to successfully restore data and restart computers. In other cases there is a legal requirement imposed either by regulators or by companies to protect themselves.

Once the data was collected, the plaintiff attorneys reviewed it minutely in order to build a case against us. They planned to use several forums to present evidence of wrongdoing: filings to the court based on directly gathered information, other submissions using our testimony in meetings where they were the examiner, and further evidence if the judge chose to have a hearing involving the defendants and plaintiffs.

On Thursday, June 15, 2011, I drove to the Washington offices of Gibson Dunn & Crutcher, the law firm that I had engaged to protect my interests in the sale of SRA. We met in a conference room with attorneys for the plaintiff in the Delaware suit, who was alleging that the purchase price did not produce the greatest possible benefit to shareholders. Also present was an attorney from Kirkland & Ellis representing the SRA special committee, and an attorney for Providence from Debevoise & Plimpton.

After brief introductions, a court recorder asked me to raise my right hand and pledge to speak the truth. Then the plaintiff attorney began the deposition examination. He was a modest, unassuming man, average height, and probably in his fifties. He started by taking a paper from a folder, handing copies to the court recorder and the other attorneys, asking the recorder to label it as "Exhibit 1," and giving me a copy to read. Then he asked, "Do you recognize this paper, Dr. Volgenau?"

After a meeting, I often dictate notes that my executive assistant transcribes. I edit the result, the executive assistant retypes it, and I usually put a paper copy in my files. I do this so I can consult the notes before the next meeting with that person, which might occur weeks, months, or even years later. I want an accurate reminder of what was said, and I don't want people to question my word or say that I do not fulfill commitments.

My files also contain draft outlines of talking points or brief concept papers on a specific subject for a future planning meeting. I began this process when I was in the military many years before, and did not anticipate that these papers would be used as evidence in a court trial by a clever attorney who could present them out of context and exploit ambiguities. But I hated to give up a system that had served me well for a very long time. In any case, the first obligation of an executive is to the company, and such papers are often necessary. He cannot spend a lot of time trying to phrase sentences perfectly or argue with an attorney about working papers.

Many of the exhibits were immediately recognizable to me and the questions easy to answer. But occasionally, the plaintiff's attorney would hand me a document that I appeared to have written but was undated, not easily identifiable, or contained information I could not precisely recall or understand what I had meant when I wrote it.

The attorney would direct me to a particular sentence or paragraph in the document and ask me to interpret it, even when I would say I didn't recall what I meant when I had written it.

"Objection!" my attorney would interject, "The plaintiff is asking the witness to speculate."

And so it went for nearly seven hours, with several short breaks and a brief lunch of sandwiches in the conference room. At the end, my feelings were mixed. I knew I made several mistakes, but at other times my replies were good.

Ultimately, the request for an injunction of the shareholders' meeting made by the Virginia plaintiffs was denied, and the Delaware complaint did not prevent our shareholder meeting and vote scheduled for July 15, 2011. Michael Klein chaired that meeting. Sara and I were in Oregon with our three daughters, their husbands, and nine grandchildren at a family reunion that had been scheduled a year in advance. This was the first board or shareholder meeting I had missed in twenty-five years, since the creation of our advisory board.

It was held at SRA headquarters, in a large presentation center. I was told the magnitude of planning leading up to the meeting was considerable. In a series of meetings SRA people from security, legal, facilities, and other areas pored over every potential scenario. Were special signs necessary? What about reserved parking? What would the policy be for media and recording devices?

I participated in some of these preparations but was not worried. We had many board meetings over the years and, even in the worst of times, hardly anyone outside the company ever attended. I offered to bet anyone a meal in a fine restaurant that there would be less than ten outside shareholders.

Seven outside shareholders attended, adding their votes to those that had already been submitted by proxy. The majority of the minority question dissolved. The transaction was approved by 99.7 percent of the voting minority shareholders. The meeting lasted nine minutes. Michael Klein and the special committee had done a good job.

22

A New Beginning under Uncertain Conditions

⋯⦂ Occasionally a company may pass
through periods in which its assets can
be harvested to benefit shareholders.

⋯⦂ Be prepared for market changes;
no market grows or declines indefinitely.

O n July 20, 2011, SRA International had a new beginning. The purchase contract was consummated, and the new owners took over. I was one of them. Providence Equity Partners was the primary owner with about 80 percent of the equity. I held about 20 percent, which is roughly the same percentage as when SRA was a public company, despite the fact that I had donated to charity more than half of my previous shares. How this happened is a testimony to the wonders of financial leveraging.

Near the end of the process of selling the company in 2011, a reporter asked me questions that I found difficult to answer. He began, "In May 2002, SRA had a very successful IPO, during which you, General Atlantic, and other shareholders made a lot of money. Your argument then was that an IPO was good for the company. Nine years later, you announced an intention to take the company private. Now you and the executives of SRA will make a lot of money. Your arguments seem inconsistent. Why was it such a good idea to become a public company in the first place, and now, why is it wise to go private?"

He had my attention, and I replied, "During the IPO, I did not sell much of my holdings and, in fact, the great majority of my wealth is going to charity."

"Okay," replied the reporter quickly. "I won't accuse you of personal greed, but my question remains, 'Why is it that going public caused the SRA stock price to increase greatly; and now a private equity firm, and other potential buyers, have bid the stock price higher in anticipation of going private?'"

It was a good question, and I was stuck for an answer, replying rather lamely, "Free market forces determine the value of our stock. I didn't design the financial systems in this country, but I would be foolish not to take advantage of them."

Rolling over (reinvesting) a substantial portion of my previous shares was a condition imposed by both of the final two firms that wanted to buy SRA during the last week of the competitive bidding process in March 2011. The lenders in the leveraged buyout insisted that there be a substantial investment in the transaction. It was somewhat similar to the purchase of a new home. The bank requires a down payment from the purchaser and provides a loan for the rest of the price. I could brag about still owning a substantial percentage of SRA stock, but I was analogous to someone who owns part of an expensive house that is heavily mortgaged. Visitors might marvel at my wealth, but the bank has first claim on it. If SRA cannot pay the mortgage, I can lose a great deal (perhaps all) of my down payment.

The concept of a leveraged buyout like ours provides a partial answer to the reporter's question concerning why the SRA stock price increased when it was publicly listed in 2002 and why, nine years later, the stock went up again when SRA became a private company. The answer in both cases concerns harvesting the latent value of the company.

Prior to going public in 2002, our stock price was below that of comparable, but publicly listed, firms. SRA was potentially much more valuable if listed on a major exchange. By having a public offering, our company was able to put this unused value to work by selling stock and using the money for acquisitions. Prospective investors could not buy stock in the private firm but, for the higher public price, could become part of the SRA team and benefit from our success. They did well until we ran into difficulties six years later.

The problems began late in 2007, became much worse in 2008, and continued for three years. Our stock price fell rapidly to less than half of its previous value and recovered only slightly. The company continued to grow and generate profit, but investors apparently could see no path to the luster of former years. However, private investors recognized that there was unused value that could be leveraged through bank loans. They could own the entire company by taking out loans and investing cash for only about 30 percent of its value. By changing strategy and the CEO, they believed that the company would grow more rapidly. After a few years, they would have paid down a substantial portion of the loans and then could sell part or all of their equity in a much more valuable firm through some financial event—perhaps another public offering. The partial answer to the reporter's question then is that the two events, the IPO in 2002 and the privatization nine years later, in effect harvested some of the unused value of SRA.

Providence wasted no time in asserting strong leadership over their new acquisition. Julie Richardson, Chris Ragona, and I were an informal partnership that decided immediate next steps, although I was a minority shareholder. We told Stan that he would not be part of the SRA future, and we engaged Korn Ferry International in a search for the new CEO. Stan was gracious in the decision. He continued leading the company and maintaining a positive attitude while the replacement process took place.

With the help of Korn Ferry, we developed criteria for the new CEO and narrowed the list to five well-qualified candidates. All of them had great respect for SRA and wanted to compete for the position. It soon became evident that two executives appeared most likely to meet our needs. Our preliminary reference checks and meetings with them were positive. Both appeared sincere in their intent to maintain the name, values, and culture of SRA. Julie, Chris, and I debated for several weeks about what to do while Korn Ferry made further reference checks.

On Monday, July 25, Julie Richardson and I sent out messages announcing William Ballhaus as the next president and CEO of SRA International, Inc. Bill received a master's degree and PhD in aeronautics and astronautics from Stanford, and an MBA from UCLA. He came from a family steeped in the aerospace industry. His grandfather had been chief engineer at Northrup Grumman and then CEO of a California firm that developed medical diagnostic and research instruments. Bill's father was an executive at NASA, who led two businesses within Lockheed Martin and then served as CEO of Aerospace Corporation. When Bill was growing up, dinner conversations revolved around aerospace systems, management philosophies, and the importance of making contributions and doing the right thing.

Bill was not searching for a job. He had already been the CEO of another company, Dyncorp, which he grew from $2 billion to nearly $4 billion and privatized in 2010. When Korn Ferry introduced us to Bill, he was working with a successful private equity firm. Later, he told me that he became interested in SRA when our conversation turned to values and culture. His first engineering job was at Hughes Electronics, which reminded him of our company. People were carefully selected and values were emphasized. As we talked in several meetings and I learned more about him, I became confident that Bill would focus the company and steer it to a new course of success. However, Bill had a challenge that was bigger than we realized at the time and would grow larger during the next several years.

Business decisions often seem much clearer in retrospect. As events unfolded, I occasionally lamented the mistakes we made. Today, better decisions seem obvious. However at the time, there were many distractions, and we could not fully understand the true state of our company, the market, and how both were changing. My initial inclination was to blame most of those problems on Stan Sloane, but the issue was more complex. Some of our weakness began to emerge before he arrived. He was a good man who made a few mistakes that made the situation worse.

During our IPO in 2002, and for three years afterward, I proudly proclaimed to investors that we almost never lost a competition to extend a contract when the original expired. Our customers loved our work, and we understood their problems intimately. As a result, we were usually in the best position to prepare a new proposal that did not merely extend the current job; rather, we suggested innovative ways to improve the work. Many of our traditional rivals (CACI, SAIC, ManTech) did not bid in some of our re-competes or did not put their first team on the proposal. Instead, they often tried unsuccessfully to beat us with a lower price.

Then the situation gradually changed. After years of exceptional growth, our organic growth rate began to slow beginning in 2007. This problem was reflected in our ability to win contracts. During fiscal years 2001 through 2007, we won two thirds of all contracts that we bid on. For the period 2008 through 2011, our average win rate had declined to 52 percent, and in fiscal year 2012 it was only 40 percent. As with many corporate challenges, there was no single deficiency that, if remedied, would correct the problem.

Stan's principal mistake lay in the strategic direction that he began shortly after arriving in April 2007. He began to redesign our firm as a system engineering company in the mold of large companies, like Lockheed Martin and General Dynamics. This was in anticipation of acquiring more technical work. He purchased a system engineering and product company called Era and hired people who knew less about IT and professional services work and more about the requirements that contractors must follow when building large government systems. They, in turn, began adding new infrastructure, standards, and procedures. However, Era lost substantial amounts of money, and the rest of SRA was unable to win any significant work of that type.

This was the classic mistake of placing form before substance. Money and management attention was diverted to military products and the development of engineering services to support them. These resources could have been better spent on our IT services business to build business development capabilities and to train and motivate our customer-facing teams. The Era acquisition alone cost us $150 million over five years.

Another problem was the mismatch between Stan's management style and the SRA culture. His somewhat introverted personality may have been exacerbated by his many years of experience in the disciplined hierarchy of large aerospace companies. SRA, on the other hand, was much more collegial. People were encouraged to speak out under the mantra "The best ideas win." As a result of this incompatibility, we lost key people. By the time Stan left in 2011, several senior talented executives had resigned and half of the top two hundred SRA executives had been with the company less than two years. One effect was that some people in our customer-facing units lost motivation and skills in client cultivation.

Just when business seemed to be particularly bad, the entire management team was distracted with the sale of a company. A special committee of the board engaged an investment banker to develop strategic alternatives for the company. Selling SRA moved to the top of the list, and bids were solicited. This led to a great deal of work for the senior management team—a significant distraction at the very time when we needed remedial action for our previous mistakes.

Nearly six months passed before the company negotiated a deal with Providence Equity Partners as the ultimate winner of the auction for SRA. An additional three months was required to prepare regulatory forms, conduct a shareholder vote, and complete the details for the sale. Once Providence took over, a new CEO (Bill Ballhaus) had to be hired, and he needed a few months to become familiar with the company and begin to diagnose our problems. Therefore, about a year of distraction elapsed after the special committee was formed and before remedial actions began.

By mid-2011 (about the time when Bill became CEO), the slow economic recovery from the 2008 recession had stalled and global economic news was threatening. Unemployment remained above 9 percent, and a bitter partisan debate erupted between Democrats and Republicans regarding the growing U.S. debt. The market for the type of work that SRA performs peaked in 2010 and was declining for the first time in a decade. One factor was the uncertainty associated with the federal budget deficit. Another cause was the end of the Iraq war and the gradual disengagement from Afghanistan. Companies like CACI, ManTech, and Lockheed Martin were losing work supporting military units overseas; therefore, they began to bid more IT services contracts. It gradually became clear to most people that government expenditures would continue to decrease; contracting would decline. Despite some successes, we lost, rather than gained, business. In order to address these problems, Bill and the board had to diagnose the causes and prescribe remedies, and we had to be careful not to over-react to current events. Since our decline from previous successes had begun at least five years before then, it was not logical to expect that the problems could be corrected in a few months.

SRA was similar to a once fine athletic team that gradually lost its conditioning and some of its best players. Our mental outlook suffered even more. Some people wondered whether we had grown too big and bureaucratic and might not ever recover and once again lead the pack.

As 2012 progressed, Bill returned our focus to the core information technology and professional services business where we helped government agencies solve significant problems related to their missions. He sold Era and Global Clinical Development. The former had been a terrible distraction. The later was part of another acquisition by Stan (Constella), other parts of which complemented our basic business.

Calendar year 2012 would prove to be very challenging and probably the worst in our history for re-competes. June 30 marked the end of the fiscal year; revenue had declined for the first time in our history. We reduced costs by laying off people who were not working directly for customers. We won some important re-competes such as the National

Practitioner Data Bank, but then we lost two significant contracts: one for the Military Sea Command and the other for the National Guard, but ultimately recovered both contracts after protesting. Discouraged but undaunted, we focused on a competition supporting the Federal Deposit Insurance Corporation (FDIC). We had held the job for eight years; it was one of our largest and most important contracts, and had been ably managed by Steve Tolbert for much of that time.

Shortly after arriving at SRA in July 2011, Bill detected problems with the contract and soon took steps to correct them. He replaced the SRA team leader and met regularly with the customer, who also was new to the project. Although the client was experienced, some of our people regarded him as opinionated.

It was clear that FDIC, like many of our other customers, was under pressure to achieve more with lower funding. This motivated us to find new approaches to the work. When the RFP came out, we put some of our best people on the proposal. Don Hirsch and his project team worked very hard, frequently over the weekends. With eager anticipation, we submitted the proposal. A few days later, we defended it in an oral presentation. Our answers to the customer's questions seemed to go well. Then we waited . . . and waited.

Finally, we received the call. SRA had lost! Surprisingly, we were defeated by Computer Sciences Corporation, which had experienced significant problems in recent years. While our proposal was judged acceptable, theirs was rated excellent, and their cost was slightly less.

How could this have happened? Bill had been on the job more than a year and seemed to have taken all the right steps. The executive team was strengthened; cost reductions allowed us to bid at lower rates; and new vibrancy and enthusiasm were beginning to permeate our workforce. Although we engaged in substantial introspection regarding losses on these three important re-competes, there seemed to be no simple answer.

Someone suggested that the highly competitive market at the time was stacked against incumbents when it was time for a new competition. A typical major contract runs three to five years. During that time, members of the incumbent team gain seniority. Their compensation increases and their hourly rates go up, making it difficult for the incumbent to compete from a price standpoint with other contractors who can offer new, younger teams at lower cost. Customers expected their budgets to decrease because of the large federal deficit and were strongly tempted to award the contract to the lowest bidder, who had a technically acceptable proposal. Meanwhile the competitors tried to portray the incumbent as set in its ways and lacking innovative ideas, which were needed by the federal government to do more with less. This theory seemed relevant to our FDIC competition. An added factor was the change in the FDIC people who managed the contract when there was only about a year remaining until the new competition. Our old customers loved our work; the new ones seemed to have a predilection for another firm.

Investors understood the dynamics of the declining market for government information technology services. The values for companies like SRA decreased. While our decline in value and loss of several important contracts was uncomfortable and frustrating, the board, which included Julie Richardson and Chris Ragona, remained calm and continued to ask logical, insightful questions concerning the strategy and operations of the company. I knew very well that Providence and I had substantial investments that depended on the success of SRA, but I was confident that Bill Ballhaus and his team were taking the right steps.

In September 2012, Julie Richardson announced her retirement from Providence. She had spent more than two years studying SRA and cultivating our people, and she strongly supported our values and culture. Moreover, her keen mind, excellent intuition, and pleasant personality contributed substantially to the cohesiveness of our board and its relationship to the rest of the company. Fortunately Chris Ragona, who was equally talented, but in different ways, remained on the board.

One of the assumptions in the Providence financial model was that a private company can be operated at a lower cost than a public firm, which has the burden of substantial regulatory activities. We had to decrease expenses. But the company's stagnant growth meant that even further reductions than initially anticipated would be necessary. At the same time, we needed resources to reinvigorate our growth.

The task of turning around the company was, indeed, formidable. Late in 2011, nearly 150 indirect positions had to be eliminated. Whenever possible, people were moved to direct contract work, but others were laid off. Even though the latter group represented less than 2 percent of the workforce, it was a difficult decision for a new CEO who was trying to establish a reputation for enlightened leadership and care for people. Another similar reduction was required less than a year later.

Debra Alderson joined us from SAIC and served for about eighteen months, first as executive vice president and later as chief operating officer, before departing to be CEO of a smaller company. Jeff Rydant, who was head of our growth organization, left to hike the Appalachian Trail. He was succeeded by Max Hall who left in November 2013. Jeff and Max had contributed to our company for many years.

In February 2013, Charles Gottdiener, a managing director for Providence Equity Partners, was elected to the board of directors. Prior to joining Providence, he held leadership positions in the Boston Consulting Group, CSC Index, Cap Gemini Ernst & Young, and Dun & Bradstreet.

Bill consolidated the management team and reduced costs, which was possible because while SRA's public debt is registered and we are a voluntary filer with the SEC, SRA was no longer a public company. More challenging and longer-term tasks were to restore revenue growth while assuring that all of our jobs were performed properly. We also needed to reinvigorate our culture of working together. These ambitious objectives were made much more difficult as the market continued to decline.

We protested our losses of three major re-competes. In December 2012, our FDIC award protest was sustained and a new competition would be held. In the meantime, our work on that contract was extended. This was a small amount of good news because we could try again to win the competition, although the odds seemed to be against us. Furthermore, it was clear that protesting contracts would not restore our company to its previous eminence.

March 2013 passed, the political stalemate continued, and sequester occurred; arbitrary budget reductions automatically took place in all government organizations. The Republicans presented a budget and the Democrats replied. The two seemed far apart. It appeared that political posturing might continue indefinitely. The market was declining because budgets had to be reduced, but the political uncertainty made the situation much worse.

These were difficult times and all the companies in our market were feeling the effect. Many were reducing costs incrementally to remain competitive. Bill tried a different approach. We would take the medicine all at once through more layoffs and other cost decreases and then invest some of the savings in business development. These painful measures would not only keep SRA cost competitive, but also free resources to allow the company to grow. If we were able to do this, the layoffs would end, new opportunities would open up, and everyone would benefit.

The objective was to gain an annual growth rate of 5–10 percent, despite the market. In order to do this, Bill set a goal of a threefold increase in proposals between FY 2012 and FY 2013. There were an adequate number of RFPs. Whether we would actually achieve the relatively low assumed win rate (20 percent) remained to be seen. Meanwhile our customers continued to lower their annual spending rates on many of our jobs, and SRA became smaller. The situation was not that bad, of course; but from the time that Bill arrived at the end of July 2011, through March 2013, we lost about 1,200 people and our rate of decrease approached 10 percent per year.

A particularly controversial cost reduction measure changed the system for paid time off, which had been designed many years earlier when the company was prospering. The leave policy was far more generous than market norms. A new policy reduced the accumulation of annual leave by about 20 percent and limited the amount that could be retained each year. The most controversial part of the new policy required employees to draw leave from their banks of saved time off before they could begin to accumulate additional leave. This in effect decreased compensation for some longtime staff members. Emily Crespin, who had held key roles in Touchstone and in our capabilities center, described the phases that most employees experienced in response to the austerity measures: surprise, anger, frustration, and grudging acceptance. In the vernacular of the times, they had to suck it up and do their jobs. But there was risk that we would lose more capable people.

As a result of business reviews and individual meetings, Bill concluded that while getting costs under control in a problematic market was certainly one of the first steps, an equally high priority was to return to the basic values that had helped make SRA great. Late in 2012, he launched a program called "Leading with Honesty and Service." There were many meetings. Each involved about fifty senior executives and began in the afternoon. Bill and the executive team described the declining market and our response to it and answered questions. Informal conversations occurred at a reception afterward. The following morning the attendees were divided into groups of about ten and addressed basic issues such as their feelings and how the company should respond to the challenges. This was an opportunity for people to think creatively and also speak frankly about their motivations and frustrations. Bill and his key executives listened patiently to the report of each team and then responded. Each attendee was asked to convey the message to at least five others under their supervision. The meetings ultimately reached about 1,200 people over a period of about nine months. In this way, Bill hoped to communicate more directly, through first line supervisors, with roughly six thousand employees.

Bill and the board also implemented a long-term incentive program for several hundred of the most senior executives. Cash would be awarded—and in some cases, stock—to those who remained with the company several years. Since SRA was declining, bonuses were nonexistent, but the long-term program was intended to reward hard work and loyalty.

23

Painful Decisions as the Market Declines

⋯⋗ Be prepared for market changes;
no market grows or declines indefinitely.

⋯⋗ Continuously improve company business
development, contract execution, and other
processes to respond to changing markets.

As the summer of 2013 progressed our decline continued. Fiscal year 2013 ended on June 30. Revenue had decreased 10 percent to $1.5 billion. A lot of this reduction was caused by budget cuts in existing contracts or jobs that were not renewed because our customers wanted to save money; however, re-competes continued to be a problem. They were smaller and increased competition made win rates lower. We won nearly $100 million in new business in FY 2013, but it was not enough to offset these other factors. When the board met in late August to discuss FY 2013 and upcoming FY 2014, the outlook was challenging. We had just learned that SRA lost the FDIC competition for the second time; the hill to climb would therefore be much harder.

There were, however, some successes. In the fall of 2012 we won an important health care accounting system job from the Centers for Medicare and Medicaid services as the result of the good work of a team led by Rebecca Miller. One year later we won two important IT support contracts at the National Institutes of Health (NIH), thanks to the good work of Kamal Narang and the talents of other SRA professionals.

Meanwhile our civil group had to be substantially restructured under the leadership of Paul Nedzbala, a process that would require months before the group could thrive again. We had other challenges in the defense sector where customers tended to make awards on the basis of lowest price, technically acceptable proposals. The result was frequent price shootouts in which the winner was able to best decipher the lowest cost that appeared believable to the customer. This approach was not our forte. Our strength was in delivering the best value, which is to say, the most cost-effective solution; this is the way we won NIH contracts. We believed that many of the low costs bids for Department of Defense (DoD) IT contracts would eventually get into trouble and those customers would change their policies, but for the time being, we had to endure the present procedures.

During the first quarter of FY 2014, SRA won more new business than in all of FY 2013. The company was still shrinking but if we could keep up the pace, our decline would flatten and the prospects for growth in FY 2015 would be good. Then there was another setback. On October 1, 2013, the government was partially shut down, placing SRA and other companies at substantial risk. The problem was caused by a stalemate between the Republican-led majority in the House of Representatives, and the President. The Republicans wanted concessions on the Affordable Care Act (sometimes referred to as "Obamacare") that had been passed by a Democratic majority three years before. The President said that once the new budget was passed by Congress, he would negotiate these issues, but until then, he would not be held hostage.

Most government employees were put on furlough except for those deemed essential to government operations. About 70 percent of our employees on contracts were working on essential government functions that were not impacted by the shut-down, and we told them to continue. We told the others they could use leave. They could even run a small negative balance; otherwise they were on leave without pay. We adopted a similar policy for people on indirect jobs (such as accounting and finance, human resources, and administration) because with much smaller income, the company could not afford large indirect costs.

Temporarily putting people on leave was contrary to all our policies about treating people well, but we had no choice. Furthermore, there was a much more ominous development. The government stopped paying its bills because the people that processed our invoices were required by the law to stay home.

The board met to consider alternatives one week after the shutdown began. We discussed cash flow projections and concluded that, if by October 18 the stalemate between the Congress and President was not mitigated to allow payment of the debt and end of the government shutdown, we would be forced to furlough even more people, and they would run out of leave.

We engaged the support of several professional organizations where we were a member, and we asked their senior corporate executives to make calls to express concern, particularly to the Republicans in the House and to the President. We wrote letters to local members of Congress, and I had lengthy conversations with our two Virginia senators, Mark Warner and Tim Kaine, both of whom were well respected and had served as effective governors of Virginia. Mark had helped fund and manage a successful business earlier in his career. In a speech before an important Senate committee hearing, he cited our experience and plight without mentioning the name of our company.

We frequently followed news reports, which were generally bad. On Friday, October 11, 2013, Republican House leaders made a proposal to the President. They would extend the debt ceiling for six weeks but leave the government partially shut down. This was one of the worst possible scenarios for us because the arguments would likely continue, and we would remain unpaid, except for a small trickle of funds from the DoD, which had recalled some of its employees. The two primary stockholders (Providence and I) could invest more money, but our original investment was already at risk with no end to the national problem in sight. Furthermore, under such a scenario, the stock and bond markets would be depressed and there was a limit to what I could offer. It was a major challenge, at a time when we seemed to be correcting our problems and managing the company well.

The President once again rejected the House Republican offer saying that if a faction of one party or another threatened to throw the nation into default because its demands were not approved, a dangerous precedent would be established threatening the future governance of the country. According to pundits, the small faction was about thirty so-called "Tea Party" Congressmen and a few other sympathizers who were elected in solid Republican districts, saying they would work hard to lower growing government costs while reducing entitlements and abandoning Obamacare (the Affordable Care Act). Although there appeared to be enough Democratic and moderate Republican votes in the House to raise the debt limit and reopen the government, Speaker of the House Boehner stood solid with the Tea Party activists and refused to allow the bill to be voted by the full House. At that point, the House leaders gave up and turned the problem over to the Senate.

With national default only five days away, Senators Harry Reid and Mitch McConnell began negotiations on a new bill. Progress seemed painfully slow and even if successfully negotiated, there was always the question concerning whether Boehner would allow a House vote. Meanwhile we reviewed our analysis and discussed plans in case the stalemate continued indefinitely.

Then on October 16, one day before default was due to begin, there was a breakthrough. The House and the Senate approved the bill, and the President signed it. The problem was not solved but only deferred to mid-January. We had three months to accumulate cash in case the issue began again at that time. Furthermore, we had to assess the damage that had been done to our company. Profit from the second quarter of 2014 (ending December 31, 2013) would be lower because of lost income combined with fixed costs, but other problems were harder to define. We probably lost momentum and time associated with capturing new business because customers would be preoccupied with restarting their activities.

Meanwhile, the SEPTA vs. Volgenau, et al. lawsuit concerning the sale of SRA was like a mosquito flying around our heads; we did not know where it would land and bite. We had done nothing wrong to warrant its attention, and therefore the wound would likely be benign, but there was always the very small chance that it carried West Nile virus and the threat of a severe infection. However, we were preoccupied with much more significant challenges: the market decline, increased competition, shrinkage of our company, consequent cost reductions, and retention of our best people.

The plaintiff submitted for consideration by the judge a large number of bogus, complex, and arcane allegations against the board, me, and Providence: that I manipulated the transaction to gain an advantage, that Michael Klein helped me in the process and gained advantage for himself, that the special committee was negligent in its duties, that Providence improperly participated in the process, and as a result public shareholders suffered.

The SRA board had made specific efforts to have a fair, legal transaction. The special committee formed by the board examined all potential alternatives. The committee included two experienced business attorneys on the board (Michael Klein and Miles Gilburne), and excluded me to preserve its independence and demonstrate its sole commitment to reaching the most value for SRA shareholders. Then they hired a law firm to represent the special committee and the company. On strong advice from virtually everyone, I engaged a firm to protect my interest. The board then took special measures to keep the process pristine. As a layman, I could not imagine any grounds for legal objection, and I certainly had a clear conscience.

During key parts of the transaction and at the request of bidders, two of my decisions made the transaction possible and put me at a substantial disadvantage compared to all other shareholders. The first and most substantial concession was to guarantee a large loan to Providence using some of my stock. The loan was secured by sale of SRA subsidiaries Era and Global Clinical Development. Those assets ultimately sold for less than half the value of the loan. The second concession was to roll over, that is reinvest, a substantial amount of my stock in SRA after its acquisition by the auction winner; as such I became a partner with Providence. All the other shareholders were allowed to cash out, and I had been repeatedly warned that too much of my personal portfolio was in SRA stock. The fact that the great majority of my estate was going to charity made my obligation to protect the assets all the more important.

Another allegation of the plaintiff against me was that I wanted Providence to win the bidding contest because they seemed more likely to preserve our values and culture. However, the evidence showed that the allegation was wrong. At the very early stages of the sale process, I did have concerns that certain possible buyers (in particular big companies) would homogenize SRA into their bureaucratic systems, which was not my preference. However, I subsequently learned that my fears in that regard were wrong. All of the four bid finalists, which included two big companies and two private equity firms, said that the SRA name, values, and culture had market value, and they would be foolish to eliminate them. SRA would remain as a quasi-independent entity in any sale, no matter who ultimately prevailed in the auction. I was certainly relieved by this, particularly because I did not participate in the recommendation to sell the company to any bidder, which was presented by the special committee, or in the final board vote on Providence's proposal. For the shareholder vote, I agreed that the final decision on sale of the company would be made by the majority of the minority shareholders. This vote turned out to be overwhelmingly in favor of the transaction.

Vice Chancellor Noble in the Delaware Court of Chancery saw through all of the plaintiff's unsubstantiated innuendo and rhetoric, and in a summary judgment ruling on August 5, 2013, dismissed every one of the plaintiff's allegations. In reading Judge Noble's seventy-page opinion deciding the case, I was amazed at his ability to sort through the arguments of four groups of lawyers to accurately determine the facts. It was a complex case filled with numerous allegations and each had to be evaluated. It amazes me to think that throughout the year, he must encounter a variety of other cases and that they all are likely to be far different from ours. This experience gives me a new respect for the court system in our country. The news media occasionally reports about corrupt lawyers or incompetent judges, but a small percentage of poor performers make the news, while the hardworking competent professionals do not.

I hoped that the Vice Chancellor's decision, strongly in our favor, would end this distraction, but the plaintiff appealed to the Delaware Supreme Court saying that the SRA board violated its charter and that the wrong standard of review had been applied by the lower court. On May 13, 2014, the Delaware Supreme Court ruled in our favor; and so, after three long years, the case was over.

I wonder what public good was accomplished through this case and the many others that occur each year in our country. I am proud of the way we conducted the sale of SRA. Many people (in addition to the board and its lawyers) were involved in the process and any substantive allegation by them or others would have been investigated by an independent organization. We spent a substantial amount of money, and the time of some of our most talented executives, defending ourselves against spurious claims. We spent even more time and money many months beforehand making sure that the transaction was well documented, honest, and fair to all shareholders. This case seems to be an example of why litigation reform is needed in our country.

As we entered calendar year 2014, we were disappointed to observe that, despite the budget compromise reached in the previous fall, government decision making was still quite slow. New RFPs were delayed beyond their scheduled release dates, and award decisions were similarly extended. The market had begun to decrease three years before then and all of the companies in our sector were shrinking.

In the nearly three years, Bill had done a good job revising the strategy that his predecessor had followed and reducing costs accordingly. As the market declined, he found novel ways to further reduce costs and concurrently increase the amount of money that could be devoted to bids. He reemphasized our honesty and service ethic and met regularly with a wide variety of employees. As a result, he became respected and well liked.

Faced with market declines and painful cost reductions, Bill was unable to give his full focus to improving our new business capture. The challenges in this area began to emerge about four years before Bill arrived at SRA, when our organic growth rate (revenue increases exclusive of acquisitions) began to slow. When the market began to decline in 2011, these issues became even more evident.

It seemed to me that the problem was caused by weakness across the entire company, beginning with program and project managers, extending though our business developers, business area managers, group directors, and culminating in the growth organization where most of the large bids were prepared. We still had very capable people, but many of our project and program managers, and their supervisors, were less seasoned or new to the company. They did not realize that while good work for customers is essential, it is by no means sufficient. They must constantly assess the needs of their customers and be absolutely sure that their projects are within cost and schedule, the work is outstanding, and the customers are pleased with the progress. But the SRA managers must go far beyond this. They must find new opportunities to make customers successful. This creative process often, but not always, leads to more work for SRA, but that is not the primary objective. Our program and project managers and the executives above them had to become trusted confidants whose customers know that SRA people will place the interest of the government and job above those of the company.

Some of these managers routinely practiced this ideal, but others were not sufficiently trained in this important aspect of the SRA culture. As a result of this lack of leadership, some customers, who our people thought were highly satisfied, actually had ambiguous views of our performance. Another problem was new RFPs that we did not begin to pursue until a few months prior to issuance. A new large job usually requires eighteen to twenty-four months of customer cultivation in order to be competitive. Over the years we had developed a procedure called the Step Process to ensure methodical and thorough preparation for competitions, but all of our organizations did not follow this process. As competition increased, these deficiencies became more evident.

During 2012 these deficiencies were manifested in a disagreement between Deb Alderson and Jeff Rydant. Deb believed in bidding a lot of jobs. This would lower our win rate, but the extra volume would make up for it. Jeff wanted to focus his talented team on a small number of important proposals. In retrospect, neither approach worked well, and we had to work to strike a balance between a broad bidding strategy and maintaining high win rates.

Our discussions in the board meetings were friendly rather than hostile; we were all trying to improve the company, and the issues were often nuanced rather than clear. It sometimes seemed to me that we spent too much time on quantitative issues rather than business building. The group directors did provide revenue estimates and how they hoped to achieve them and they included a pipeline of likely bids with a discussion of each large job. But these quantitative estimates were hard to verify.

The Providence Equity board members and their supporting staffs were primarily numbers people and very good at those types of calculations. After all, that is what private equity firms do. They find companies that are performing below their inherent value, replace the managers as necessary, and then verify that the company is improving while making other adjustments as necessary. They generally have little line management experience and leave that job to others.

We sometimes discussed whether Providence was trying to achieve a certain profit level because earnings before interest, taxes, depreciation, and amortization (EBITDA) is one of the best measures of a company's value. They were not. Rather, being realists, they recognized that, in a declining market, revenue was likely to decrease and a good tactic is to reduce costs faster than the overall shrinkage so that EBITDA decreases at a slower pace. It was hard to argue against this logic; however, if costs were reduced too fast, we ran the risk of losing good people who would become discouraged with decreases in pay and the loss of corporate capability.

If my assessment about the overall decline of revenue building capability was correct (that is, the entire system for capturing business was weak), then hiring or promoting a few good people into key positions would not be sufficient. Other changes involving a broader segment of the workforce would also be necessary. As time passed, competition became more intense, and Bill took further action to improve our new business capture. In November 2013 he reduced the number of operational groups from four to two and the number of business areas from fifteen to seven. These changes were driven in part by cost reductions but also improved our focus. The health and civil group was led by Paul Nedzbala and the national security group by George Batsakis. Paul Nedzbala graduated from Virginia Tech, with a BS in management science. He worked at the Washington Consulting Group, United Information Systems, and Constella, joining SRA when we acquired that company in 2007. George Batsakis graduated from Hillsdale College, became an Army infantry officer, and later worked at Electronic Data Systems, Teledyne, Northrup Grumman, and SRA in 2007.

Bill named Tom Nixon as director of our central growth organization. Tom replaced Max Hall, who had made many contributions to our company but was not well suited for a position that required a strong but collegial personality to restore discipline in our corporate business capture processes. Tom had successfully led teams at Southwestern Bell, Unisys, and other companies before joining SRA.

Bill, the group directors, and Tom selected two people to lead group business development: Doyle Choi, for national security, and Rebecca Miller, for health and civil. Doyle had a good career at Northrop Grumman and after only a few months at SRA, was highly regarded for his wisdom in business development. Rebecca had distinguished herself at SRA with several notable proposal wins. This revised team then proceeded to staff the groups with business developers, capture managers, and system architects supporting the business areas. Bill also created a cohort group of thirteen promising executives (business area managers and a few others) in order to cultivate new leaders.

The other members of Bill's team were also capable. Some were longtime employees with whom I felt a special kinship because of their contributions and loyalty over many years. I fondly recall personal vignettes for each of them.

Tim Atkin joined SRA in 1999 after twelve years in the Coast Guard, a stint with the NSC as a White House Fellow and two years as a member of the Senior Executive Service at the Department of Labor. Tim performed well in a variety of assignments. After doing double duty as chief operating officer and acting head of human resources (HR), Tim was happy to welcome John Reing, the new head of HR, who had compiled a strong record while at BAE North America.

In 1988, Rick Nadeau was a young Arthur Andersen audit partner newly assigned to our account by his boss Bob Grafton. In 2009, Rick became our chief financial officer and did a good job for many years; however, once we became private and slowed acquisitions in order to fix the organic growth problems, he missed the work of a being a public company CFO. Therefore, he left in May 2014 to become the CFO in a public company that has had a greater volume of merger and acquisition/divestiture work that he enjoys. Bill appointed a promising young executive, David Keffer, as acting CFO.

In 1990, Anne Donohue joined SRA, a graduate of the University of Michigan, working for Jerry Yates in our administrative organization. Jerry was a tough task master, but continually praised her. I encouraged Anne to pursue MBA studies, but she attended law school at night, passed two bar examinations, and became the first in-house counsel at SRA. We hired Mark Schultz, a talented Harvard Law School graduate, as general counsel in 2008. Mark, Anne, and the rest of his team did an excellent job during the sale of SRA but, when we became a private company, our legal needs changed. Mark left, and Bill Ballhaus selected Anne as general counsel. I still tease Anne about not taking my advice to study business.

Bill appointed Pat Burke as chief technology officer. Pat joined SRA in 1989 after twenty years as an Air Force pilot and a final assignment in command and control for the Joint Chiefs of Staff. He managed SRA projects successfully, including one that involved conversion of government computers for the year 2000 and a job for the U.S. Postal Service (USPS). For two consecutive years SRA was named Quality Supplier of the Year for USPS, despite competition from thousands of other firms.

Under this group of leaders emerged stalwarts, who had served our company well on many occasions, and others who arrived more recently. Many of them received SRA awards; they are listed in appendix B. I hesitate to mention any because there are so many and no clear place to stop.

This account of the SRA history ends in mid-2014, which also marks three years since Bill Ballhaus arrived. He took over a company that was ailing from problems that began to gradually become evident in 2007 and were aggravated by a market that started to decline in 2011. When a company has problems years in the making, it is not reasonable to expect that they can be corrected in a year or two. And this was the case for SRA. In FY 2012 our revenue was $1.68 billion; by FY2014, it had declined to $1.39 billion.

In my view, the principal problem afflicting SRA in recent years was our inability to bring in business, and this weakness was aggravated by occasional failures on big jobs. A firm that cannot get enough business to keep from declining, must continually reduce costs, and the struggle is enervating and distracting. On the other hand, if a company can get work from customers and perform it well, then everything else becomes much easier. The firm has less difficulty retaining capable people and can invest in initiates that make it more competitive and profitable.

As FY 2015 got underway, there was reason for cautious optimism. While the company had declined in size over the previous three years, for the first time it was bringing in more business than it was consuming. In FY 2014 we won $2 billion in business compared to $1.6 billion in FY 2013. This was despite the government shutdown late in the first half of FY 2014 and the final loss of the big FDIC job. One measure of business awards is the ratio of new business brought in, compared to old awards that are used: the so called book-to-bill ratio. In FY 2014 this ratio was 1.4 compared to ratios of .8 in FY 2012 and 1.0 for FY 2013.

Bill Ballhaus created many useful initiatives but, in my view, the most important involved improving the entire system for winning business. This initiative began shortly after he arrived in 2011 when he changed our strategy to focus on core information technology services rather than the broader system engineering and products market pursued by his predecessor. Two years later he focused even more narrowly, by reducing the number of groups from four to two and the number of business areas from fifteen to seven.

Another initiative involved cost reduction in order to make SRA more competitive and free more resources for business development. This effort began because the cost to manage a privately held company can be less than that to operate a public firm. However, the market was declining and more painful reductions were necessary, particularly in benefits and people working in the least essential indirect jobs. We used some of the savings to bid more proposals; however, our win rate declined because we had not invested enough time determining what the customers actually needed and making sure they were properly informed concerning our capabilities. This led to an effort to hire business developers, capture managers, and system architects; and to improve our capability to cultivate prospects long before they became formal requests for proposal and all the way through the preparation and submission of proposals.

Cost reductions continued, and one of the most innovative was examination of our most important jobs to make sure all of the costs were essential and the right people were on each task. This increased profit but also worked to the advantage of our customers. The effort provided the opportunity to meet directly with most of our program and project managers and explain what was expected of them. As Kevin Wardlow (our head of job quality) said, "We should have been doing this all along." The initiative reminded me of the early years of SRA when upper level managers had close relationships with our customer-facing leaders and everyone knew what to do. Evidently we had lost some of this capability in the previous seven years because of many distractions.

Another positive sign was our profitability. As previously mentioned, a common measure is earnings before interest, taxes, depreciation, and amortization. EBITDA is one of the most important measures of a company's value. Despite the decline in revenue it remained at about 12 percent, which was one of the highest in our industry.

Bill instituted many other constructive changes: for example, he worked to nurture a culture of ethical leadership and the concept of Best Teams. At times I wondered if we were trying to do too much, but the initiatives were all useful.

As 2014 progressed, it was too early to declare victory. We had learned that the path to success is frequently bumpy. Nevertheless, there were enough positive signs to be encouraged. A new vibrancy seemed to be taking hold in SRA International.

24

Epilogue

look forward with hope to the future, while reflecting on the past thirty-six years. We can not return to the SRA of old, but we can restore its values and create a culture that is based on the best of the past and yet is suitable for a much larger company. In the early years, our success was driven by a small group of leaders. The alchemy of our teams—an inexplicable ingredient—was always at the root of our achievements. SRA was never perfect. We often struggled with issues of growth and change, but we persevered because our key executives were talented and devoted to the company and relished the privilege of contributing in many ways to the nationally important missions of our government clients. Most were hard workers, but some were completely over the top, far exceeding the standards that any employer could expect. I have often wondered why they did it.

Why did Jeffrey Westerhoff drive an hour to work, arriving at 4 or 5 a.m., and spend twelve to fourteen hours deeply absorbed in his tasks before heading home? Why did he continue this regimen, even after having been diagnosed with terminal cancer, until a week or two before his death? Why did Dick Hunter spend nights and weekends on proposals and jobs? Why did he continue, while confined to a wheelchair, after being injured in an automobile accident because of overwork and too little sleep? Why did Bob Day, who at age eighty could have been comfortably retired, continue to work a few days a week and whose devotion was such that he would be buried in Arlington National Cemetery wearing a shirt with the SRA logo? He was the SRA Everyman, representing the best of our middle managers.

Those people were inspired by the leadership of a more senior group: Ted Legasey, Bill Brehm, Renny DiPentima, Jeffrey Rydant, Barry Landew, Gary Nelson, Stuart Rubens, Sherman Greenstein, Ed Mc-Gushin, Steve Hughes, on and on. And now there is a new generation of leaders (personified by Bill Ballhaus) who are picking up the baton in the race to greatness.

The answer to the question of their dedication lies in the values of our company. History is filled with stories of groups of people who sacrificed and achieved a great deal because they had a higher calling. Today they are evident in our elite military forces: Navy Seals, Marines, and Green Berets. Capable people want to be part of something special. In business and in life, values inspire us. The best leaders in government, military, and business understand that and create a suitable vision, and they choose people who share their values and vision and work together to reach their goals.

In our first decade, when the word began to get out about SRA ethical standards and business success, an increasing number of talented people wanted to be part of it. This momentum carried our firm to even greater accomplishments. We made mistakes and sometimes became quite discouraged, but the sacrifices of our heroes and the positive change we strove for in our government work inspired us and provided resiliency.

I sometimes talk to old-timers from SRA, and I see Ted Legasey two or three times a year. He still consults for us, and I wish we used him more often. During the first twenty-five years, Ted more than anyone else helped me build a company that was universally admired for its ethics and business success. We have often discussed ways to restore and preserve the SRA business model. About two years after Barry Landew left the company he said, "You know, we built a special company—a business success that stood for something."

"You and a few others were a big part of it," I replied.

Then he said, "You can never restore the SRA of old. Almost all of the original superstars are either dead, retired, or have left for other work; and over the last five or six years the company has slipped from its former status." He paused, and I knew his next remark would be important but enveloped in irony and wit, "Do you still believe in the perfectibility of humankind?"

I smiled and replied, "No. But we can strive for perfection and be fulfilled in the journey."

Although he did not know it, Barry's remark had particular relevance to me. While at the Naval Academy, I was selected to participate in a two-semester course of great books. It was a welcome respite from the challenging regimen of engineering, physical conditioning, and military discipline. One of the books we discussed was *Candide* by Voltaire. Published in 1759, the satire centered around two young lovers (Candide and Cunegonde) and their professor (Dr. Pangloss), who traveled to many countries and experienced some of the worst depravity of humankind. Dr. Pangloss had a frequent refrain, "All is for the best in this best of all possible worlds." And he had an absurd explanation for the bad things that happened to them.

In the 1960s, Leonard Bernstein composed a clever musical that used some of Voltaire's settings. When the show opened on Broadway, Sara and I had two friends (Victoria and Tom Pyle) with principal roles. In the final scene, the two young lovers, Candide and Cunegonde, return to their home, apparently unfazed after suffering indignities that would have put most people in a mental institution. They now recognized that the world is far from perfect and conclude, in a final duet, that they will settle on a small farm, have children, and "make our garden grow."

My life has always been characterized by idealism, and I have suffered many setbacks in an imperfect world. SRA International, Inc., is admittedly an idealistic initiative. It suffered failures and will never reach perfection, but the fulfillment of its voyage is well worth the effort. Each year after giving up the CEO officer role in 2005, I have become less relevant to the future of the company, but the ideals that SRA stands for are a garden that needs to grow. Perhaps one day our company will serve as a model for corporate America and other countries where free enterprise is practiced—a successful business that embodies high ethical standards, genuine care for its customers and employees, and service to society.

BUSINESS LESSONS LEARNED
IN MORE THAN FIFTY YEARS
OF LEADERSHIP

A. PEOPLE, VALUES, AND CULTURE

1. People

Business success is all about people. As an old military expression goes, "Care for your people, and they will care for you." And business success also depends on how you treat customers, business partners, and the general public. Hiring and motivating capable professionals is absolutely essential. Relationships are vital within the company and in dealing with customers, suppliers, and even competitors. Do not tolerate organizational or personal conflicts. Develop a sense of comradeship and company unity. If you or your team criticizes others, eventually some of them will seek revenge. If, on the other hand, you treat everyone with dignity and respect (even those whose personalities or actions offend you), then you will be much more likely to achieve your goals.

2. Values and Culture

Values are vital; capable people want to be part of something great. Focus on a clear set of values and a culture that supports them. Articulate these values and culture in a way that is inspirational. "Honesty and Service" remain the values of SRA today; the corporate culture evolved from that theme. Honesty implies highly ethical performance. Service has three components: doing high quality, useful work and ensuring customer satisfaction; taking care of employees; and serving society in other ways. Having clear statements of corporate values and culture is just the beginning. Actually achieving these ideals requires continuous management emphasis. Train employees in ethical behavior, other values, and the company culture. The board, CEO, management team, and line managers must walk the talk; their behavior must reflect company values.

3. Leadership

Noblesse oblige implies leadership for the good of society. Never miss an opportunity to show that you care about people. It is essential to the success of an enterprise and requires continuous attention. Mechanistic and bureaucratic procedures cannot replace leadership. Noblesse oblige is a good concept to help inspire leadership everywhere. Humility is a vital ingredient.

4. Selecting People

Hire bright, energetic people, who will bring long-term value to your organization. While the people you employ should usually have capabilities in the market that you serve, resist the temptation solely to fill positions on current jobs. All should share your idealism. Do not give preference to your relatives and friends. Capitalize on the power of diversity; never underestimate the potential of women, minorities, and new young employees.

5. Cultural Incompatibility

Cultural incompatibility can cause businesses to suffer. When hiring anyone for a company (director, executive, lower-level employee), be sure to consider cultural compatibility. Many young people are inspired by lofty values and a distinct culture; but some people, who have worked in other organizations, are products of their environments, and it is difficult for them to adapt to a new culture. This happened to us on many occasions, not because SRA was right and the experienced employees wrong; rather, the two were fundamentally different and, therefore, incompatible. A talented senior candidate may be worth this risk, but it is important to assess the degree of potential incompatibility.

6. Incentive System

Make rewards proportional to output, not input or seniority. Be aspirational in your goals; stretch the executives and the organization. The incentive system should be heavily oriented toward results; simply working long hours is not enough. Create an executive system that reinforces the business vision, values, and culture. Do not pit executives against one another. Sometimes people must sacrifice a personal or organizational objective for the greater good. Make the incentive system as transparent as possible so that all employees have the opportunity to clearly understand how incentives are earned.

7. Quality Work and Customer Satisfaction

Quality work and customer satisfaction are essential. Encourage employees to exceed customer expectations, create value for customers, and not simply satisfy the terms of a contract. Strive to do more important work. To empower employees in this way requires careful selection, extensive training, and job progression so that promising professionals can stretch in their personal development but not be assigned to jobs beyond their capabilities. Even when work goes well, continuous communication with the client is essential to avoid misunderstanding because sometimes customers have unrealistic expectations.

8. The Best Ideas

In an entrepreneurial company, the best ideas win. Continuous dialogue is necessary to find the best solutions to problems, and this inevitably leads to disagreement. Instill in your organization the habit of listening to everyone's idea regardless of his or her position. When you disagree, do it with dignity and respect, and do not be paralyzed by indecision. Committees do not manage successful companies.

9. Succession

When the founders retire, watch out for problems. Plan for succession (the loss of key executives). The more successful a company, the more important it is to develop leaders for the future management team. Successful firms tend to be dominated by the CEO and other senior leaders. When they retire or are recruited to other companies, there is often a power vacuum. Recruiting a new CEO from outside the firm is always risky. He or she will require time to learn about the company and its markets and will ultimately demand the right to select the management team. During this process, key people will leave, and the firm may falter. It is far better to plan for succession of the entire team (not just the CEO) than to deal with such problems spontaneously.

10. The Board

Hire a capable board that provides more than fiduciary oversight. The board should demand that good systems for performing corporate functions exist and are followed. Accounting and finance are particularly important, but other processes also deserve attention: job execution, human resources (particularly compensation), protection of corporate information, and overall governance. The management team may conscientiously follow good processes, yet the company can be headed for trouble. For this reason, the board must also insist on a good strategic plan and a table of key performance measures. Hire board members who have had first line management experience, who understand your business, and who operate effectively as a committee. Planning for succession is particularly important. Start with an advisory committee so you can find out who is really effective.

11. Criminals in the Company

Be vigilant because, sooner or later, a crook will join your team. Idealism may blind you to criminals in your company. Others may not share it. Trust but verify; ensure appropriate business controls are in place, and expect someone to commit larceny. Practice healthy skepticism.

12. Hard Work and Perseverance

If you want to be successful, expect long hours of very hard work. If you are not willing to contribute a lot of time, sometimes at the expense of your family or social life, then being an entrepreneur is probably not for you. Despite your best efforts, there will be times when everything goes wrong, and you just want to give up. You can quit your job or sell the company, and life won't be too bad. However, if you really crave the satisfaction of success, then you will continue when most rational people would not. If you can persevere while working hard under duress and still maintain a positive attitude, then you are truly unique.

13. Other Personal Virtues

Cultivate your personal virtues, including self-discipline; without it, you will court professional disaster. Be organized; you can save a lot of time and money. Write and speak simply and directly. Demonstrate humility. Continue your education; it is vital to success and the process never ends.

B. BUSINESS

14. Business Vision

Your business vision must fulfill a definite market need. The SRA vision was to create value for customers by providing professional services in computing and communications at a time when those technologies were expanding substantially. Our differentiating focus was to fuse knowledge of the customer's business with expertise in information technology.

15. Planning

Plan ahead, influence destiny. Do not embark on an endeavor without careful preparation, or you may become a victim of chance. Stick to a successful strategy. Do not be distracted by interesting opportunities that occasionally emerge but are not consistent with the strategy. On the other hand, the plan is a guide, not a controlling device. There may be occasions when you must adapt to unforeseen dangers or opportunities. Planning extends to daily activities. Before an important meeting, visualize potential scenarios. Estimate the objectives of the other party and what they will say. Plan your response.

16. Serendipity

Chance favors the prepared mind. Some people regard success as a matter of luck. Chance does influence destiny, but an organization that is prepared and motivated is much more likely to recognize and exploit an opportunity than one that is not. Planning is part of this process, but serendipity comes to those who are constantly alert for it.

17. **Business Growth and Profitability**

Idealism is academic if you neglect the bottom line. Public and private markets value a company based on its likelihood to produce consistent future profit growth. While having high corporate ethics is essential, this idealism will not matter if the company is not a business success.

18. **Marketing and Sales**

Good business development is essential to the culture of a successful company. For many years, we said that everyone in SRA was a marketer for the company, and this precept was one of the most important factors in our success. Many companies have a marketing and sales organization that tracks the emergence of large bid opportunities and coordinates the preparation of proposals. The viability of such a group is essential to success, but the most important type of business development occurs where the work is performed, on individual contracts. If the company delivers value to clients on each project, then customers will often be receptive to constructive expansion of the work, and they will provide good references to potential new clients. Therefore, project managers and team members must be motivated and trained to develop additional, useful work. Business development is the responsibility of everyone.

19. **Focus and Distraction**

A management team without focus invites chaos. We were at our best when we concentrated on four things: ethics and culture, growth and profitability, quality work and customer satisfaction, and taking care of our people. When we faltered, it was because we took our eyes off those four precepts. There are many ways that a management team can become distracted and lose focus. Acquisitions are a prime example.

20. **Acquisitions**

Acquisitions are a double-edged sword; they can lead to new opportunities, but most do not live up to expectations. A company often acquires another firm in order to grow into a new market or gain an additional technical capability. But acquisitions are difficult. Firms are often put on the market because of some shortcoming; the stated reason for listing a company is often different from the actual latent deficiencies. The listing statement is phrased to attract buyers; for example, "We want to be acquired by a larger firm in order to grow more rapidly." When acquiring a company, insist on thorough due diligence aimed at disclosing deficiencies and a tight purchase contract with an escrow fund in case deficiencies become evident in the first year or two. Good integration of the acquired firm and employment conditions (particularly compensation) are also important because key executives tend to leave firms that have been acquired. Motivate them to remain and help make the combined company a success.

21. Diversifying

Moving to a new market or offering can be risky. Staying power is required to successfully diversify, but recognizing when to persevere and when not to is a challenge. Many initiatives will fail; cutting losses is often the best policy.

22. Products

If you provide services, forget products. Evolving real products from a services business is much harder than it would logically seem to be. Creating a successful product is far more than having a good idea or producing a prototype. Bringing a product to market requires substantial business knowledge and capital. Successful products are beyond the capabilities of most services firms. The lightbulb, telephone, television, and digital computer required business knowledge and years to develop as successful businesses.

23. Government and Commercial Work

If you are a government contractor, forget commercial work. The reverse of this is true as well. The two markets are substantially different, and expertise in one does not translate to the other.

24. Information Technology

Information technology will always be a growing endeavor. Humans have survived as a species because they steadily improved their ability to communicate and cooperate. Information technology fifty thousand years ago was symbols sketched in dirt; today it is enabled by computer and communications technology, but the idea is the same. IT fosters advancement and, therefore, will always be important.

25. Market Variables

Be prepared for market changes; no market grows or declines indefinitely. While the information technology industry has experienced phenomenal growth over the past sixty years, there have been periods of decline and displacement that have put many companies out of business. Early examples were the decrease in the mainframe market caused by mini-computers and their replacement a few years later with personal computers and servers. Then there was the mass extinction of dot-com companies around the year 2000 and, ten years later, the decline of personal computers caused by applications on cell phones and cloud computing. These same factors influenced the government sector, but included the added complexity of budgetary problems, a political stalemate, and decreases in defense spending between 2010 and 2014.

26. Technological Euphoria

Technological euphoria can be expensive. People often overestimate the potential impact of new technology on society. However, social processes usually change slowly. The result is sometimes great disappointment and wasted time and money.

27. Raising Money

Get money when it is available; it may not be there when you really need it. As the old saying goes, bankers do not want to lend money to people who really need it. They are happy to provide money to prosperous organizations that are not likely to forfeit their loans, but are suspicious of those who desperately need money.

28. Financial Leveraging

Occasionally a company may pass through periods in which its assets can be harvested to produce value for shareholders. Financial leveraging is closely related to arbitrage, which is a condition that occurs when an asset does not trade for the same price in several markets. SRA experienced arbitrage twice. In the first instance, the company was privately held in 2002; listing it on a public exchange raised the price substantially. The second case occurred in 2011. SRA had been publicly listed for nine years but was trading at a low price due to leadership mistakes. A private equity firm recognized this and leveraged a purchase of the company through loans. The purchase price was substantially higher than the public listing, but the investors hoped to complete arbitrage by fixing the company and selling it later for a much higher price.

29. Infrastructure

Continuously improve company business development, contract execution, and other processes to support a changing organization. While winning contracts and performing them well are vital, the entire organization should be viewed as a whole so that one part of it does not inhibit the rest. Accounting and finance, human resources, and IT infrastructure are examples of segments that could limit corporate growth, particularly if they become focused on the goals of their individual organizations, as opposed to their mission, which is to support the entire company.

30. Conserving Resources

Frugality is more than a virtue. Conserving resources begins on contracts, where customers appreciate products delivered on time and within cost. They also respect a contractor that does not suggest marginally effective work or products. The most expensive resource is time; therefore, limiting time spent on indirect projects is a high priority. Instilling a sense of frugality in all company activities is just as important: consumption of supplies, use of office space, cost effectiveness of subcontractors, and virtually every aspect of office life.

SRA AWARDS RECIPIENTS

President's Award

1997 Jeffrey Westerhoff—
*All Time Business
Development Award*
Jerry Yates—*Perseverance
Despite Adversity*

Leadership

1992 Chuck Perry
1993 Ray Leahey
1994 Joan Osborne
1995 John Hillen
Ellen Moyer
1996 Jim Jones
1997 Jim Badger
Raelene Wagoner
1998 John Quinlan
Linda Skelton
1999 Andy Cohen
2000 James McCollough
2001 Kevin Fagan
Bruce Gilbert
2002 Bob Evarts
2003 Steve Roerig

2004 Bob Day
Mitch Miller
2005 Jennifer Buchanan
Dave Wallen
2006 Brian Michl
2007 Carla Saia
2008 Ian Fetterman
2009 Bryan Polk
Courtney Rodi
2010 John Cordone
2011 Ben Badami
Tom Oliver
2012 Scott Barnhart
2013 Mike Curry

Honesty and Service

2008 Diane Pulliam
2009 Karen Amato
2010 Al Bornmann
2011 Steve Wiley
2012 Lester Sauble
2013 Kevin Brunner
Rebecca McHale

New Business Development

1992 Howard Mosley
      Jeffrey Westerhoff
1993 Rob Smith
      Joe Hsu
1994 Kevin O'Connor
      Jeffrey Westerhoff
1995 Richard Berger
      Charles Groover
1996 Anirudh Kulkarni
1997 Larry Martin
      Jeffrey Westerhoff
1998 Pat Burke
      Lisa Rau
      Michael Reingruber
1999 Denise Lee
      Jim McCoy
      Year 2000 Services
2000 Eileen Clark
      Mike Yocom
2001 Mary Ellen Condon
2002 Pricing Team
      David Wallis—*Pricing Manager*
2003 Steve Erlich
      Dan Newton
2004 Bill Carden
      Steve Lindblom
      Karen Holloway
      John Ludecke
2005 Brian Collins
2006 Jim McClean

Quality Assurance

1992 Howard Moody
1993 Sue Jones
1994 Sharon Bowen
1995 Michael Sydla
1996 Documentation & Curriculum Maintenance Team
1997 Mij Strange
      St. Clair Wyre
1998 Nick Caramanica
1999 Helen Horner
      Doug Million
      Phil Pau
2000 Sandra Nickerson
      Leslie Bainbridge
2001 Joe Collins
2002 Lee Defibaugh
2003 Paul Hansen
2004 Nancy Van Balen
2005 John Blair
2006 Chris Longe

Technical Excellence

1996 Chinastu Aone
      Kevin Hausman
      George Krupka
      Jim Scharen–Guivel
1997 Larry Fobian
      Brian Fogg
      Gena Threatt
1998 Raymond Good
      John Young
1999 MUC Team
2000 Andy Cornell
      Peter Halverson

2001 David Garfield

2002 Allen Deitz

Technical Achievement

2007 David Dikel
     Stanislav Stoliarov

2008 Dan Gross

2009 Adam Meyers
     Dan Kimball

2010 John Corbin

2012 Emerson Brooks
     Jon Cummings
     John Ferguson
     Brian Ore

2013 Dan Kimball

Company Improvement

1996 Knowledge Center Team

1997 Chris Zegal

1998 Laura Luke

1999 Susan Infeld
     Lisa Provance

2000 Officers of the
     Toastmasters

2001 David Kane

2002 Online Open Enrollment
     Team
     Mahesh Kaka—*Project
     Manager*

2004 Kourtney Walker

2005 Get F.I.T. Team
     Kay Curling—*Program
     Director*

2006 Deltek Implementation
     Team

Excellence

2003 Brian Cross
     Janet Norris
     Bill Scherer, Jr.

2004 James Christopher
     David Kane
     John Luongo
     Brian Michl
     Cindy Wilson

2005 Cathleen Myers

2006 Ryan Schaeffer
     Len Discenza

Staff Achievement

1992 Alfreda Clark
     Stuart Davis
     Khanh Vu

1993 Mary Lou Palmer
     Seth Salmon
     Mary Beth Terry

1994 Brian Cross
     Brian Fogg
     Les Lynnes
     Sue Morgan
     Jennifer Mullin
     Susie Regnier

1995 Albert Brooks
     Jeff Cobb
     Shirl Mack

1996 Janice Hall
     Brenda Howell
     Kip Hyde
     Siew Ng
     Alvin Queen

1997 Samantha Armstrong
     Beryl Castello
     Tim Kroll

Jenny Menna
Cylina Pulliam
Steve Rathert
David Tatum
Belinda Vines
1998 Connie Birkland
Mike Martin
Tammy Smith
Cleopatra Von Ludwig
1999 Yovanda Alexander
Robert Boucher
Jill Caballero
Danielle Kobasa
Jennifer Kurzhals
Sarah Martin
Brian Michl
Sue Morgan
Eleni Pecjak
Daniel Sheehan
2000 Elizabeth Case
Jeaneen Chaffin
Frank Durso
Dan Fleck
Lorie Shaull
2001 Jeff Bielot
Tammie Bowen
Tao Tran
Gary Watts
2002 Debbie Cioletti
Tonya Cox
Dana Pittman
Paul Reeder
2003 Scott Buffardi
Lucia Caron
Angela Davis
Jennifer Russ
Courtney Salthouse
Susan Schneider
Rhoda Williams

2004 Rebecca Hamil
Deborah Kalmer
David Keffer
Dave Kelley
Rhonda Pekelo
Tony Woods
2005 Jason Adolf
Tracey Culbertson
Cale Dunn
David Grant
Travis Janson
Pedro Ramirez
2006 Gina Thansom
Jodi Wharff
Nyree Waters

Individual Excellence

2007 Lance Jones
2008 Rebecca McHale
2009 Joann Heck
2010 Marc Melkonian
Kim Doner
2011 Cathy Beykzadeh
Fawzi Al Nassir
2012 Ray Baskerville
Marcy Jacobs
Will Watts
2013 Robert Andres
Paula Harper
Marci Newsome
Kate Welch
Carl Willis-Ford

Integrator Mindset

2013 Marcy Jacobs

Vision

1992 Sherman Greenstein
1993 Karl Wilhelm
1997 Scott Bennett
2000 Susan Lilly
2001 Kathleen McCormick
2003 Laurence Newcome
2006 Steve Newburg–Rinn

Entrepreneurship

2007 Susan Castillo
2008 Gary Celli
2009 Vladimir Knezevic
2010 Susan Pearson
2011 John Levy
      Kamal Narang
2012 Michael Calvert
      John Patrick
2013 Damon Bramble

Community Service

1992 Joyce Reeves
1993 Marge Hodgen
1994 Brenda Howell
      Wendy Huber
      Mary Lambert
      Chris Zegal
      Chris Paulen
1995 Chris Zegal
1997 Stephanie Glasser
1998 Jennifer Greene
2000 Arlene Gatchalian
2001 Jim Huang
      Bill May
2002 Alan Shultz
2003 Silent Auction Team

2004 TSD Community Action
         Group
2005 Andrea Pacley
2006 Frank Durso
2007 Mary Keeser
2008 Sean Connelly
2009 New Directions Alternative
         Program
2010 Kevin Brunner
      Kathy Fruge
2011 A.J. Jablonsky
      SRA O'Fallon Cares
         Committee
2012 Johanna Culbertson
2013 Matt Raymond
      Natalie Worrell

Rookie of the Year

1999 Jean-Paul Boucher
      Michael Gross
2000 David Ahern
      Matt Hodge
      Vivian Lin
2001 Erin Duffy
      Andrew Graham
      Peter Hewitt
2002 Scott Kidder
2003 Matt Gann
      Adam Meyers
2004 Pat Bohan
      Eliot Harris
      Stephen Mathieu
2005 Pouya Eftekhari
2006 Erin Speck
      John Dewar
2007 Rachel Bowman
2008 Amanda Post
2009 John Collier

2009 Condylia Heliotis
2010 Jason Williams
2011 Patrick Boebinger
      Alan Jackoway
      John Miller
      Kathleen O'Malley
2012 Matt Radolec
2013 Jenny Madorsky

Special Recognition

2011 Charles Dye

Operational Excellence

2010

Talent Solutions Group
Dana Pittman, *Director*

2011

- **SRA Procurement Team**
  Courtney Pugh, *Chief Procurement Officer*
- **FDIC ISC Client Services Team**
  Bryan Polk, *Project Manager*

2012

- **Air Force Distributed Common Ground System Team**
  Troy Hithe, *Project Manager*
- **ITS Information Security Compliance Team**
  Jeanne Alley, *Project Manager*

2013

- **Workday Team**
  Bryan Polk, *Project Manager*

Project Team Excellence

1992

DPLDC Information System
Scott Little, *Leader FEMA Logistics*
Chuck Perry, *Leader*

1993

- **OPES D&I Operations Division**
  Jeff Rydant, *Team Leader*
- **Joint Computer–Aided Acquisition and Logistics Support (JCALS)**
  Paul Cynewski, *Team Leader*
- **Technology Insertion Project (TIP)**
  Gene Frank, *Team Leader*

1994

- **Medical Planning and Execution System (MEPES)**
  Ron Beatson, *Team Leader*

1995

- **Scheduling and Movement Team**
  Terri Sipantzi, *Leader*

1996

- **Pentagon Renovation Team**
  Jim Badger and Charles Payne, *Leaders*

1997

- **FDA Smart**
  Joan Osborne, *Program Manager*

- **GCCS Data Base Team**
  Erik Kurzhals, *Leader*
- **Troutman Sanders Team**
  David Brown, *Program Manager*
  Dan DePuy, *Project Manager*

- **Federal Parent Locator Service (FPLS)**
  Larry Wilson, *Project Manager*
- **HCFA Minimum Data Set (HCFA MDS)**
  Gary Newell, *Project Manager*
- **NASD Advanced Detection System(NASD ADS)**
  Jim Hayden, *Project Manager*

- **National Practitioner Data Bank/Healthcare Integrity and Protection Data Bank (NPDB/HIPDB)**
  Kevin Fagan, *Project Manager*
- **National Association of Securities Dealers Order Audit Trail System(OATS)**
  Chuck Rounds, *Project Manager*

- **Housing Operations Management System (HOMES)**
  Eric Kurzhals, *Project Manager*
- **Personal Information Carrier Integration Management Support (PIMS)**
  Ray Leahey, *Program Manager*
  Raymond Good, *Project Manager*

- **Pilot Transportation Operational Personal Standard System (PTOPS)**
  Jim Hopson, *Project Manager*

- **Best Execution Analysis and Monitoring System**
  Bill Brooks and Sue Jones, *Project Managers*
- **Presidential Intelligence Dissemination System**
  Lauren Halverson, *Project Manager*
- **White House Tape Restoration Project**
  Zorana Ilic and Joseph Miller, *Project Managers*

- **Brownfields Analytical & Technical Support (BATS and COMMITS)**
  Colleen Morgan, *Project Manger*
- **DISA Medium Grade Services (MGS) Public Key Enablement (PKE)**
  Ed Bouton, *Project Manager*
  Steven Kerr, *Technical Lead*

- **HHS Portal**
  John Keller, *Project Manager*
- **GAO ISTS**
  David Brown, *Project Manager*

- **Laboratory of Molecular Pharmacology**
  Susan Castillo, *Project Manager*
- **GuardNet XXI**
  Robert Gentili, *Project Manager*

2004

- **ENERGY STAR**
  Sheri Neeley, *Project Manager*
- **mAdb**
  Susan Castillo, *Project Manager*
- **Installation Support Modules (ISM)**
  Linda Burak Chappell, *Project Manager*
- **USXPORTS Phase 3**
  PJ Kirkegaard, *Project Manager*

2005

- **Army National Guard Active Directory Project**
  Ed Bouton and Maurice Mathews, *Project Managers*
- **Air Mobility Command A38 Web and Portal Support Team**
  Jim Curtis, *Program Manager*
  Doug Hurd, *Project Manager*
- **U.S. Agency for International Development**
  Kenneth Rohrer, *Project Manager*

2006

- **Advanced Information Technology Services Program/Army National Guard Exchange 2003 Team**
  Don Edwards, *Project Manager*

- **FEMA Individual Assistance/ Public Assistance Hurricane Response and Recovery Team**
  Ron Davison, *Project Manager*
- **Disaster Credit Management System Team**
  John Keller, *Project Manager*

2007

- **Defense Advanced Research Projects Agency, Tactical Ground Reporting Network (TIGRNET)**
  John Perry, *Project Manager*
- **National Institutes of Health, Enteropathogen Resource Integration Center (ERIC)**
  John Green and Matt Shaker, *Project Managers*
- **U.S. Agency for International Development, Health Policy Initiative (HPI)**
  Sarah Clark and Nancy McGirr, *Project Managers*

2008

- **Defense Personal Property System**
  Don Tindall, *Project Manager*
- **Federal Deposit Insurance Corporation**
  Steve Tolbert, *Program Manager*

2009

- **Enterprise Support Services National Security**
  Jim Curtis, *Business Program Manager*
  Scott Ready, *Program Manager*
  Deb Hagstrom, *Account Manager*

2010

- **Enterprise Operations & Security Services**
  Mark Barnette, *Program Manager*

2011

- **Extended Tether Program**
  Troy Hithe, *Project Manager*
- **Gulf Study Team**
  Matt Curry, *Project Manager*
- **New Campus East Deployment Planning & Execution**
  Ben Badami, *Project Manager*

2012

- **The Cancer Genome Atlas Data Coordinating Center Team**
  David Pot, *PhD Project Manager*
- **NIH Center for Information Technology Customer Service Portfolio Team**
  Neal Moskowitz, *Project Manager*

2013

- **COIC IWAS**
  Doug Days, *Project Manager*
- **HIGLAS**
  Tom Park, *Project Manager*
- **MSC Afloat**
  Ben Badami, *Project Manager*

SRA MILESTONES

1978–1980

- Ernst establishes SRA headquarters in the basement of his home; he organizes the company and searches for contracts and employees; wife (Sara) keeps the books and serves on the Board.
- American Management Systems (AMS) awards SRA a small contract to study maintenance management using computers on U.S. Navy ships.
- Ted Legasey joins the firm; wife (Tricia) does the typing.
- Company leases an office at 2425 Wilson Blvd., Arlington, VA, from Association of the U.S. Army.
- SRA is awarded a contract to help design and evaluate the largest military mobilization and deployment exercise since World War II (Nifty Nugget).
- SRA adopts "Honesty and Service" as the basis for its values and culture.
- Company implements a college recruiting program.
- Staff expands to twenty-five employees and revenue approaches $1 million.

1981–1985

- SRA has many small jobs but wins its first large prime contract (U.S. Army exercise support) in 1981.
- Company begins to move from consulting to systems development by supporting a large Army command and control system called AWIS.
- Based on recommendations of a senior panel formed by SRA, the Federal Emergency Management Agency (FEMA) is formed; SRA is

awarded a contract to help implement the new agency and eventually becomes a leader in emergency management.

- Penguin becomes the SRA mascot in 1982.
- SRA originates the concept of a Joint Operation Planning and Execution System (JOPES) and receives a contract to design it from the Office of the Secretary of Defense in 1983.
- Partnering with American Management System in Westboro, MA, and San Bernardino, CA, SRA opens first field offices.
- SRA launches a telecommunications network design practice—its first engineering specialty.
- Company forms a strong corporate development group to prepare proposals.
- SRA is named to the "Inc. 500" list of fastest growing, privately held companies in the United States and remains on the list for four consecutive years (1984–1987).
- SRA headquarters moves to a beautiful new building called Arlington Plaza. Company also opens an office in Heidelberg, Germany.
- Company publishes first annual report in 1985. Revenue is nearly $15 million; 182 employees.

1986–1990

- Company governance is changed; SRA International is created and Systems Research and Applications Corporation is its primary operating unit. Performance-oriented stock options are granted to key employees.
- SRA develops Natural Language Processing (NLP), software that can read, summarize, and index text in a variety of languages—another engineering specialty that helps differentiate the company.
- Company combines NLP and expert systems in an artificial intelligence initiative.
- In a planning offsite, executives decide to transform SRA into a systems integration company.
- SRA wins a multimillion-dollar contract in 1989 to provide systems integration, design, development, operations and maintenance support (SIDDOMS) to the DoD Health community.
- Employees create the community assistance program.
- Revenue triples in this period to $47 million and over 500 employees.

- Company opens new office in Fairfax, VA (Fair Lakes); headquarters remains in Arlington.
- SRA receives two of its largest contracts in the same week: JOPES Design & Implementation and CIM.
- Commercial business continues to grow including law office automation and technical support to BellSouth.
- Well ahead of most competitors, company prepares for a dramatic shift in how IT services are procured: Government Wide Acquisition Contracts (GWACs) and (GWACs).
- SRA wins coveted prime contracts, FEDSIM 9600 and NIH CIOSP—two of the first GWACs. Company ultimately books more than $1 billion of work under each of these contracts and their successors.
- DoD requests a tenfold increase in the CIM/Business Process Reengineering contract, making SRA the biggest business process reengineering contractor for the federal government.
- SRA embarks on an open office design experiment at Fair Lakes; two years later, the cube farms are removed and private offices are rebuilt.
- First annual Awards Banquet is held.
- A new full-time proposal facility (PF2000) opens to increase productivity and efficiency.
- SRA receives an award from Government Computer News as one of the top federal government system integrators.
- Company starts Navisoft for online publishing with David Cole and Miles Gilburne. It is later sold to America Online and is cited as a milestone in the development of the World Wide Web.
- SRA establishes a board of advisors.
- Revenue nearly triples again to over $134 million and nearly 1,000 employees.

1996–2000

- Work begins on the Treasury Information Processing Support Services (TIPSS) contract for the U.S. Treasury and IRS.
- By 1996 company employees more than 1,000 people.
- Services and Solutions take on an Internet, intranet, and e-business focus.

- Company introduces a new corporate logo, the letters SRA surrounded by an elliptical swoosh.
- U.S. Postal Service awards SRA a large Year 2000 contract.
- Company makes its first acquisition, a small French IT firm, but sells it in less than two years.
- In 2000 SRA is named to *Fortune* magazine list of the "100 Best Companies to Work For" and remains on the list for ten years in a row.
- Board of advisors becomes board of directors.
- Revenue is over $312 million and more than 1,700 employees.

2001–2005
- SRA rebuilds the U.S. Navy command center, which it originally constructed; but it was destroyed in the September 11, 2001, terrorist attack on the Pentagon.
- Company acquires Marasco Newton Group, an environmental consulting firm, in January 2002.
- In May 2002 SRA International stock begins trading on the New York Stock Exchange as SRX. The stock is oversold by a factor of eighteen and is one of the top performing IPOs of the year.
- SRA acquires Adroit Systems for $40 million in January 2003.
- Company holds a secondary stock offering of $91 million in 2003.
- SRA celebrates twenty-fifth anniversary with revenue of $450 million and over 2,600 employees.
- Company wins Government Accountability Office and National Guard contracts, each potentially worth more than $100 million.
- SRA acquires Orion Scientific Systems (specializing in counterintelligence, counterterrorism, and law enforcement) in January 2004.
- Company is awarded a $341 million task order for USAID (Prime 2.2) under the GSA FEDSIM contract.
- In 2005 Renny DiPentima is named as CEO, replacing Ernst who remains chairman of the board.
- SRA acquires Touchstone Consulting Group in January 2005, Galaxy Scientific Corporation in July 2005, and Spectrum Solutions Group in November 2005.
- SRA is named "Government Solution Provider of the Year" by Government VAR magazine.
- Company announces a 2 for 1 stock split.
- Revenue exceeds $880 million.

- SRA acquires RABA Technologies in October 2006 to expand its intelligence portfolio.
- Company is awarded Enterprise Operations and Security Services (EOSS) contract by the Army National Guard.
- Stanton Sloane is appointed president and CEO in April 2007, replacing Renny DiPentima who retires.
- Company acquires Constella Group (health consulting services), Era Systems Corporation (aircraft flight tracking), and Interface & Control Systems (command and control) in July 2008.
- SRA named to *Fortune* magazine's list of the "100 Best Companies to Work For" for the tenth consecutive year.
- Company acquires PQA (environmental consulting) in February 2010, Sentech (energy management) in July 2010, and Platinum Solutions (software development) in November 2010.
- Revenue is over $1.6 billion and more than 7,000 employees.

- Company is sold in July 2011 to a group led by Providence Equity Partners and is no longer publicly listed.
- William Ballhaus replaces Stanton Sloane as CEO.
- The market that SRA serves (information technology and mission support services) begins in 2011 its first extended decline in more than a decade due to increasing national debt and political stalemate.
- Company reduces costs in increments to remain competitive; some of the savings are added to business development.
- For the first year in its history SRA experiences a revenue decline (-2%) to $1.68 billion in FY 2012.
- The decline continues to $1.39 billion in FY 2014, but also in that year, SRA wins $2 billion in awards, the largest amount in three years.

Index

Accenture, 41

accidents: at nuclear power plants, 24, 50–51, 56–57; oil spills, 57

acquisitions: of Adroit Systems, Inc., 141–43, 174; of Constella, 146, 147, 164–65, 167; costs, 201; of Era, 146–47, 165, 167, 201; of Galaxy Scientific Corporation, 144–45; growth influenced by, 146; GWACs, 151–53; lawsuits with, 181, 185, 193; of MNG, 139–41; of Orion Scientific Systems, 143, 174; of RABA Technologies, 145; of Spectrum Solutions Group, 145; by SRA International, 138–47, 164–65, 167, 174, 182, 201; SRA International acquired by Providence Equity Partners, 173, 179–207; of Touchstone, 144

Adams, Kathy, 133, 155–57

Administration for Children and Families, 97–98

Adroit Systems, Inc., 141–43, 174

Advanced Information Technology Services (AITS), 150

Advanced Logistics System (ALS), 12–14

AEC. *See* Atomic Energy Commission

Affordable Care Act, 209–11

AFIT. *See* Air Force Institute of Technology

AFLC. *See* Air Force Logistics Command

AI. *See* artificial intelligence

Air Force, U.S., 35, 61; AI and, 77–80; bases, 6, 7, 12, 14, 15, 30, 41, 150; with mobilization exercises, 30; Volgenau, Ernst, in, 6–8, 11–17

Air Force Institute of Technology (AFIT), 6

Air Force Logistics Command (AFLC), 12–14

Air Force Space Systems Division, 7

AITS. *See* Advanced Information Technology Services

Albright, Bill, 83, 119–20

Alderson, Debra, 205, 215

ALEXIS, 80–81, 82

ALS. *See* Advanced Logistics System

Amato, Karen, 116–17

American Management Systems (AMS), 26, 27, 31, 39, 42, 47; business problems at, 159–60; leadership at, 158–60; SRA International and, 59, 60, 61, 63, 65, 139, 158–59

America Online (AOL), 126, 174

amortization. *See* EBITDA

AMS. *See* American Management Systems

culture, 9, 16–17; software, 12, 14, 53, 91; technology and systems analysis, 27, 41; U.S. Naval Academy with, 5–6. *See also* artificial intelligence

Computer Sciences Corporation (CSC), 33, 47, 94, 123, 151, 152, 203

Conetsco, Dave, 83

Congress, 23, 35, 192, 209, 210

Congressional Budget Office, 43

Congressional Medal of Honor, 130

Constella, 146, 147, 164–65, 167, 202

Continuity of Government (COG) program, 56

contracts, 38, 42, 151–53, 209. *See also* indefinite delivery/indefinite quantity contract; *specific contracts*

Control Data Corporation, 12, 28

Cooke, Tim, 156

CORA. *See* Center for Response Ability

corporate information management (CIM), 87, 89, 91–92

costs: acquisitions, 201; bloat, 16; of embezzlement, 107–8; IPOs, 130; operating, 37–41, 46, 56; of technology, 15–16, 27, 75

credit lines, 37–38, 72–73

Crennan, Bill, 48, 78–79

Crespin, Emily, 206

Crestar. *See* SunTrust

Crockett, E. David, 171

Cross, Brian, 153

Crotty, Chuck, 135, 167

CSC. *See* Computer Sciences Corporation

culture: business, 46, 55, 71, 73–74, 91, 104, 105–7, 112, 124, 142–43, 153–54, 166; computers in popular, 9, 16–17

Culture and Values courses, 106, 108, 109

Curling, Kay, 115–16

Danzig, Richard, 28, 29

DARPA. *See* Defense Advanced Research Projects Agency

data, 12, 28; data-mining software, 121–22; EDS, 94, 129–30; Federal Parent Locator Service database, 97–99; management, 101; NPDB, 96, 97, 203

Davis, John, 21

Davis, Stuart, 135, 136

Day, Barbara, 179, 183

Day, Robert (Colonel), 178–79, 183, 220

Deadbeat Dad Database. *See* Federal Parent Locator Service database

decline: in growth, 162–63, 165; in revenue, 208–19

Defense Advanced Research Projects Agency (DARPA), 83

Defense Contract Audit Agency, 38

Defense Information Systems Agency, 89

Deitz, Allen, 113, 149, 150, 151, 156; leadership of, 163; with USAID, 153–54

Denison, Ann, 109, 113, 114, 115, 117, 133

Denning, Steve, 173–74

Department of Defense (DoD), 28, 31, 34, 43, 51, 86; audits, 38; CIM and, 89; contracts, 42, 209; health, 87, 94; IDEF and, 88

Department of Health and Human Services (HHS), 94–95

Department of Homeland Security, 144

depreciation. *See* EBITDA

detonations, space and nuclear, 7

DiPentima, Renny, 105–6, 123, 133, 136, 165; with acquisitions, 141, 142; leadership of, 158, 160, 161–63, 220

dishonesty, 106–9

DoD. *See* Department of Defense

Donohue, Anne, 156, 190, 217
downsizing, 204, 205–6
Dozier, Linda, 120–21
drugs, 81, 95–96
Duffy, Mike, 69–70, 71, 98, 113, 133
Durso, Frank, 156

earnings before interest, taxes,
 depreciation, and amortization.
 See EBITDA
Eastman Kodak International, Inc., 119
EBITDA (earnings before interest,
 taxes, depreciation, and amortization), 215, 219
EDS. *See* Electronic Data Systems
education, 3–8, 42
Edwards, Don, 150
Electronic Data Systems (EDS), 94,
 129–30
Ellis, Larry, 184
emails, 85, 122, 193–94
embezzlement, 107–8
emergencies: FEMA, 51–57, 86, 96;
 planning systems, 22–24, 57–58
employees, at SRA International: with
 acquisitions, 139–43, 144, 145; aptitudes of, 69–70; awards, 113; business success with focus on, 103–6,
 111–17; with Culture and Values
 courses, 106, 108, 109; *In Depth*
 magazine, 117; downsizing, 204,
 205–6; with embezzlement, 107–8;
 geeks, 9, 28, 104; health insurance,
 115–17; hotline for, 172; mush
 heads, 9, 28, 103–4; numbers, 1,
 42, 53, 71, 111; recruitment of, 26,
 32–34, 41–44, 47, 48, 52, 54, 63–64,
 69–71, 83–84, 100, 111–12, 113,
 139; sick leave, 114; stock options,
 130, 207; with succession planning,
 159–69. *See also specific employees*
energy, 20, 21, 99

Energy Research and Development
 Administration (ERDA), 20
enterprise resource planning (ERP),
 145
Enthoven, Alain, 8
Environmental Protection Agency
 (EPA), 139–40
Environment and Organizational Ser-
 vices (EOS), 141
EPA. *See* Environmental Protection
 Agency
Era: acquisition of, 146–47, 165, 167,
 201; sale of, 189, 202, 212
ERDA. *See* Energy Research and Devel-
 opment Administration
ERP. *See* enterprise resource planning
Errol, 123–24
EUCOM. *See* U.S. European Command
executive compensation, 191–92
exercises, 52, 53. *See also* mobilization
 exercises, military and
Exxon Valdez, 57

FAA. *See* Federal Aviation Administra-
 tion
failure rate, of businesses, 37
Fargo, JoAnn, 68
FDA. *See* Food and Drug Administra-
 tion
FDIC. *See* Federal Deposit Insurance
 Corporation
Federal Aviation Administration
 (FAA), 145, 146
Federal Deposit Insurance Corpora-
 tion (FDIC), 154–57, 203–4, 205
Federal Emergency Management
 Agency (FEMA), 51–57, 86, 96
Federal Parent Locator Service da-
 tabase (Deadbeat Dad Database),
 97–99
Federal Retirement Thrift Board,
 159

FEMA. *See* Federal Emergency Management Agency
Fisher, Rolland, 41, 53, 56, 60, 95, 96
Flannery, Steve, 152
Food and Drug Administration (FDA), 95–96
Fortune, 113, 115, 128, 157
Fox, Mike, 64, 154, 156, 163
Frank, Gene, 64, 89, 156
frugality, 40, 56, 68–69, 77, 185

Gagnon, Neil, 136
Galaxy Scientific Corporation, 144–45
Garbin, David, 122
GD. *See* General Dynamics
GE. *See* General Electric
geeks (wire heads), 9, 28, 104
General Atlantic Partners, 173
General Dynamics (GD), 34, 60–61, 136, 174
General Electric (GE), 84, 168
genomes, 99–100, 101
Gentili, Rob, 149
George Mason University, 182, 191
Gibson Dunn & Crutcher, 194
Gilburne, Miles, 120–21, 174–75, 177, 184
Giumti, Phil, 159
Global Clinical Development, 188–89, 202, 212
Goldwater-Nichols Act of 1986, 35–36, 172
Google, 9, 83
Gottdiener, Charles, 205
government: audits, 38, 39, 109; COG program, 56; Innovations in American Government Award, 98–99; Millennia and, 151–52, 153, 154; with RFPs, 151; shut down, 209–11. *See also specific government agencies*
government-wide acquisition contracts (GWACs), 151–53

The Graduate (film), 1
Grafton, Bob, 167, 184, 217
Graves, Kevin, 114, 115
Greene, John, 100, 123
Greenspan, Alan, 118
Greenstein, Sherman, 34, 61; AI and, 76–83; leadership of, 221; at SRA International, 68–69, 70, 71, 97, 98, 104–5
Groover, Charles, 42–43, 44
growth: acquisitions influencing, 146; decline in, 162–63, 165; "Hot Growth" companies, 157; of IT, 14, 17, 28; of SRA International, 54–55, 67–74, 86, 135, 138–47, 148, 157, 162–63, 165, 169, 174, 200, 206, 218; of technical services, 27
Grubbs, Wayne, 135
GTE Corporation, 47, 60, 61–63, 64, 90
GuardNet XXI, 148–50
GWACs. *See* government-wide acquisition contracts

Hadelman, Lew, 63, 64, 89–90
Hall, Max, 205, 216
Harris, Bill, 73
headquarter staff bloat, 16
health, 102, 123; Affordable Care Act, 209–11; DoD and, 87, 94; HHS, 94–95; insurance, 115–17; NIH, 92–93, 95, 97, 100, 101, 151, 208, 209
Healthcare Quality Improvement Act, 96
Hertzog, Jon, 47, 53, 60
HHS. *See* Department of Health and Human Services
Hill, David, 87
Hirsch, Don, 203
Hoffman, Dustin, 1
Hogan, Anna, 142–43
Honesty and Service, 3, 5, 17, 25, 67,

103, 106, 109, 135, 139, 164, 206, 214, 223

honesty, 3, 25; dishonesty, 106–9; service and, 5, 67, 103, 106, 109–10, 135, 139, 164, 206

"Hot Growth" companies, 157

hotline, for employees, 172

Houlihan Lokey, 185, 190

Hughes, Steve: IPOs and, 135; leadership of, 158, 161, 162, 166–67, 221; with "The Road Show," 131–33, 136; at SRA International, 164

human genome, 99–100

Hunter, Dick, 69, 88–89, 95; leadership of, 105; with SRA International, 152, 220; with vision statement, 103

Hunter, Lauris, 89

Hutton, Tom, 57

IBM (International Business Machines), 6, 28, 82, 129

ICBMs. *See* intercontinental ballistic missiles

idealism, 9, 67

IDEF, 88

ID/IQ contract. *See* indefinite delivery/ indefinite quantity contract

Ilisevich, Dan, 126

iLumin Software Services, Inc., 127

indefinite delivery/indefinite quantity (ID/IQ) contract, 92–93, 95, 97, 100, 151

In Depth magazine, 117

information, 99, 150; CIM, 87, 89, 91–92; Defense Information Systems Agency, 89; SCIF, 29, 54, 81

information technology (IT), 9, 14, 17, 28

initial public offerings (IPOs): for EDS, 129, 130; for SRA International, 125–26, 128–37, 199

Innovations in American Government Award, 98–99

insurance: FDIC, 154–57, 203–4, 205; health, 115–17

intelligence. *See* artificial intelligence

intelligence community, 29, 54, 80–82

interaction, with technology, 14

intercontinental ballistic missiles (ICBMs), 8, 60–64

International Business Machines. *See* IBM

Internet, 83, 84, 118, 120–21

IPOs. *See* initial public offerings

Iran, 129–30

Iraq, 35, 57, 202

IsoQuest, 83, 122

IT. *See* information technology

ITOP II, 152

Jacobs, Paul, 84

JCS. *See* Joint Chiefs of Staff

Jeopardy (television show), 82

JNIDS. *See* Joint National Intelligence Development Staff

Johnson, Gene, 122

Joint Chiefs of Staff (JCS), 35, 44, 171–72

Joint National Intelligence Development Staff (JNIDS), 80–81

Joint Operational Planning and Execution System (JOPES), 44–45, 47, 64, 89–90, 91–92

Joint Operations Planning System (JOPS), 30, 44

Jones, David C. (General), 28, 35–36, 171–72

JOPES. *See* Joint Operational Planning and Execution System

JOPS. *See* Joint Operations Planning System

Kaine, Tim, 210

Kalergis, James, 64

Kaplan, Judy, 71
Keffer, David, 217
Kennedy, John F., 152
Kerwin, Walter "Dutch" (General), 29
Kirkland & Ellis LLP, 185, 188, 189, 194
Klein, Michael, 166, 173, 179; with SEPTA vs. Volgenau, et al., 195, 211; with SRA International sale, 182–84, 188, 189, 190, 195–96
Knapp, Lauren and Andrew, 115
Kodak Legal Systems, 119–20
Korn Ferry International, 199, 200
Koshoggi, Adnan, 65
Kriegman, David, 70–71, 133, 152–53; with FDIC, 156; leadership of, 161, 162
Krupka, George, 84
Kurzhals, Eric, 150–51, 154

Lambert, Mary, 98
Landew, Barry, 42, 47, 53; with acquisitions, 142, 143; IPOs and, 133; leadership of, 158, 161, 162, 166, 167, 220–21; SMART system and, 95; at SRA International, 70, 71, 88, 112, 124, 151, 153, 164; with weapons work, 60–63, 65, 66
Lane, John, 79
Lane, Sara Glen. *See* Volgenau, Sara
Langstaff, David, 174, 180–81
language. *See* natural language processing
lawsuits: with acquisitions, 181, 185, 193; AMS, 159; emails in, 193–94; SEPTA vs. Volgenau, et al., 192–95, 211–13
layoffs. *See* downsizing
LBO. *See* leveraged buy-out
leadership: at AMS, 158–60; awards, 113–14; at GE, 168; problems, 176;

at SRA International, 9, 26, 46–47, 53, 57, 71, 92, 103–4, 105–6, 113–14, 150, 158, 160–69, 176, 179, 199–207, 214, 216, 217–19, 220–21; Stockdale Center for Ethical Leadership, 130; with succession planning, 159–69
Leading with Honesty and Service, 206
Leahy, Ray, 96
Legasey, Ted, 12–13, 14, 21, 159; with acquisitions, 139; FEMA and, 51–52; IPOs and, 133; leadership of, 26, 46, 104, 158, 160–61, 164, 220; logos and, 67–68; at NRC, 22, 24, 27; with "The Road Show," 131–33, 136; at SRA International, 26–27, 39, 40, 41–42, 46, 47, 51–52, 67–68, 71, 123, 151, 221; with vision statement, 103; with weapons work, 60, 61, 64, 65, 66
Legasey, Tricia, 22, 27
legislation: Affordable Care Act, 209–11; Goldwater-Nichols Act of 1986, 35–36, 172; Healthcare Quality Improvement Act, 96; Sarbanes Oxley Act, 172
leveraged buy-out (LBO), 180–82, 198
Lilly, Susan, 112
Liu, Edison, 123
Lockheed Martin, 151, 152, 168, 170, 182, 202
logos, 68
Luongo, John, 150–51, 155, 156, 163

Macy, John, 51
Mail2000, 122, 126
Mantas, 121–22, 125, 126
ManTech, 134, 200, 202
Marasco, Amy, 139–40, 141
Marasco-Newton Group (MNG), 139–41

Marine Corps, U.S., 3, 30, 35
market, needs of, 16
Martin, John C., 4
Martin Marietta, 79, 170. *See also*
  Lockheed Martin
McClave, Jim, 143
McConnell, Mitch, 211
McGrane, Cathy, 95
McGushin, Ed, 81; leadership of, 106,
  221; at SRA International, 52–53,
  55–57, 58, 69–70
McGushin, Sandy, 57
MCI Corporation, 123
McKinsey, 41
McNamara, Robert, 8, 43
Medicaid/Medicare, 101, 208
medical service, military, 87
memorial scholarships, 92
Merrill Lynch, 6, 122
Mertin, Alan, 191
Mestrovich, Mike, 87
methodology, of business. *See* busi-
  nesses
Michl, Brian, 150
Midas, 145
military, 80, 171, 221; AI and, 77–84;
  automation in, 27, 30–31; bases,
  6, 7, 12, 14, 15, 30, 41, 94, 150;
  chain of command in, 35; with
  emergency planning systems, 22;
  medical service, 87; with mobiliza-
  tion exercises, 28–31, 44, 87; SANG,
  64–65; SDI, 60; Selective Service
  System, 31; WWMCCS, 30, 47. *See
  also* Air Force, U.S.; Army, U.S.;
  Department of Defense; Marine
  Corps, U.S.; National Guard, U.S.;
  National Guard Bureau; Naval
  Academy, U.S.; Navy, U.S.; *specific
  military associations*
Military Sea Command, 203
Millennia, 151–52, 153, 154

Miller, Rebecca, 208, 216
missiles, 6, 8, 57, 60–64
MNG. *See* Marasco-Newton Group
mobilization exercises, military and,
  28–31, 44, 87
Moyer, Ellen, 98
Murasaki, 82–83
Murray, Russell II, 34
mush heads, 9, 28, 103–4
Mutryn, David, 186
MX Command, Control, and Commu-
  nications system, 60–61, 62, 64
Myers, Richard, 133

Nadeau, Rick, 167–68, 186, 217
Narang, Kamal, 208
National Association of Securities Deal-
  ers (NASD), 84, 121
National Association of Truck Stop
  Operators, 42
National Cancer Institute, 100, 123
National Communications System, 44
National Guard, U.S., 2–3, 87
National Guard Bureau, 148–50
National Institute for Allergies and
  Infectious Disease (NIAID), 101–2
National Institutes of Health (NIH),
  208, 209; Cancer Genome Atlas,
  101; ID/IQ contract, 92–93, 95, 97,
  100, 151
National Practitioner Data Bank
  (NPDB), 96, 97, 203
NATO, 29, 44
natural language processing (NLP),
  120; AI and, 76, 78–85; Assentor™,
  85, 122, 126, 127
Naval Academy, U.S., 3, 89; with
  computers, 5–6; with honesty and
  service, 5; Volgenau, Ernst, at, 4–6,
  128–30, 221–22
NaviSoft, 83, 121, 126, 174

Westerhoff, Jeffrey, 92, 97, 156; with Business Development Award, 114; Federal Parent Locator Service database and, 98; with SRA International, 152, 220
White, John, 119–20
Whiz Kids, at Pentagon, 8, 11, 26, 32, 43, 60, 159
Wilhelm, Karl, 121
wire heads. *See* geeks
work ethic, success and, 2, 86, 92
world. *See* black world
World War II, 2–3

World-Wide Military Command and Control System (WWMCCS), 30, 47
World Wide Web, 83, 120–21
WWMCCS. *See* World-Wide Military Command and Control System

Yates, Jerry, 108, 114–15, 217
Yates, Nancy, 114, 115
Yeager, Chuck, 7
Yocom, Mike, 149
Young, John, 122